Continuity and Change in the Westphalian Order

Editor
James A. Caporaso

Published by:

Blackwell Publishers, Inc.
350 Main Street
Malden, MA 02148 USA

Blackwell Publishers, Ltd.
108 Cowley Road
Oxford OX4 1JF
United Kingdom

Library of Congress Cataloging-in-Publication Data

Continuity and change in the Westphalian order / editor, James A. Caporaso.
p. cm.
"ISSN 1521-9488."
Includes bibliographical references.
ISBN: 978-0-631-22145-6
1. State, The–History. 2. Legitimacy of governments–History. 3. Nationalism–History. 4. Power (Philosophy) I. Caporaso, James A., 1941–

JC137 .C66 2000
320.1–dc21 00-062131

Continuity and Change in the Westphalian Order

Acknowledgments

I want to give special thanks to Tom Volgy and Anne Jones who first suggested this project to me. Volgy has been an exemplary leader in his role as Executive Director of the International Studies Association and Anne Jones has provided excellent guidance and judgement as an Editor for Blackwell. My greatest intellectual debt goes to Bob Denemark of the University of Delaware. The roots of the ideas for this special issue go back to the planning for the 1998 annual meeting of the International Studies Association in Minneapolis, Minnesota. Denemark not only organized and put together the entire program but also directed his considerable energies into elaborating a central theme. That theme had to do with the transformation of the Westphalian system. The 1998 convention marked 350 years since the signing of the treaties that established the Westphalian state. Denemark did his best to channel the interests of a large and diverse international studies community into this central theme.

I also want to acknowledge the support of the University of Washington during the period of time when we were trying to get this issue off the ground. Resat Kasaba of the Jackson School of International Studies provided support for a small workshop to give us the opportunity to "brainstorm" for two days. Several people participated in that workshop who did not write a paper. In particular, I want to recognize Joseph Jupille of Florida International University and Stephen Krasner of Stanford University. The discussion and contributions of both are gratefully recognized. Finally, I want to thank Steve Olswang, our Provost at the University of Washington, for his generous support and encouragement of my research.

Contributors

David L. Blaney is Associate Professor of Political Science, Macalester College.

Bruce Bueno de Mesquita is Senior Fellow, the Hoover Institution, Stanford University.

Kurt Burch is Associate Professor of Political Science and International Relations, University of Delaware, on leave at the Department of Political Science and the Center for Conflict and Change, University of Minnesota.

James A. Caporaso is Professor of Political Science, Department of Political Science, University of Washington.

Naeem Inayatullah is Assistant Professor of Political Science, Ithaca College.

Karen Litfin is Associate Professor of Political Science, University of Washington.

Walter Mattli is Assistant Professor of Political Science, Department of Political Science, and a member of the Institute on Western Europe and the Institute of War and Peace Studies, Columbia University.

Hendrik Spruyt is Associate Professor of Political Science, Arizona State University.

Changes in the Westphalian Order: Territory, Public Authority, and Sovereignty

James A. Caporaso[1]

Department of Political Science, University of Washington

In 1648, with the signing of the treaties of Munster and Osnabruck, the Westphalian order came into existence. Depending on one's critical viewpoint, this order either defined the central architectural principle of the modern state system or provided a very misleading "origin myth" about its evolution. The universal ideas that gave cohesion to the medieval world—a cohesion no less important because it contradicted great diversity—gave way to separate states and nations, each capable of defining its own goals and cultural mission. The idea of sovereignty took root, though not immediately, and provided the ideological justification for ultimate control within a specific territory at the same time that it provided a basis for recognition from other states. Sovereigns made treaties with other sovereigns, forged policies to rule inside a territory, attempted to exclude other authorities from interfering in "domestic politics," developed stronger controls over their own borders, and actively participated in the construction of citizenship and nationalism. In short, the politics of "inside-outside" began their active construction (Walker 1993).

The above represents at least the canonical version of the origin and development of the modern state system. I recognize that the Westphalian order is an ideal type from which there are enormous departures in practice. Agnew's "territorial trap" (1994) and Krasner's "Westphalian compromises" (1995/1996) both point out the dangers of conceiving the Westphalian state as overly bounded in territorial terms. But for better or worse, the Westphalian model has served

---

[1]I am very grateful to Robert A. Denemark for his suggestions concerning the organization of this volume. Indeed, the central theme of this special issue of *International Studies Review* comes from Denemark's work as program chair for the 1998 annual meeting of the International Studies Association.

Published by Blackwell Publishers, 350 Main Street, Malden, MA 02148, USA, and 108 Cowley Road, Oxford OX4 1JF, UK.

as a point of departure and baseline against which the more complex empirical world is compared. The Westphalian order renders a powerful influence even if it is honored in the breach. The basic idea is one of a system of territorially organized states operating in an anarchic environment. These states are constitutionally independent (sovereign) and have exclusive authority to rule within their own borders. They relate to the population within their borders as citizens (*Staatsangehoerige*, those belonging to the state) and to other states as legal equals.

Kenneth Waltz's (1959) famous three levels of analysis—the individual, the national state, and the international system—build implicitly on this inside-outside distinction. The second level, that of the nation-state, is almost by definition a Westphalian state and the systemic level refers to the distribution of capabilities (of power, variously defined) among nation states. Waltz carries the logic of the territorial state to its limits by exhorting us to ignore second-image factors in favor of the systemic distribution of capabilities. These capabilities are in effect the aggregations of distinct national powers, even if their sources rest physically within the territory of another country.[2] Even studies of dependency, hardly part of the research core of realist theory, use the nation-state along with a heavily idealized notion of an autonomous national economy as counterfactual reference points. While heavily influenced and penetrated by "foreign" capital, which rears its head "internally" as part of the comprador domestic bourgeoisie, peripheral countries are presumed to be frustrated political, economic, and cultural communities struggling to realize their distinctive potential. This potential is defined in terms of an autonomous state, nationally unified, and in control of its own economic policy. Here the Westphalian model serves as an ideal from which dependent countries have departed in the face of global economic pressures.

Numerous research questions can be organized around the Westphalian order. To what extent was the Westphalian moment really a turning point of significance? Such a question does not assume that a new system was born overnight. Instead, we can ask if this date (or temporal region) constituted an inflection point in the trajectory of the evolution of the state system. The notion that the state system came into existence full-blown in 1648 has been under constant attack, but the brunt of the attack has come from those who think that the territorial state was put in place, and consolidated, much later. Thus, Janice Thomson's (1994) research on the consolidation of the means of violence demonstrates that the state's much-touted monopoly of legitimate violence did not arrive until the middle of the nineteenth century.

---

[2] For example, the economic resources of subsidiaries of international and multinational corporations may be mobilized by the parent state for use in warfare, economic negotiations, and sanctioning.

The growth of nations and nationalism was a phenomenon that took off during the eighteenth and nineteenth centuries. How did the growth of nations and nationalism relate to the development of the Westphalian system? We take nationalism as a critical part of the modern landscape. Yet in the seventeenth century states could hardly be said to rest on anything like the cultural groups that developed much later. How did states and nations come to their present level of congruence that, while far from perfect, is much closer than we might expect? Can this process of mating between nations and states be accurately described as a Deutschian (Deutsch et al. 1957) demand-side phenomenon, with communities of feeling and common identity forming and then choosing their own sovereign institutions—in short, their own states? Or is the Tilly (1992) formulation a better approximation? In Tilly's approach, aspiring state leaders are engaged in a struggle for the reins of state power. As part of the part of the project of consolidating this power, states create loyal subjects and citizens, teach civic pride, and inculcate numerous symbols in the minds of their subjects. For Tilly, nationalism is partly a by-product of the struggle for state power.

While many have noted that the Westphalian state did not look very Westphalian until centuries after 1648, others argue (Hinsley 1986; Spruyt 1994) that what was alleged to have taken place in the middle of the seventeenth century in fact took place much earlier.[3] If sovereignty is exclusive property rights exercised over a definite territorial space, then something like this came into being five centuries earlier with the Concordat of Worms. Bueno de Mesquita argues (in this volume) that the modern state structure emerged from a struggle between religious authorities and kings. So Westphalia is denied any dramatically different status, at least in qualitative terms, from the world that existed before it and the one that followed.

While a lively research program exists, progress is impeded by the lack of clarity and agreement on basic concepts. As a result, we often speak past one another. Separate research fails to accumulate and individual efforts do not add up. Unless one believes that knowledge is incommensurable, creating a conversation is perhaps the first order of business (Burch, this volume). In turn, dialogue is most likely to succeed if it proceeds from a sound diagnosis of the problems. Here, unfortunately, it is difficult to speak with any certainty. I can only offer hunches for the current state of affairs and proceed to outline a program that I hope leads to progress. Epistemological hunches are contingent in the same way that substantive hypotheses are.

What reasons can be offered for our current condition? Of course, the central concepts with which we deal are difficult to say the least. If we run through the

---

[3] Hinsley (1986) and Spruyt (1994) can actually be put on both sides of the divide, since each argues that Westphalia occurred both before and after 1648.

roster of concepts—territoriality, authority, sovereignty, power, legitimacy—we can immediately see that we are dealing with concepts at a high level of abstraction, very different from say, seniority in the Senate, gross national product, or even party fragmentation. However, to say that the concepts are difficult does not get us very far. Everyone is likely to agree, but so what?

Three additional reasons can be offered to explain the disarray in studies of international system change. These reasons have to do with 1) the highly abstract nature of our concepts; 2) the dichotomous conception of many key variables; and 3) the overly aggregated nature of many terms. I will try to convince that these three points are separate, that they are genuine problems, and that good analysis can lead to improvements. While efforts to convince the reader along these three lines are related, each point stands alone. In the sections that follow, I briefly review the problems and then move to possible strategies to deal with them. In the "remedial" section, I concentrate mostly on the aggregation issue.

Abstract nature of the concepts. All concepts are abstract. Indeed, the root of the word means to draw out or away from what Harry Eckstein called "the relentless particularity of experience." Concepts attempt to draw together elements of concrete experience that can be grouped in a fruitful way, so as to improve our understanding. Thus, the point is not to avoid abstraction, but to build fruitful concepts. Again, no one will disagree with so anodyne a statement. The challenge is to pitch concepts at the right level so as to connect both upward (towards general theory) and downward (towards the empirical data). The mix of concepts associated with the Westphalian order (sovereignty, authority, autonomy, control, territoriality) have fallen down on the latter criterion, that is, on the connection between abstract concepts and empirical observations.

Dichotomous nature of concepts. Concepts such as sovereignty and territoriality have been treated as if they could take on two possible values—present or absent, sovereign or not sovereign, territorial or nonterritorial organization. While some concepts are inherently dichotomous, many so treated are at bottom continuous. Even types of political systems, such as presidential and parliamentary, can be conceptualized as having more or less of these properties measured on some underlying continuum (Shugart and Carey 1992:2–3).

Defining our concepts in either/or terms has caused us to labor needlessly about whether certain states are sovereign or not, whether emerging international unions such as the European Union (EU) possess sovereignty or not, and if they do, whether such sovereignty is shared with the constituent nation states. Dichotomous conceptions of sovereignty have also prevented us from conceptualizing "sovereignty bargains" (Litfin 1997). Disputes over sovereignty and who possesses it are bound up with the notion that sovereignty is the ultimate right to decide. Sovereignty in this sense implies a hierarchy of both norms and power. Many institutions within (and outside) society may possess both competencies and normative support, but when they are in conflict with one another—when "the chips are down" as the saying goes—the important question is who has final authority? Since the ideas of normative conflict and hierarchy of norms are central to much legal reasoning, lawyers tend to adopt this view of sovereignty as located in final authority. Since the law is about adjudication among competing norms, lawyers are supremely well placed to shed light on sovereignty so defined. Yet the idea of sovereignty as the ultimate right to decide has seriously retarded progress. Dichotomous conceptions of sovereignty do not allow much observable variation, cannot be untangled from other important concepts, and are not easily assimilated into the language of political exchange (compromising sovereignty, sovereignty bargains) and sovereignty practices.

Almost all of the concepts related to the Westphalian model—territory, control over borders, authority, autonomy, legitimacy, and sovereignty—can be thought of in continuous terms. While phrases such as "more or less sovereign" may sound odd, I suggest they do so because of the ingrained notion that sovereignty is the ultimate right to decide. While this point is straightforward, it is not uncontroversial, and finding areas of agreement with respect to definitions is an important first step.

The aggregation of concepts. Concepts such as territoriality, sovereignty, and authority obviously exist at a very high level of aggregation. To some extent, this is unavoidable. We are dealing with macroconcepts that often cannot be factored down into more specific, microlevel representations. Anarchy is a structural characteristic of the international system, not a characteristic of states. States are not anarchic, yet placed in relation to one another they form an anarchy. And individual states are not bipolar or multipolar but the system as a whole may be. Information about components is used to construct systemic properties (how could it be otherwise?), but once assembled in relation to one another, the system takes on meanings of its own. Composition counts. The placement of elements makes a difference. Waltz (1979) has gone to great pains to establish the independence of third-image (systemic) theory. If Waltz is correct—and I think he is on this point—systemic theory cannot be reduced to its components. A theory of the market is different from, and not reducible to, a theory of firms, just as a theory of international relations is separate from a theory of foreign policy.[4]

Lest I sound as if I am defending what I want to criticize, I note that the aggregation issue takes two forms. The first, discussed briefly above, concerns

---

[4] This is a separate question from whether systemic theory by itself is underdetermined and therefore requires a theory of foreign policy as a complement.

the spatial outlines (boundaries) that the concepts of international relations theory trace. Here we simply have to follow the instructions of the concepts themselves. Anarchy is an organizing principle of the international system; sovereignty a characteristic of states; legitimacy a relation between ruler and ruled, and so on. The second form of the aggregation issue has to do with compound concepts—the grouping of concepts under broader umbrella terms. The use of compound terms shows up in the definition of authority (power wielded legitimately), power (asymmetric resources, conflict of will, compliance of one to the wishes of another), and territoriality (physical space and public authority).

The use of compound terms may reflect an elective affinity among components, an affinity so strong that we can think of certain things as bonding naturally, almost by definition. Certain elements of the periodic table go together in such frequent and stable fashion that the compounds themselves are treated as "real" things, having a stable existence of their own. Or we may wish to treat certain properties together because we suspect that the whole is greater than the sum of the parts, that strong interactions exist among the components and that viewing each in isolation from the other runs the risk of missing these essential interactions.

Neither of these cases provides a good defense for starting and finishing at a high level of aggregation when studying the territorial state. It is true that state, border, citizen, national, territory, and authority have come together with such regularity that we are likely to recognize the whole more easily than the parts. Nevertheless, the components associated with sovereignty do not always come together; indeed, they are arguably increasingly detached from one another. States and corporations attempt to extend their authority outside their own territory, the International Criminal Court (ICC) extends its jurisdictional reach within the domestic boundaries of recognized states, and postnational (post-state) forms of citizenship are emerging in which identifications are in part detached from territory. The extent and significance of these decouplings are debatable, and they are debated in this volume. Here I am just trying to establish that the bonds and linkages are not so tight as to warrant a definitional fusion of separate properties into one overall concept. To do so would cannibalize potentially interesting propositions.

Two important examples of compound terms are authority and territoriality. In Weber's (1947) famous definition, authority is power wielded legitimately. Authority refers to the structure of rule (Herrschaft) in which the commands of the ruler are accepted as legitimate. In this formulation, power, which is already a complex concept, is attached to legitimacy to form a conceptual compound, authority.

The term "territoriality" has been used in numerous ways (see Ruggie 1993). It is used to signify that nearly all the landmass of the world is carved up into spatially exclusive units. With few exceptions (The Order of Malta, foreign embassies), states do not have overlapping jurisdictions regarding territory. It is doubtful that subsidiaries of international firms are competing authority structures in the full sense of the word. They are without question extremely important extraterritorial islands of power and influence. As Hatch and Yamamura have argued (1996), when Japan directly invests in a foreign country, its presence is not limited to physical structures of investment. It is also exporting *keiretsu* and the organizational habits of Japanese management culture. Territoriality is also used to denote a principle of political organization that delimits the spatial scope of public authority. In this usage, the reach of public authority is coterminous with the physical boundaries of the state, that is with its geographic borders. Finally, territoriality is used to remind us that states have borders that serve to physically protect from outside threats, to enhance a range of economic objectives, and to preserve cultural autonomy.

It is not just that territoriality can mean many things when used by different analysts but rather that it inherently means several things at the same time, even when used carefully by the same person. Territoriality brings together physical space and public authority. In this sense, territoriality is a function (a hypothetical relationship) rather than an attribute.

One way to deal with overly aggregated concepts is to unpack them. Sovereignty as a complex concept should be broken down and analyzed. Among several scholars who have urged this approach I single out the work of Krasner (1995/1996, 1999), Litfin (1997), and Ruggie (1993) as especially productive. Krasner identifies four properties associated with sovereignty—territory, recognition, autonomy, and control—and proceeds to examine the combinations that occur. He flatly states that "only a very few states have possessed all of these attributes" (1999:220). Trade-offs and compromises abound. As Jackson and Rosberg (1982) noted long ago, many of Africa's weak states persist not because of state capacity to rule internally and to control borders, but because of the stabilizing force conferred by international recognition. Also, the rulers of states can enter into international treaties that may limit their own authority. The member states of the Treaty of Amsterdam recognize that the European Court of Justice (ECJ) can overrule states on certain matters of domestic law and practice. For example, while the United Kingdom is a system of parliamentary sovereignty, laws of Parliament can be overridden by judgements of the ECJ in certain areas. Thus, without repealing the United Kingdom Accession Act of 1972, by which the UK entered into its obligations with the European Union (EU), Parliament does not always have the ultimate right to decide. Other states, such as Taiwan, may have the capacity for domestic rule, as well as the capacity to exclude external authority structures, and yet not enjoy international legal recognition (Krasner 1999:4). The permutations and combinations are limited only by the number four.

In "Sovereignty in World Ecopolitics" (1997), Karen Litfin makes two important conceptual moves. The first move is to shift the focus from sovereignty as ultimate right to decide to sovereignty as a set of ongoing norms and practices. Sovereignty immediately becomes more differentiated, more observable, separable, and variable. The second move is to unpack sovereignty into three constituent elements: autonomy, control, and legitimacy (1997:169). Although these elements commingle in practice, Litfin argues that it is important to distinguish them analytically. If autonomy, control, and legitimacy were perfect indicators of a perfectly homogenous concept, they would always move in an identical way in relation to other variables. By contrast, we find that these core conceptual elements are imperfectly related; indeed, sometimes they are at odds with one another. This leads Litfin to engage in the analysis of "sovereignty bargains."

While my formulation of sovereignty and the Westphalian order differ somewhat from Litfin's and Krasner's, they have nevertheless pointed the way by breaking with the legalistic approach, conceptualizing sovereignty as continuous rather than discrete and absolute, and breaking down overly aggregated concepts into more primitive components. By doing so, they have permitted, indeed encouraged, the analysis of the complex ways in which the components of sovereignty move.

In the remainder of this paper, I attempt to build a taxonomy of key concepts relative to the Westphalian order, relying upon power, authority, and territory as primitive terms. I then attempt to apply the conceptual scheme to an empirical illustration of how territory and authority have increasingly become separated (not merely separable) from one another in the present European context.

Conceptual Clarification

A full understanding of the Westphalian order requires at a minimum attention to four concepts: authority, sovereignty, territoriality, and citizenship. In this section, I will attempt to clarify these concepts and show how they function together, as a coherent ensemble, as part of the overall concept of the Westphalian order. It follows from this that changes in the Westphalian order are not so much changes in the component concepts as changes in relationships among them. Nevertheless, analyzing the components is essential to understanding the overall relationships.

Authority. The significant aspect of authority from my perspective is "right to rule" or "recognized right to rule." Since politics is about systems of rule, claims about the right to rule are distinctive claims about both legitimacy and capacity to govern.

However, while authority claims rest partly on acceptance and legitimacy, our collective understanding of legitimacy seriously overstates the importance of notions of political support, informed by modern theories of public opinion. Weber's famous definition of authority as "power wielded legitimately" was not intended to imply that authority exists only when a democratic citizenry actively supports the policies and governance structures of the state. Instead, authority is best conceived as a relation of command and obedience, as a set of claims "to the exclusive right to make rules" (Thomson 1995:223). The success or failure of these claims rests on a variety of bases, including active political support, a generalized acceptance of the rules of the game, deference to experts, fear of retaliation, and sheer indifference to the process and outcomes.

The concept of authority raises serious definitional difficulties that will not be solved in this short article. One difficulty may be summarized by pointing to the Parsonian tradition in sociology, which more or less equates authority with voluntary consent of the subject to the "holder" of power, and contrasts this voluntary dimension with naked force and coercion (Parsons 1967). As Dennis Wrong (1979:38–39) perceptively points out, this view of the relation between force and authority seriously overestimates the amount of consent in society and also fails to see alternatives to coercion and active legitimacy (an aware, informed acceptance of rule) as foundations of compliance. The rules of governments may be obeyed because of fear of reprisal, because of inducement, because of a belief that the "authorities" are competent experts (e.g., independent central banks), and because they are deemed to be legitimate. My definition of authority comes closest to Arendt's use of this concept.

> The authoritarian relation between the one who commands and the one who obeys rests neither on common reason nor on the power of the one who commands: what they have in common is the hierarchy itself, whose rightness and legitimacy both recognize and where both have their predetermined stable place. (Arendt 1961:93)

Thus the distinctive characteristic of authority is the presumptive right to rule, which is a structural relation joining both rulers and ruled. The above definition of authority makes it clear that "private authority" is not a contradiction in terms nor is the phrase "sovereign authority" redundant. These two concepts are separable in principle and in practice. And since authority rests on numerous foundations, this definition recognizes authority in authoritarian systems, an impossibility if authority relations imply the voluntary acceptance of and democratic compliance with rules.

Sovereignty. While sovereignty and authority are related, the latter can exist without the former. A religious leader may exercise authority over believers, a doctor over patients, and a parent over a child. Different authority structures may function in their own space. If these separate structures are "scheduled" so as not to conflict with one another, no question need arise as to which is supreme.

I will argue below that the territorial principle forces the issue of which authority is controlling.

Sovereignty has to do with relations among authority structures. The sovereign authority—the state—is the final authority, the authority that claims the ultimate right to decide. As Hinsley (1986:21) points out, sovereignty did not evolve in perfect synchrony with the state. It lagged the emergence of the Westphalian state by several centuries. Sovereignty, as a claim about ultimate rule within a territory, came after the state itself, even if we today confusingly define the state as sovereign. This definitional tangle of separate properties masks a complex historical interaction between states and systems of rule.

The view of sovereignty as final and exclusive rule cuts through the subtle and more differentiated discussion of the concept by Krasner and others (Krasner 1999; Thomson 1995). Krasner identifies four broad uses of sovereignty: control over borders, external recognition, ultimate right to decide, and capacity to exclude external authority structures. I rely on the last two closely related uses—sovereignty as the ultimate right to decide and as capacity to exclude external authority structures.

Territoriality. Territoriality refers to the organization of political space, in particular to the principles underlying the way political space is organized. Political organization is territorial when the legal reach of public authority is coterminous with certain spatial boundaries, such as those of the national state or of federal jurisdictions within a state. Territoriality links politics as authoritative rule with the geographical reach of this rule. Other principles of political organization exist: rule by and over tribe (which might be dispersed in different territories), rule over believers (say over Catholics worldwide), and rule in terms of administrative task (e.g., independent regulatory agencies that are not limited to state borders) (Ruggie 1993).

The emergence of the territorial principle, of rule over territory by a single ruler or political institution, is subversive of multiple claimants of authority. It is possible to imagine separate authority structures existing side by side. Indeed, the medieval principle of organization in which multiple authorities exist within the same territory, each authority making claims based on use, customary rights, and personal relations, provides a case in point. However, the persistence of competing claims and the absence of sovereignty depend on nonterritorial forms of organization. When the territorial principle emerges, it immediately raises the issue of rule over space, regardless of substantive domain. When conflict occurs, it is more difficult to resolve by more finely honed specialization of function or by exit.

The territorial state is of course a state with physical boundaries, and a well developed sense of inside-outside and us-them. As Bartolini (1997) has persuasively argued, the modern state has closed off boundaries, thus altering the relative incentives in favor of voice against exit. The rise of political parties, the expansion of the electorate, the growing importance of formal representation and parliaments, and the development of interest group lobbying may be seen as indicators of this selective but powerful tightening of the borders of states. With the movement of people and capital more restricted, and with claims to rule by the state more pervasive, "domestic" mobilization became inevitable.

In short, territorial organization implies rule over a distinct space, the subjects in that space, and the economy within that space. It also implies drawing together (consolidating) scattered islands of authority into one hierarchy or separating authority into separate territorial spheres, as in federal systems. The territorial principle implies neither total control nor absolutism. The authority of the territorial state can be quite limited and carefully circumscribed. Constitutions, formal and informal, may spell out the precise range of authorities of the state and may divide the powers of the state among several institutions. But whatever the boundaries of the state with respect to the society, when conflicts among authorities occur, the sovereign state can claim final right to rule.

Citizenship. The meaning of citizenship centers on membership in a political community and is incomprehensible apart from it (Brubaker 1992; Wiener n.d.). In the Westphalian order, citizenship is based on membership in states. This membership implies certain rights and responsibilities. Membership in cosmopolitan associations and transnational markets (as tourist, as guest worker) may provide resources and opportunities but these areas are not institutionally entrenched in the same way that citizenship rights are.

The territorial state has served as a container for our understanding of citizenship, so much so that a distinguished international relations scholar has asked if multinational citizenship is possible (Aron 1974). The boundaries of the state have traditionally set limits to the range of rights and responsibilities with which we are familiar. Yet state-centric citizenship displays its limits as integration among countries increases. The flow of goods and factors, especially labor, across national lines, pointedly raises questions about rights regarding the market and beyond. Tensions build between the scope of benefits supplied by the territorial state and the practical needs of people moving across state borders. Unemployment insurance, pensions and social security, dependency allowances, and rights to move spouses and children all take on new and problematic aspects in an integrating context. In Western Europe at least, the tensions between state-centric citizenship and regional markets are prompting an examination of postnational conceptions of citizenship (Curtin 1997; Shaw 1999).

The Westphalian Syndrome

Authority, sovereignty, territory, and citizenship are distinct concepts in the sense that none both logically entails and exhausts the meanings of the others.

True, sovereignty is a type of authority but it is also more than that. Territory involves the merging of physical space and public authority but the congruence between the two is far from perfect. It is precisely this variability in fit that provides leverage for research. A central question is what accounts for changes in looser or tighter levels of fit. Citizenship has been closely identified with membership in the Westphalian state but there has always been some deviation from a perfect territorial interpretation of citizenship. Citizens abroad may vote by absentee ballot in their own domestic elections, and foreign workers may have rights (to medical treatment, for example) beyond their own borders. Nevertheless, these four concepts are coupled to a sufficient extent so that we can refer to their relationships as a syndrome—the Westphalian syndrome. Since these concepts are empirically correlated at the same time that they are conceptually distinct, it makes sense to disaggregate them and investigate their empirical interrelationships. For the most part, it is changes in these relations, rather than component properties, that we have in mind when we refer to the Westphalian order.

Table 1 sketches four "types" of relationships based on two polar values of territoriality and salient principle of rule. Regarding territory, I refer simply to the inside-outside dimension. Regarding principle of rule, I distinguish between authority and power. The cells of the table thus are formed by the intersection of form of rule and the territorial principle: politics within or among states.

Cell 1 directs our attention to authority relations inside the state, that is, domestic politics. The salient basis of governance is recognized right to rule,

Table 1. Types of Domestic/International Systems

		Form of Rule	
		Right/Authority	Power
Territory	Inside	(1) Domestic rule Legitimacy Final authority to rule within a territory	(2) Autonomy Freedom from external influence State capacity to rule State strength
	Outside	(3) Control over borders External recognition Capacity to enter "game" of international politics Hegemonic order	(4) Control over borders Power over others Agenda power Go-it-alone power

that is, authority relations. There is a significant component of a generalized acceptance of rule and of the right of political institutions to make laws within a territory. This is the classical locus of government seen as legitimate rule, as a structured hierarchy of command and obedience. Cell 2 shifts attention to power relations, which while not completely distinct from authority, focuses us more on the capacity to mobilize resources and to use them—to resist or to achieve positive goals—within a territory.

Perhaps the most fundamental power-oriented goal relates to autonomy and self-determination. A state that is penetrated from the outside, that is subject to every push and pull of the global political economy, may not even be able to form its own goals. Such is the sorry state of affairs painted by dependency theory: a weak "domestic" economy, where the label scarcely applies; widespread presence of "external" actors such as MNCs and comprador classes whose internal presence also cannot be denied; and fragmentation of the nominal domestic economy, which is not strongly linked by Leontieff input-output processes or connected via the movement of aggregate economic functions (savings, investment, production, consumption).

The third cell brings us back to the dimension of right to rule, though now in its external significance. I hasten to add that these boxes do not represent qualitatively distinct relations. Instead, they refer to different mixes of raw power and authority. Immediately below the horizontal line appears "control over borders." States regulate exchanges between inside and outside. Such exchanges include trade, capital flows, drug traffic, immigration, migrant labor, and tourism. There is a greater consensus on how to manage some of these border exchanges (e.g., trade) than others (e.g., migrant labor). Also in this cell are international legal recognition (Jackson and Rosberg 1982), diplomatic recognition, and playing by the norms and rules of the game of international politics.

There is another side to the external aspect of legitimacy. Authority relations may extend from inside the state to relations among states. There are fragments of authority as part of the United Nations' peacekeeping activities in many parts of the world; in normative movements such as the drive for international racial equality (Klotz 1995); and more controversially as part (and only a part) of the International Monetary Fund's programs in the less developed world. Hegemonic power is also, inevitably, hegemonic authority.[5] The

[5] Again, I am not suggesting that hegemony, especially the hegemony of the IMF, is legitimate in the corrupted modern sense that it is viewed as welcome and in the interest of those on behalf of whom the power is wielded. But it is also more than raw power, or even power with a fig leaf of ideological justification. It would be difficult to imagine the programs of various international organizations, as well as the international projects of many states, without an appeal to external constituencies and some support for these hegemonic projects from receiving countries.

British Empire, the IMF, and the visions of world order projected by France and the United States are all based in part on a claim to authority that goes well beyond raw power and material capabilities.

Finally, Cell 4 points us towards the traditional realist content of international politics—the use of power across national borders. The full range of power applies: the power to control the actions of others, the power to control outcomes, the power to structure agendas, and the power to "go it alone" (Gruber 2000), that is, the capacity either alone or in coalition to pursue a path upon which others must follow. Germany and France formed such a coalition in the first two decades of the European Union's existence. Perhaps Germany, France, and the United Kingdom form such a coalition today.

While this discussion hopefully clarifies my main concepts, it does little to address the issue of change. If the Westphalian order involves congruence among territory, scope of public authority, and citizenship, then a weakening (strengthening) of this system involves a loosening (tightening) of these bonds. If contemporary states decrease their capacity to resist external authority (not influence) or, conversely, if they succeed in projecting their authority outside their borders, this indicates a change in the parameters that govern the Westphalian order.

In the remainder of this article, I attempt to demonstrate what a change in the Westphalian order entails. It should be clear from the above discussion that the Westphalian state system is not necessarily altered by increasing levels of interdependence, loss of control over borders, decreased policy autonomy, or inability of particular states to exert control over international outcomes. These things tell us something about power, autonomy, influence, and dependency but little about the pillars of the territorial state, which have much more to do with the congruence between territory and authority structures.

In order to highlight territory and authority, I focus on a distinct case, the reception of European Union authority into the United Kingdom's constitutional order. The force of the example stands or falls on the claim that it is the exclusion of external authority, rather than the capacity to resist an external force, that is at issue. The central failing of most of the attempts to study changes in sovereignty involves the confusion of constraints on state power and autonomy with constraints on and sacrifices of sovereignty itself (the latter quite a different thing). The time frame of this empirical example runs only a couple of decades (from 1973 to the present), a mere dot (actually a short line, representing about 7 percent of the temporal spectrum of Westphalia) in the *longue duree'* of the Westphalian order from 1648 to the year 2000. This temporal mismatch works against my example by placing the burden of plausibility (forget about proof) on a few decades when clearly a much longer time frame would allow these deep changes in international system structure to develop, if indeed they were occurring. But plausibility is all I am trying to show, not proof. If the reader is convinced, even curious, that a thin wedge of change in the nature of the territorial state is taking place, I will have accomplished my purpose.

In what follows, I argue that territorial boundaries and domestic authority structures have increasingly decoupled, that external authorities routinely intrude on the UK legal order, that a significant component of economic citizenship is given operational content by authority structures physically outside the UK, and that key aspects of the domestic constitutional order—Parliamentary sovereignty—are threatened by "alien" political practices such as judicial review. While I am aware that I cannot provide a convincing case for so ambitious an agenda in the few remaining pages, I hope the following is suggestive.[6]

The European Union and the United Kingdom: A case of fragmented and shared sovereignty.[7] Since becoming a member of the EU in 1973, the UK has experienced difficulties adapting to European policies and institutions. While the policy dimension is most often emphasized (e.g., social policy, monetary policy), the institutional implications of UK membership may be of more lasting importance for the territorial nature of authority. One critical aspect of the UK institutional order relates to Parliamentary sovereignty, the doctrine that the laws of Parliament are supreme. Yet this important institution, the core of the British constitution, is being compromised by judicial processes emanating from an external body, the ECJ.

To tell this story, I will first describe how an international treaty (The Treaty of Rome, and later treaty amendments) was transformed into a constitutional document, how that document was then used to interrogate domestic legislation, and how this legislation (Acts of Parliament) is overturned on the basis of conflicts with European law, conflicts which are of course not objective but interpreted by the ECJ itself. Few clearer clashes between domestic and external authority structures are likely to be found.

Before judicial review of Parliamentary legislation could take place in the UK, important changes had to transpire in the nature of the Rome treaty. The Treaty of Rome defined a traditional, treaty-based international organization limited to the resolution of interstate conflicts. Mancini and Keeling (1994), reflecting on the early years of the European Economic Community (EEC), noted that the Treaty of Rome was forged as a compact among states, with no

[6] These matters are taken up in more detail in my work with Joseph Jupille (Caporaso and Jupille 2000). Also see "Sovereignty and Territoriality in the European Union: Defending the UK Institutional Order," manuscript, University of Washington, Seattle, Wa., 2000.

[7] In this section I rely on Caporaso and Jupille, "Sovereignty and Territoriality in the European Union: Defending the United Kingdom Institutional Order," University of Washington, Seattle, Wa. 2000. Pp. 11–15.

vertical lines between the institutions of the EEC and individuals. Individuals had no status, no legal standing before courts (domestic or international) under the Treaty. The term "Community" referred to a community of states, not individuals (Mancini and Keeling 1994:176).

Thus, from the standpoint of developing individual rights under Community law, the architecture of the EU seemed weak. Before domestic legislation could be called into question, the Treaty had to be transformed from a decentralized compact among states into something like a domestic constitution, providing entrenched individual rights, which are not easily reversed by simple acts of Parliament (see Mancini 1991; Stone Sweet 1995). The process by which this historic transformation has been (and continues to be) accomplished is referred to as "the constitutionalization of the Treaty system" (Mancini 1991). This term "refers to the process by which the relevant treaties have evolved from a set of legal arrangements binding upon sovereign states into a vertically integrated regime conferring judicially enforceable rights and obligations on all legal persons and entities, public and private, within EU territory" (Stone Sweet and Caporaso 1998:102). This process involves no less than a transformation from a classic international organization based on state-to-state relations into a partly domesticated system of governance founded on law directly applicable to individuals.

This process of constitutionalization, while Court-led, has been driven by deeper social, economic, and political forces, in particular by the linkages among private litigants, national courts, and the European Court (Stone Sweet 2000). The most important jurisprudence was laid down in 1963 and 1964, with the cases of *Van Gend en Loos* and *Costa v. E.N.E.L.* The *Van Gend* case established the doctrine of direct effect, whereby Community law can confer rights upon individuals, who can invoke those rights in making claims against states. That is to say, the Court asserted that provisions of the Rome treaty created rights and responsibilities for individuals even without supplementary actions by national institutions to translate Treaty doctrine into domestic law. The Court propounded an important doctrine, eroded a standing partition between domestic and international law, and created a mechanism by which individuals could claim judicial remedies before international courts (Stone Sweet 1995:2–4).

This legal move was so important because it empowered individuals in an area of obvious self-interest to them. By doing so, it set up a mechanism for the law to become relevant to individuals while at the same time it did not require a huge bureaucratic apparatus to enforce the law. The latter factor was facilitated by the Article 177 procedure, whereby individuals could appeal to their national courts, which in turn could ask the ECJ for a preliminary ruling if the matter in question raised elements of European law.

Important as the doctrine of direct effect was, it could not very well work by itself in the face of contrary domestic law. It is not surprising that in the year following *Van Gend* the Court grasped the nettle and confronted the issue of the relationship between municipal and international law. In *Costa v. E.N.E.L.*, the Italian courts first heard the case where an Italian citizen refused to pay his electricity bill because he asserted his rights under the Rome treaty had been violated. Since Italian law governing the case (a law nationalizing an electricity company) came into existence after the Rome Treaty, the Italian Constitutional Court decided against Mr. Costa, citing *lex posteriori*. The case then was appealed under the Article 177 procedure, and the ECJ, while agreeing that Mr. Costa had to pay his $3 electricity bill, quietly added that Community law was supreme. In the process, in a most off-handed manner, judicial review was brought into being.

It is difficult to exaggerate the importance of direct effect and supremacy. Indeed, they make up what many now think of as the constitutional pillars of the EU system. In announcing direct effect, the Court provided individuals with legal standing under an international treaty, and by so doing, it considerably closed the gap between treaty law and municipal law. A transnational legal space was created within which individuals could seek redress for complaints before domestic courts relying on Community law.

The ideas of direct effect and supremacy led naturally to judicial review. If individuals were to have rights that could be exercised under European law, and these rights were to hold up even under conflicting domestic provisions, a judicial body had to exist to adjudicate claims. Judicial review involves the assessment (review) of the laws of one level of government in light of laws (including the constitution) of another level. Some hierarchy is implied in the very idea of judicial review.

When the ECJ set forth the doctrines of direct effect and supremacy, it implied that the European Court would have the ability to review and overturn domestic laws. Thus, it is no surprise that supremacy was not easily accepted. Numerous countries, France, Italy, and the UK among them, resisted and continue to resist. Nevertheless, today judicial review is variably accepted in almost all of these states. The legal innovation that made this transformation easier had to do with the fact that it was domestic courts using the preliminary reference procedure that served as agents of this change. The triumph of the judiciary and judicial review, therefore, does not appear so much as a triumph of external forces (the ECJ) over domestic institutions, as a triumph of the rule of law in the form of constant scrutiny of domestic legislation in light of European law (Alter 1998:121). Nevertheless, it is clear that the role of Parliament in the domestic constitutional order has changed, and that it is no longer supreme in the sense that it previously was.

To give focus to these macro changes in the nature of territorial authority in the UK, I will first discuss changes in British gender equality legislation brought about by litigation under European law. Gender equality legislation, particularly as it applies to the workplace, is a fascinating case study, since both the UK and the EU have their own equality provisions. The possibility for conflict between laws at different levels has clearly existed from the very beginning. Building on this discussion I will then attempt to show that there is an emerging pattern of judicial review in which the ECJ scrutinizes domestic legislation in light of European standards derived both from the Treaty as well as secondary legislation. The result is a cross-national, transgovernmental legal process in which the authority structures of the domestic order are called into question by authorities at another level. What is at issue is not the creation of a larger state but the mingling of domestic and external authority relations and the willingness to accept a different authority depending on the issue at hand. There is both a segmentation by subject matter and a loosening of authority from the physical boundaries of the state that takes us further from the Westphalian ideal.

Gender equality legislation.[8] While the UK and the EU both have equal pay and equal treatment legislation (and Treaty provisions in the case of the EU), the provisions are not identical. The UK passed the Equal Pay Act in 1970 and the Sex Discrimination Act in 1975. While the Pay Act was passed even before the UK entered the EU (1973), conformity with European law was in the minds of legislators while the Pay Act was drafted. Since the laws at the national and European levels were not identical, this opened up the opportunity for litigation by victims of economic discrimination. In fact, the UK was put under continuous pressure by the Commission and the ECJ to redraft its domestic legislation to make it conform to the European standard.

The basic narrative is as follows. The Equal Pay Act was passed in the UK in 1970 and provided for equality in pay for like work. However, a number of serious shortcomings existed, especially where the plaintiff did not have a comparator, that is, someone in a similar job in the same establishment. Since most of the inequality was between job categories rather than within them, this was a serious matter. Women could be prevented from claiming discrimination simply because there were no men doing the same job.

Thus, potential victims of discrimination faced a difficult situation. If women performed the same jobs as men, and were paid less, discrimination would be easy to demonstrate. But in the more common case where women and men worked at different jobs, and women were paid less, they would have no male equivalent, that is, no one doing exactly the same work with whom to be compared. Clearly, unless equal value (not just equal pay) standards were admitted, no progress could be made. Women's groups and others within Britain pushed

---

[8] In this section I draw heavily on Caporaso and Jupille (2000).

for amendment to the 1970 act so as to admit the phrase "work of equal value." However, little happened until the EU acted and passed the Equal Pay Directive in 1975. This Directive explicitly included the "equal value" language and imposed a deadline for its enforcement of February 1978. After this date, and upon its 1979 review of domestic measures implementing the Directive, the Commission felt that the UK had not properly implemented the Directive (primarily because of the shortcomings enumerated above) and instituted infringement proceedings.

The case was brought before the Court and the UK was found in violation of the Directive (Case 61/81, [1982] ECR 2601). In response, the Department of Employment came up with proposals for amending the Act. Women's groups, the Equal Opportunities Commission, and the House of Lords met the proposals with stiff resistance, objecting in particular to the one-year delay they would have created before giving effect to the ECJ judgment (Clarke 1984). In 1984 the Equal Pay (Amendment) Regulations were passed. This is certainly not the end of the story, as the Equal Opportunities Commission (EOC) and women's groups have continued throughout the 1980s and 1990s to invoke European law in compelling the UK government to amend domestic legislation. Domestic law in the UK was brought in line with European standards largely at the behest of an external authority structure.

Changes in the British constitution. The preceding material on gender equality legislation is provided to show that an external authority structure has intruded into the UK's domestic institutional (indeed constitutional) order. The fact that this external authority was accepted on "right to rule" grounds rather than imposed by force makes it no less compelling as an example of a change in the nation-state's territorially organized authority structure. Indeed, for this series of events to qualify as a case of authority change, rather than change in autonomy, requires acceptance by the UK of the legitimacy of the higher legal order. Gender equality is not alone as an example of external authority nor is the manner in which the ECJ operates with respect to domestic politics unique. Analyses of conflicts among legal orders in the areas of free movement, migrant labor, competition, and social security would likely yield similar results.

Just as important as these authority changes are in gender equality policy are the implied changes for the UK judicial style (Levitsky 1994). Three aspects of the British legal style may be singled out: parliamentary sovereignty, the absence of judicial review, and the absence of constitutionally entrenched rights. All three institutional properties are being subjected to intense pressure to change and in some part (though not completely) that pressure emanates from Europe.

Parliamentary sovereignty means that laws of Parliament are the supreme law of the land. As Dicey put it, the British Parliament has ". . . the right to make or unmake any law whatever, and no person or body is recognised by the law of England as having the right to override or set aside the legislation of Parliament" (from Dicey 1959, quoted by Levitsky 1994:349). The laws of Parliament are supreme and no other institution can overrule them, including the courts. Thus, the function of judges is to "limit themselves as much as possible to the literal words, avoiding constructions that are not true to the statutory text" (Levitsky 1994:350). Further, a more recent act of Parliament trumps an earlier one. In principle, the only thing that the Parliament may not do is to limit the law-making capacity of a future Parliament.

Parliamentary sovereignty implies, with little room for discretion, the absence of judicial review. If laws of the Parliament are supreme laws of the land, no other body may interrogate them and overturn them. In response to the query "but aren't there always exceptions and ambiguities," the answer is "yes but" it is the function of Parliament to draft legislation precisely, to fill gaps, and to make continuous amendments. And according to Levitsky, British statutes are drafted in a very precise manner, simultaneously limiting the scope of judicial discretion and placing a burden on legislators to write comprehensive laws. (1994:350)

Contrary to established British tradition, the ECJ has reviewed and continues to review British legislation. Community law is much more open-ended and vague than UK law and the ECJ's judicial style is correspondingly more discretionary and creative. Judges within the UK no longer have to limit themselves to narrow and literal interpretations of the law, the "plain meaning of plain words," but can rely on purposive interpretations about what the legislator must have meant and can rely on debates within the Parliament to inform their reasoning. In *Pickstone v. Freeman* (1988), an equal pay case, the House of Lords argued in favor of the plaintiff, Ms. Pickstone, on grounds that her rights had been violated by the Equal Pay Act and amendments to this Act in 1983. By 1988, the substance of the Court's judgment was not so surprising as the means by which it made its arguments, namely, the purposive interpretation of relevant Acts of Parliament. The plain words of the Equal Pay Act and the amendments failed to provide the "correct" result, that is, the result that yielded compliance of the UK law with its own European obligations. "It is plain," argued Lord Keith, "that Parliament cannot possibly have intended such a failure" (Bradley 1988). After *Pickstone*, the use of judicial review becomes even more pronounced in the Factortame cases (1990, 1991) and the Equal Opportunities case in 1994.

The web of practices lacing together European law, the changing practices of the British Parliament, and the role of courts at both the European and national levels also have an implication for the constitutional entrenchment of rights in the UK legal order.

The entrenchment of rights, the guarantee of their provision in the face of popular pressures to the contrary, hence their insulation from the changing fortunes of public opinion and legislatures, has long been considered an important aspect of democracy. It is ironic that the UK, perhaps the earliest and longest-lasting democracy, does not have an entrenched system of rights. Why is a constitutional guarantee of basic rights so difficult in a parliamentary system? The usual answer given to this question is that while a particular Parliament could pass a series of fundamental rights as part of ordinary legislation, a later Parliament could as easily repeal it. Later acts of Parliament trump earlier acts.

Judicial review alters the balance of forces in favor of constitutional entrenchment. One non-obvious implication of judicial review is that it requires that the UK Parliament cannot overturn an earlier Act of Parliament that is implied by the legal order of the EU. This has important results. The doctrine of implied repeal, by which recent Parliamentary acts overturn (repeal) earlier ones is now restricted to areas to which EU law does not apply. For example, without specifically repealing the UK Accession Act, Parliament cannot pass a new law on equal pay or equal treatment that conflicts with its obligations under EU law. Thus, the UK Parliament not only accepts judicial review but must reject UK statutes passed after accession if they conflict with EU law. The result of this chain of events is a partial constitutional entrenchment of rights (if particular policies become defined as rights based in the Treaty) for citizens in the United Kingdom (Levitsky 1994:355). These rights, limited but growing, are insulated by several layers of institutional protection, all the way up to UK repeal of the Accession Act of 1972. This in turn would imply withdrawal from the EU

The growth of judicial review and the changing balance between Parliament and the courts has profound implications for the UK domestic institutional order. Parliamentary statutes were without equivocation the law of the land and were not subject to scrutiny or repeal by any other institution. In this process of deep institutional change, an external authority structure has become centrally important.

Conclusion

Territory, authority, and sovereignty. This is the triad of concepts on which this article seeks to build. The purest expression of territory is Newtonian space. By itself it tells the politically interested person little. But melded to a particular kind of authority structure—sovereign authority structures—the political content of space takes on significance. The fusion of sovereign public authority with physical space defined by exact borders is the fundamental organizing principle of the modern world. These three properties, together, define the territorial state.

A presumption of this article, something assumed rather than demonstrated, is that the territorial state is a historical phenomenon. The medieval world was not organized according to this principle (Ruggie 1993; Spruyt 1994; and Reus-

Smit 1999). In the medieval world authority was parcellized, personalized, and despatialized. Parcellization implied no overarching rule for all matters in all contexts. The particular issue and the context provided the rules. The medieval world was characterized by a multiplicity of discrete issues with distinct rule systems and codes of conduct. Inayatullah's (1995) fascinating account of the multiple uses of landed property in eighteenth-century Bengal and the changes brought about by the British attempt to fuse habitation, work on the land, and responsibility for tax revenue, illustrates the transforming effect of "modernizing colonialism" in South Asia. In the modern world, consolidation of functions, or the fusion of different functions with a politicized space, is typical. In the medieval world, the proliferation of authorities within a common space was normal. It was not unusual for the governance of a group of people to depend on thousands of separate authorities, thus confusing the distinction between inside and outside and making the concept of "external affairs" itself problematic (Kratochwil 1986:33).

Personalization implied that rights and duties were individual, that is, attached to particular persons, rather than to institutions. The aspatial ontology of this world implied that rule was not organized over a demarcated territory. To be sure, rule took place somewhere; it had its sites. But the idea of rule was not limited by a conception of permanent borders within which such rule applied and outside of which it did not apply. The habitual, accepted, taken-for-granted aspect of rule was not organized by a conception of a bounded territory.

The Westphalian turn provided movement on all three dimensions: from parcellization to consolidation; from personalization to rationalization; and from an aspatial social ontology to one that is territorial. Our modern understanding of society and politics, and related concepts of citizenship, nationalism, political development, and the franchise, are thoroughly conditioned by the overarching framework of the territorial state.

The development of the Westphalian state involved a consolidation of rule, a pulling together of separate, semifeudal domains of rule into one single framework of public authority. Today we take for granted a centralized state with vertical lines of authority, a normative hierarchy adjudicated by courts or enforced by the powerful, and a stilling of those voices who would make policy (especially foreign policy) on their own. When the United States Supreme Court renders a decision that the state of Massachusetts may not make a law controlling the foreign economic relations of firms inside its borders, we do not blink an eye. When Arafat is told he must control the violence of all the factions within the Palestinian movement before statehood can be successfully claimed, we also do not think that anything is amiss. Centralized consolidated rule is taken for granted.

Rule has become increasingly depersonalized. It has become rationalized, normalized, more a matter of routine and role than personal traits. Authority is thought to flow from the office. Governing implies rule by law and procedure rather than by particular people. To a certain extent, the modern state—particularly the democratic state—is composed of a bundle of procedures. This is the aspect of rule emphasized most strongly by Bobbio in *The Future of Democracy: A Defense of the Rules of the Game* (1987).

Finally, over the *longue duree'* considered here, rule increasingly takes place within the territorial container of the state. Authority over believers or members of one's tribe outside the borders of the state is weak at best, and nonexistent often in fact. The term *diaspora* refers to a group of people who are separated from their fellow nationals by a territorial border. Citizenship is defined by membership in a territorially marked community. Laws are applied within state borders though extraterritorial application does take place. The distinction between the people inside and outside, between us and them, is strong. Agnew (1994) warns us to avoid the "territorial trap" of thinking that bounded territory provides a perfect container for organizing public and private affairs. It is just as important to avoid backgrounding the territorial aspects of the state, thus underestimating its power and authority.

To test such a broad thesis, broad in terms of temporal sweep and the comprehensiveness of social, economic, and political forces, is well beyond the scope of this article and the volume as a whole. At best, we as a group attempt a series of probes to tease out the meaning and logic of parts of the overall Westphalian phenomenon. My own contribution to this volume focuses on the significance of a short experience of one of the earliest states—the United Kingdom—within the context of its membership in the European Union. Persuaded to enter due to increasing economic ties to the EU countries, along with the decline in the importance of the Commonwealth and the European Free Trade Association (EFTA), the UK found itself ensnared from a most unlikely source, the legal authority of the European Court of Justice. In preserving its sovereignty, the national veto in the Council of Ministers was of no help. And opting out of the thickening system of European law proved more than difficult. Defenders of the European legal order could point out that the good justices in Luxembourg were not a bunch of radicals; they were merely reminding the British of the full content of the document signed in 1973.

The British position—that it has delegated to the EU the authority to be overruled in certain matters within the scope of Pillar One, and so retains ultimate authority—seems less and less an effective response. Under pressure from the ECJ, the UK has rewritten domestic equality legislation, amended numerous domestic acts, and altered the rights of women with regard to part-time work, pensions, and maternity rights. Fragments of European citizenship are emerging as part of a Court-inspired jurisprudence based on a European constitution (not "treaty" as it is literally called) and a distinct body of European law. Admittedly, the content of European citizenship is economic and strongly conditioned by market participation. To this extent, it can be referred to as "thin citizenship" (Caporaso 2000). But the market is a broad and powerful institution, more subtle than most allow, and it has an ingenious capacity to insinuate itself into spheres of social life thought of as noneconomic. Only time will tell how broad the impact of the market will be but my bets are placed with the Polanyi school rather than the neoclassical "arms-length economists."

External authority, an emerging but entrenched system of rights directed from the "outside," and a mingling of domestic courts and an international court add up to a decoupling of territory and rule. The objection that external authority is accepted by the UK authorities is no objection at all. It could be no other way. An external power forcing its will or manipulating material incentives would quickly be seen for what it is—the traditional exercise of external power in the face of efforts to retain domestic autonomy. When external forces present themselves as "right to rule," even superior right to rule, we come closer to threatening the core of the Westphalian order. Transformation of rule based on a loosening of the couplings among territory, authority, and sovereignty implies a deeper change than those based on changing power configurations.

I have taken pains to show that changes in the structure of authority are occurring and that these are not reducible to changes in power and autonomy. Changes in the British institutional order are different from greater constraints on policy autonomy in the face of globalization or decreased ability to control borders. But is my argument about the intrusion of external authority different from a straightforward account of change based on external normative pressures? The short answer, which is the only one given here, is "yes." Normative change, as illustrated by Klotz's (1995) account of the battle for racial equality internationally, relies on a type of persuasion. Persuasion differs from power and inducement in that it does not involve the manipulation of positive and negative incentives. It differs from coercion in that it does not rely on force. It differs from strategic manipulation in that information is not asymmetrically distributed. And it differs from counsel in that the ends as well as means-ends knowledge are at stake. Normative change involves persuasion to certain ends and commitments to certain principles. Since persuasion and acceptance of rule are part of the intrusion of external authority, how does the latter concept differ from pure normative change?

To be sure, persuasion is present in the mix of reasons for accepting external authority. But the simple acceptance of an international norm implies little about the overall structure of public authority. The external authority of the ECJ is not total but neither is it ad hoc. The scope of its authority is set out in the Treaty, in the Court's interpretation of it, and in the patterns of resistance and acceptance of the member states. Nevertheless, when the ECJ renders a judgement, the expectation is obedience. This can hardly be said of the kinds of normative change dealt with in international relations, where often hard battles have to be fought and where outcomes are uncertain, in order to effect change. In Klotz's example, changing norms of racial equality took place through intense bargaining within the United States. Key to the changes she describes were the efforts of Black power and Black civil rights activists to forge a domestic consensus against support of the South African government.

The burden of this volume is that the Westphalian order did not come into existence overnight. The year 1648 was preceded by centuries of preparation and followed by centuries of competition among rival forms of rule, and consolidation and weakening of Westphalian parameters. If and when this system changes, in the fundamental ways of which Ruggie (1993) speaks, we will only know it long after the time has past. The owl of Minerva spreads its wings only at dusk.

References

Agnew, John. (1994). The Territorial Trap: The Geographical Assumptions of International Relations Theory. *Review of International Political Economy* **1**(1):53–80.

Alter, Karen. (1998) Who Are the 'Masters of the Treaty'? European Governments and the European Court of Justice. *International Organization* **52**(1):121–147.

Arendt, Hannah. (1961) *Between Past and Future*. New York: Viking Press.

Aron, Raymond. (1974) Is Multinational Citizenship Possible? *Social Research* **41**(2): 638–656.

Ashley, Richard K. (1988) "Untying the Sovereign State: A Double Reading of the Anarchy Problematique. *Millennium: Journal of International Studies* **17**(2):227–262.

Bartolini, Stefano. (1997) Exit Options, Boundary Building, Political Structuring. Manuscript, pp. 1–54, European University Institute, Florence, Italy.

Blaney, David L., and Naeem Inayatullah. (2000) The Westphalian Deferral. In this volume.

Bobbio, Norberto. (1987) *The Future of Democracy: A Defense of the Rules of the Game*. Minneapolis: University of Minnesota Press.

Bradley, A. W. (1988) The Courts, Community Law, and Equal Pay: A Constitutional Case? *Public Law* **32**:485–494.

Brubaker, Rogers. (1992) *Citizenship and Nationhood in France and Germany*. Cambridge, MA: Harvard University Press.

Bueno de Mesquita, Bruce. (2000) Popes, Kings, and Endogenous Institutions: The Concordat of Worms and the Origins of Sovereignty. In this volume.

BURLEY, ANNE-MARIE, AND WALTER MATTLI. (1993) Europe Before the Court: A Political Theory of Legal Integration. *International Organization* **47**(1):41–76.

CAPORASO, JAMES A. (2000) "Transnational Markets, Thin Citizenship, and Democratic Rights in the European Union: From Cradle to Grave or from Job to Job?" Paper presented at annual meeting of the International Studies Association, March 14–19, Los Angeles, California, pp. 1–18.

CAPORASO, JAMES A., AND JOSEPH JUPILLE. (1999) "Sovereignty and Territoriality in the European Union: Defending the UK Institutional Order." Paper presented at a workshop on territoriality and the nation-state, December 10–11, Berkeley, California, pp. 1–30.

CAPORASO, JAMES A., AND JOSEPH JUPILLE. (2000) "The Europeanization of Gender Equality Policy and Domestic Structural Change." In *Transforming Europe: Europeanization and Domestic Change*, edited by Maria Green Cowles, James A. Caporaso, and Thomas Risse, pp. 1–45. Ithaca, New York: Cornell University Press.

CAREY, JOHN, AND MATTHEW S. SHUGART. (1998) *Executive Decree Authority*. Cambridge, England: Cambridge University Press.

CLARKE, LINDA. (1984) Equal Pay for Work of Equal Value. *New Law Review* **24** (February):177–184.

COWLES, MARIA GREEN, JAMES A. CAPORASO, AND THOMAS RISSE, EDS. (2000) *Transforming Europe: Europeanization and Structural Change*. Ithaca, New York: Cornell University Press.

CURTIN, DEIDRE M. (1997) *Postnational Democracy: The European Union in Search of a Political Philosophy*. The Hague: Kluwer Law.

CUTLER, CLAIRE A. (1999) Locating 'Authority' in the Global Political Economy. *International Studies Quarterly* **43**(1):59–81.

DEUTSCH, KARL W. ET AL. (1957) *Political Community and the North Atlantic Area*. Princeton, New Jersey: Princeton University Press.

GRUBER, LLOYD. (2000) *Ruling the World: Power Politics and the Rise of Supranational Institutions*. Princeton, NJ: Princeton University Press.

HATCH, WALTER, AND KOZO YAMAMURA. (1996) *Asia in Japan's Embrace*. Cambridge, U.K.: Cambridge University Press.

HINSLEY, F. H. (1986 [1966]) *Sovereignty*. Cambridge: Cambridge University Press.

INAYATULLAH, NAEEM. (1995) "Retrieving Multiple and Overlapping Claims to Territory." Manuscript, pp 1–32, Syracuse University, Syracuse, New York.

Jackson, Robert H., and Carl G. Rosberg. (1982) Why Africa's Weak States Persist: The Empirical and the Juridical in Statehood. *World Politics* **35**(1):1–24.

Klotz, Audie. (1995) Norms Reconstituting Interests: Global Racial Equality and U.S. Sanctions against South Africa. *International Organization* **49**(3):441–478.

Krasner, Stephen D. (1995/1996) Compromising Westphalia. *International Security* **20**(3):115–151.

Krasner, Stephen D. (1999) *Sovereignty:Organized Hypocrisy*. Princeton, New Jersey: Princeton University Press.

Kratochwil, Friedrich. (1986) Of Systems, Boundaries, and Territoriality: An Inquiry into the Formation of the State System. *World Politics* **39**(1):27–52.

Levitsky, Jonathan E. (1994) The Europeanization of the British Legal Style. *The American Journal of Comparative Law* **42**(2):347–380.

Linklater, Andrew. (1998) *The Transformation of Political Community*. Columbia, SC: University of South Carolina Press.

Litfin, Karen T. (1997) Sovereignty in World Ecopolitics. *Mershon International Studies Review* **41**(supplement 2):167–204.

Mancini, G. Federico. (1991) The Making of a Constitution for Europe. In *The New European Community*, edited by Robert O. Keohane and Stanley Hoffmann, pp. 177–194. Boulder, Colorado: Westview Press.

Mancini, G. Federico, and David T. Keeling. (1994) Democracy and the European Court of Justice. *The Modern Law Review* **57**(2):175–190.

Marshall, T. H. (1973) *Class, Citizenship, and Social Development*. Westport, Connecticut: Greenwood Press.

Onuf, Nicholas. (1991) Sovereignty: Outline of a Conceptual History. *Alternatives* **16**(4):425–446.

Parsons, Talcott. (1967) "On the Concept of Political Power." In *Sociological Theory and Modern Society*, edited by Talcott Parsons, pp. 297–354. New York: The Free Press.

Reus-Smit, Christian. (1999) *The Moral Purpose of the State: Culture, Identity, and Institutional Rationality in International Relations*. Princeton, New Jersey: Princeton University Press.

Ruggie, John Gerard. (1993) Territoriality and Beyond: Problematizing Modernity in International Relations. *International Organization* **47**(1):139–174.

SANDHOLTZ, WAYNE, AND ALEC STONE SWEET, EDS. (1998) *European Integration and Supranational Governance*. Oxford, England: Oxford University Press.

SHAW, JO. (1999) Postnational Constitutionalism in the European Union. *Journal of European Public Policy* **6**(4):579–597.

SHUGART, MATTHEW S., AND JOHN M. CAREY (1992). Presidents and Assemblies: Constitutional Design and Electoral Dynamics. Cambridge, U.K.: Cambridge University Press.

SPRUYT, HENDRIK. (1994) *The Sovereign State and Its Competitors*. Princeton, New Jersey: Princeton University Press.

STONE SWEET, ALEC. (1995) "Constitutional Dialogues in the European Community." *RSC Working Paper*, no.95/38, pp. 1–28. European University Institute, Florence, Italy.

STONE SWEET, ALEC. (2000) *Governing with Judges: Constitutional Politics in Europe*. Oxford, England: Oxford University Press.

STONE SWEET, ALEC, AND JAMES A. CAPORASO. (1998) "From Free Trade to Supranational Polity: The European Court and Integration." In *European Integration and Supranational Governance*, edited by Wayne Sandholtz and Alec Stone Sweet, pp. 92–133. Oxford, England: Oxford University Press.

THOMSON, JANICE E. (1994) *Mercenaries, Pirates, and Sovereigns*. Princeton, New Jersey: Princeton University Press.

THOMSON, JANICE E. (1995) State Sovereignty in International Relations: Bridging the Gap between Theory and Empirical Research. *International Studies Quarterly* **39**(2):213–233.

TILLY, CHARLES. (1992) *Coercion, Capital, and European States, AD 900–1992*. Malden, MA: Blackwell Publishers.

WALKER, R. B. J. (1993) *Inside/Outside: International Relations as Political Theory*. Cambridge: Cambridge University Press.

WALTZ, KENNETH N. (1959) *Man, the State, and War: A Theoretical Analysis*. New York: Columbia University Press.

WALTZ, KENNETH N. (1979) *Theory of International Politics*. New York: Random House.

WEBER, MAX. (1947) *The Theory of Social and Economic Organization*. New York: Oxford University Press.

WIENER, ANTJE. (n.d.) The Constructive Potential of Citizenship: Building European Union. *Policy and Politics* **27**(3):271–293.

WRONG, DENNIS H. (1988 [1979]) *Power: Its Forms, Bases, and Uses*. Chicago: University of Chicago Press.

The Westphalian Deferral

David L. Blaney

Macalester College

Naeem Inayatullah[1]

Ithaca College

> *There may be no rational way to convert to our point of view people who honestly hold other positions, but we cannot short-circuit such disagreements. Instead, we should live with them, as further evidence of the diversity of human life. Later on, these differences may be resolved by further shared experience, which allows different schools to converge. In advance of this experience, we must accept this diversity of views in a spirit of toleration. Tolerating the resulting plurality, ambiguity, or the lack of certainty is no error, let alone a sin.*
>
> —Stephen Toulmin (1990:30)

Only fairly recently has sovereignty appeared to us once again as a puzzle. A review of academic and popular discourse suggests that the political and ethical certainties associated with the nation-state are under assault by, variously, the inexorable forces of globalization, the transnational mobilization of environmental and human rights activists, the progressive emer-

[1]This essay is a shortened version of a longer paper and a small part of a larger manuscript. We thank Kurt Burch, Zillah Eisenstein, Chip Gagnon, Patrick Thaddeus Jackson, Alexander Moon, Nicholas Onuf, and members of the IR Colloquium at the University of Minnesota for helpful comments on an earlier draft.

Published by Blackwell Publishers, 350 Main Street, Malden, MA 02148, USA, and 108 Cowley Road, Oxford OX4 1JF, UK.

gence of global governance, and the persuasive deconstruction of borders and identities.[2] The sense that humankind is thereby facing an uncharted future has also generated historical and theoretical interest in "Westphalia," with the expectation that critical reflection on the origins, principles, and purposes of the state system might help us identify the materials and strategies by which we can re-make the world (see Walker 1993; Spruyt 1994; Ferguson and Mansbach 1996; Ruggie 1998; Onuf 1998; and Van Creveld 1999).

We share the supposition that a return to the puzzle of sovereignty is important for political and ethical inquiry. Cutting against the grain of much contemporary academic practice, however, we believe that sovereignty—as theory and practice—remains a site of political and ethical possibilities. Rather than being simply an ethical dead end or a site of political closure, the problems posed by sovereignty contain opportunities that extend, stretch, divide, and revise more than they fully transcend sovereignty as conventionally located and understood.[3] One such problem, the focus of this paper, concerns the way the principle of formal equality among states—central to sovereignty and implied in Westphalia—intensifies the difficulties we face in responding to differences in culture, religion, and mode of life. How does this "problem of difference" emerge with Westphalia?

Perhaps ironically, differences in culture or way of life may remain less of a problem in an age of empire where the principle of hierarchy reigns supreme. As Michael Walzer (1997:15) suggests, "[i]mperial rule is historically the most successful way of incorporating difference and facilitating (requiring is more accurate) peaceful coexistence." Subjugated peoples, though excluded from the apex of the social order and usually marked as inferior, paradoxically may find a kind of sufferance of their way of life, religious practices, and distinct customs. Walzer (1997:14–16) argues that this form of tolerance is partly rooted in a sense of "minimal fairness" that the imperial center extends to the conquered, but is largely a practical matter: as long as imperial rule is respected—taxes are paid and imperial authority is acknowledged—further subordination is unnecessary, except in the case of threats to internal order. Preserving the peace of the empire may entail not only imperial sufferance, but also enforce-

---

[2]Popular accounts include Barber (1995), Greider (1997), and Friedman (1999). The academic literature is increasingly drawn to such conclusions. See MacMillan and Linklater (1995), Lyons and Mastanduno (1995), Falk (1995), Lipschutz and Mayer (1996), Weiss and Gordenker (1996), Weber and Biersteker (1996), and Shapiro and Alker (1996).

[3]Our earlier work (Inayatullah and Blaney, 1995; Blaney and Inayatullah, 1996) reflects and represents a defense of this belief.

ment of peaceful coexistence among the "authority structures and customary practices" of the various conquered groups. And, though tolerance is extended primarily to groups rather than individuals (this is not a liberal world!), individuals may to some degree escape the pressures for communal conformity in the more cosmopolitan cities of the empire.

These days we are less comfortable with hierarchy and we cannot sanction imperial practice. Relatively speaking, the rise of the principle of equality serves to de-legitimate and break the hold of the monopoly of social and political power of a restricted group. But where groups of all sorts and persuasions are placed on more equal (legal, if not social) footing, the imperial solution of sufferance of the subservient "other" is mostly foreclosed. When the equality of the "other" is acknowledged, we require the affirmation of the "other" to secure our own status. However, the presence of differences in way of life, values, and visions also challenges the givenness of our particular social practices and threatens the certainty of our sense of self (Benjamin 1988: chapter 2). Michael Walzer (1983:249–54) also points in this direction, explaining that hierarchical orders resolve the problem of recognition by giving everyone a fixed place in the social order. Whenever such a ranking is absent or breaks down, we are presented with a potential challenge to our sense of our own value and become unsure of our relations to others. In this way, the problem of difference intensifies as it emerges under modern conditions of relative equality, leading often to the re-assertion of (illicit or informal) forms of social hierarchy—the marking of the "other" as inferior and thereby less of a threat. How then should we reconcile need and threat? How do we achieve equality with difference? This problem remains central to modernity (Todorov 1986; Fraser 1997: chapter 1).

Reading back from this contemporary angle, in section two we examine the Peace of Westphalia in its historical context: as a response to the "religious cleansing" and material and psychological devastation of the Thirty Years' War. We characterize the Thirty Years' War as a crusade against difference, involving an equation of difference and inferiority that justifies efforts to assimilate or eliminate the "other."[4] Though Westphalia is conventionally understood as marking a transition to a secular and more tolerant modern order, we argue that the settlements of the time represent only an initial and foundering effort to address the problem of difference. The Peace of Westphalia, in our reading, was little more than an acknowledgement that the attempt to eradicate the religious "other" had reached an impasse. While the settlement fostered an external détente among

[4]We draw this formulation from Todorov (1986). We have examined Todorov's work at much greater length elsewhere (Blaney and Inayatullah, 1994; Inayatullah and Blaney, 1996).

states—a restraint supported by a relative balance of forces and the moral injunction of mutual restraint among sovereigns—it did little to break the conception and practical delineation of difference as an inferiority to be eradicated. Rather, the Peace was an attempt to formally contain difference within states so as to avoid the destruction of international war. The price of this move was to sanctify the continuation of conquest, purification, and conversion within a ruler's realm. More strongly perhaps, Westphalia appears as an act of evasion or deferral—less a direct effort to acknowledge, confront, and explore the diversity of human existence than an attempt to contain and manage difference within the newly erected boundaries of states. Westphalian arrangements thus have served only to secure the persistence, salience, and centrality of the problem of difference in international society: as an enduring diversity within national boundaries, as a diversity that spills inevitably across boundaries, and as conflict between "imagined" nations.

We argue that the intellectual legacy of the period is likewise limiting. As do similar fears in our own time, the chaos and destruction of the period produced a proportionately intense demand for order, safety, and certainty. An overriding demand for stability in society at large spurred the dominant seventeenth-century project of discovering unassailable knowledge of natural and social order—a social theory and practice beyond the dangers and doubts a confrontation with difference creates. Just as the Westphalian settlement attempted to sidestep the uncertainties and conflicts accompanying difference, the intellectual discourse arising under the shadow of the Thirty Years' War denigrated the positive potentials of difference, tightly tying it to chaos and strife. Thus the heritage of political thought bequeathed to us by this period—from Descartes to Hobbes, Grotius, and Locke—tends to base social order and political peace on relative religious and cultural homogeneity and a strict political uniformity.

Returning explicitly to the present, we argue in section three that we continue to live with the consequences of this deferral or evasion. The contemporary theory and practice of the Westphalian system—or "international society" as we will generally call it—functions primarily to reinforce this suspicion of difference. In international society, the "other" is located outside, beyond the boundaries of the state. Within the state, a realm of relative "sameness" is presumed—the kind of commonality we associate with the idea of political community or the body politic. But the problem of difference remains, if obscured or repressed. The "other" lurks as a perpetual threat in the form of separate political communities or as difference within, vitiating the presumed but rarely, if ever, achieved "sameness." Against the presumption of domestic commonality, difference is "managed" by some combination of hierarchy, assimilation, and tolerance in varying degrees and kinds. Difference beyond our boundaries is left to its own means, interdicted at border crossings, and balanced and deterred.

Thus, though we are unable to accept the legitimacy of the kind of eradication of difference within states originally sanctioned in the seventeenth century, the legacy of the Westphalian deferral endures in that we remain unwilling to confront fully the Pandora's box of either our own domestic diversity or the worldwide diversity of ways of life.

In large measure, this is merely a restatement of the power of the logic of "inside/outside"—a demarcation of global political space into distinct and mutually exclusive jurisdictions on which a society of independent sovereign states depends (Walker 1993). The "inside/outside" logic thereby performs an act of "splitting," excluding the overlap of "self" and "other" (Benjamin 1988:62–63).[5] Locating difference beyond the boundaries of "self" impedes our capacity to fully acknowledge and affirm the "other" that always lies within, or to appreciate and claim the "self" that exists as part of the "other" beyond these boundaries. That is, unless we can respond creatively to this exclusivity of "self" and "other," exposing and cultivating the spaces that connect "self" and "other"—the overlaps of commonality and difference—we cannot find a way to allow equality and difference to coexist. Fortunately, some theoretical and practical avenues are already present as recessive moments within various accounts of the contemporary meaning and workings of the Westphalian settlements. In the concluding section of this essay, we briefly explore these avenues and their implications.

From a Purifying Hatred to an Empire of Uniformity

Most historians consider the Thirty Years' War—and the Peace of Westphalia that brought it to a close—to be among the major events of the latter half of the millennium. Ronald Asch (1997:7) calls the Thirty Years' War "the best example of a political event which profoundly changed political and social structures, and perhaps even collective mentalities." The decisiveness of these events is sealed by the predominant view of the Peace of Westphalia as signaling the move from a religious to a modern, secular world and from the accepted, if somewhat vaporous, goal of a united Christendom to a system, or perhaps society, of independent states (Thomson 1963:814; Pages 1970:17, 250). There is nothing foreign about this interpretation: the decisiveness of

---

[5] Though Benjamin (1988:63) explains that "splitting" has a "narrow, technical use" in psychoanalytic thought, she suggests that, when applied to "supraindividual" processes, it also carries a "broader metapsychological and metaphoric meaning."

these events is asserted, if not taken for granted, by most of the field of international relations.[6]

This period is indeed notable for the central role played by religious conviction in instigating military conflict. While legal and political motivations—such as the limits of the Emperor's authority and dynastic rivalry—were certainly present, such factors took on a distinctly religious hue. Just as we today perceive the ubiquity of the economic motive (whether narrowly or broadly conceived), both the ruling classes and the masses of the sixteenth and seventeenth centuries are said to have seen the events of their time through a distinctly religious gaze (Thomson 1963:800; Brightwell 1979:418; Langer 1980:11; Lockhart 1995:1–2; Asch 1997:7). The religious conflict flaring up in the sixteenth century and all but consuming the seventeenth century found its initial spark in the Reformation's challenge to the ideological monopoly and material power of the Catholic Church (Friedrich and Blitzer 1957:10–11; Van Creveld 1999:67–84). This challenge persisted and escalated with the spread of various forms of Protestantism among the masses and the conversion of certain territorial princes in Germany. Put in terms we introduced above, the "other" demanding recognition was experienced as a pressing threat. Princes loyal to Catholicism leapt to or were drawn into a defense of the Universal Church—a Counter-Reformation led by the Habsburgs, the Holy Roman Emperor, and the Papacy. Protestants responded in kind, and both sides mobilized for war. Years of indecisive hostility were brought to a temporary halt by the Peace of Augsburg (1555).

---

[6] See, for example, Gross (1968:47), Bull (1977:27–38), Morgenthau (1967:299), Herz (1959:43–44), Ruggie (1998:188), Linklater (1998:23–24), Van Creveld (1999:86, 159–60), and Spruyt (1994:178–79, 191–92). However, two kinds of protest have arisen recently within international relations. The first, exemplified by Stephen Krasner's "Westphalia and All That" (1993), takes aim at this narrative in order to dispute the decisiveness of ideas in constituting the state system. His discussion of the ambiguities of the Peace of Westphalia—its failure to break fully with the Medieval order—is instructive, though not at all sufficient to defeat the idea that theory and practice are inextricably intertwined. His later (1999) claims that sovereignty has always been honored in the breach, accommodating various forms of rule, is similarly important. More telling is his conclusion (1999:235) that "Constitutive rules never exclude alternatives." Ironically, Krasner imagines that his dissenting views about sovereignty support IR (international relations) orthodoxy. In contrast, David Strang (1996:45) takes this contestability as definitive of a "constructivist" approach. David Campbell (1992: chapter 2) similarly makes clear that the narrative of a clear medieval-modern break is used to sanctify the identities forged by the state system. We remain intrigued (and puzzled) by Krasner's position, but more comfortable with Strang's and Campbell's views.

From our point of view, Augsburg appears as an initial and meager attempt to come to terms with the problem of difference: it "confirmed the independence of the princes from the emperor" by recognizing the principle *cuius regio eius religio*—the right of rulers to fix the religion of their own subjects (Thomson 1963:791). This worked best in practice where jurisdictions were "fractured and fragmented," such that "people of deep religious commitments need not move far to find, either a ruler who shared their convictions, or a tolerant free city." It worked less well in an "extensive, long-unified territory," where migration to a safe haven of co-religionists was more difficult (Toulmin 1990:49–50). It is the limits of Augsburg that stand out, however. The right of individual conscience was not recognized, and tolerance was established only between Catholic and Lutheran princes, excluding Calvinists, Zwinglians, Anabaptists, and other sects. In addition, even the minimal tolerance established by the treaty was seen by the signatories as an act of prudence in the face of a balance of forces, merely a pause in an ongoing struggle to eliminate the religious "other." As Asch (1997:10) describes the situation:

> Those who signed the Peace of Augsburg . . . did not yet see this principle as the essence of the settlement as clearly as the lawyers interpreting the Peace later were to do; for they had not yet given up the hope of reestablishing some sort of religious unity.

As would also be the case with the later Peace of Westphalia, the Catholic Church refused to accept the principle of tolerance among princes. The Emperors—Charles V (1519–1556) and Ferdinand I (1556–1564)—saw the settlement as undermining the special relationship of Empire and Church (or Empire and God). Protestant princes and states tended also to accept the arrangements as provisional (Thomson 1963:500–01; Pages 1970:37; Parker 1997:16–17).

The outcome seems scripted, and we are tempted to read the Thirty Years' War as the inevitable culmination of a long period of religious zealotry in which difference is translated into inferiority and an object to be eradicated, on the one hand, and as the prelude to a more tolerant modernity on the other. While the events of the seventeenth century are usually read in this way, Stephen Toulmin warns us against accepting such a view too readily. He argues instead that the sixteenth century also offered an alternative, more tolerant theory and practice than is suggested by the usual retrospective reading of the Medieval period as the antithesis and precursor of the Modern. For example, in Erasmus, Montaigne, and Shakespeare, Toulmin finds "an urbane open-mindedness and skeptical tolerance," reflecting the Renaissance's impatience with the quest for religious or philosophical certainty as well as its relative "respect for complexity and diversity" (Toulmin 1990:25–30; quotations on

25 and 29).[7] Similarly, in Henry IV of France, he finds a political practice that turns gradually towards greater tolerance of the Protestant Huguenots, despite domestic and external opposition. However, when Henry's assassination in 1610 brought his experiment to an end, the event was interpreted widely as a failure of the policy of tolerance: this was a "confirmation of people's worst fears" and "dashed the last hope of escaping from irresoluble conflicts" (Toulmin 1990:46–53, quotation on 48; see also Van Creveld 1999:72). The equation of difference and danger was seen as vindicated with savage results.

Emperor Ferdinand II's defeat of the Bohemian rebels and his intensification of religious persecution reverberated throughout Europe, irrevocably shattering the uneasy stalemate. This phase of Counter-Reformation was prosecuted as a "consuming passion" with the tools of "fire and sword" (Wedel 1991:51; Parker 1997:75–76). Though not all rulers welcomed these provocations or the eventual outbreak of open warfare, the prospect of losing a religious war and being subjected to the religious dictates of the victor generated an anxiety difficult to bear. Protestants and Catholics alike mobilized to resist this possibility; neutrality became almost impossible (Trevor-Roper 1962:39–40; Brightwell 1979:418–19; Gutmann, 1988:767–68; Parker 1997:75–76). In this context, piety was translated into a clear and certain response to difference—an attempt to eliminate alternative modes of Christian belief and practice by conquest, persecution, and purification.

The resulting conflict is infamous for the material devastation, but also the social, moral, and psychic scars it left across Europe. Trevor-Roper (1962:33) considers it the "greatest and most destructive war in preindustrial Europe." Toulmin (1990:53) is more expansive in his characterization of its effects on Central Europe:

> For thirty years, in a series of brutal and destructive military campaigns, shifting alliances of outside powers used the territory of Germany and Bohemia as a gladiatorial ring in which to fight out their political rivalries and doctrinal disagreements, most often by proxy, and turned the Czech and German lands into a charnel house.

Perhaps a better sense is provided by comparison with a more contemporary reference. Geoffrey Parker (1997:192–93) notes:

> Until 1939, the Thirty Years' War remained by far the most traumatic period in the history of Germany. The loss of people was proportionally greater than in World War II; the displacement of the people and the material devastation was

---

[7] On the importance of Montaigne, see also Richard Tuck (1988:23–24) and David Boucher (1998:23).

> almost as great; the cultural and economic dislocation persisted for substantially longer.

And, following Charles Weeks (1991:213), we might describe the events as a cataclysm foreshadowing those of our own time: the Thirty Years' War was a total ideological war, ushering in a "modernist" period in which the "unfolding disasters of war"—runaway inflation, the spiraling of continuous military engagement, and the "phalanx of disease, hunger, and chaos"—crashed down on civilian populations. John Theibault (1995:1–2) reports that the Thirty Years' War is selected (still today and by a wide margin) by Hessian villagers as "the greatest calamity to befall their villages" in the period bounded by the Black Death and World War II. We would, then, along with Herbert Langer (1980:10), emphasize the devastating psychic wounds left on populations—both masses and ruling groups.

Surely an important reason for the extremes of destruction is that armies were maintained in the field continuously for nearly the duration of the War. Troops became, in Herbert Langer's term (1980:97), "marauding baggage-trains," draining the resources of the countryside and spreading terror and epidemics in their wake (Nichols 1989:261–63; Theibault 1995:141–42, 151–60). Conscription, fed by heavy battlefield losses and the unremitting toll of disease, depopulated villages across Germany, Sweden, Finland, and elsewhere. Military service became a veritable death sentence (Lynn 1991:95; Parker 1997:186–88). However, if the length of the war helps explain the magnitude of the destruction, this factor cannot easily account for the savagery displayed by combatants.

Toulmin (1990:54) argues that the doctrinaire character of the religiosity fed the frenzy of killing:

> The longer the bloodshed continued, the more paradoxical the state of Europe became. Whether for pay or from conviction, there were many who would kill and burn in the name of theological doctrines that no one could give any conclusive reason for accepting. The intellectual debate between Protestant Reformers and their Counter-Reformation opponents had collapsed, and there was no alternative to the sword and the torch. Yet the more brutal the warfare became, the more firmly convinced the proponents of each religious system were that their doctrines *must be* proved correct, and that their opponents were stupid, malicious, or both.

We should not be surprised, then, that the barbarities were unspeakable, of a kind some trace to this time (Langer 1980:101), though recognizable in the events of our own century. The pillaging of the countryside was accompanied by torture and rape, often including children and pregnant women. No religious grouping was spared; nor were the religious dissenters less cruel than their persecutors (Lynn 1991:94; Wedel 1991:42–45; Parker 1997:186–88). The savagery reached such a scale that the inhabitants of Styria, who had contributed generously to Emperor Ferdinand's coffers, claimed that his armies has caused more destruction and suffering than the dreaded Turks (Nichols 1989:261–263). And one of the Hutterite brethren, a group subjected to perhaps the worst indignities, compared the infidels favorably to their fellow Christians: "Even Turks and Tartars . . . would have said it was too much." Thus Wedel, echoing Toulmin's analysis with which we began, takes the treatment of the Hutterites as evidence of the power of a "purifying hatred" (Wedel 1991:46–47).

Purifying hatred, one might imagine, burns with great fury but can also exhaust itself, especially when joined by an equally furious fire. Indeed, it is argued that exhaustion again led the combatants to a series of peace tables and the resulting treaties are usually labeled the Peace of Westphalia. Historian Georges Pages' view (1970:250) is emblematic of the interpretation usually ascribed to this set of events:

> The peace of Westphalia substituted the idea of independent states, a sort of international society, for the idea of a united Christendom. The peace did not openly express this idea but it did contain the idea of a society which took no account of the method of government of its component states. . . . Similarly, no account was made of the dominant religious faiths. On the international plane, Europe became a secular system of independent states. It was the dawn of the principle of nationalism.

S. Harrison Thomson's account of the events (1963:814) likewise portrays the Peace as a marked step forward for religious tolerance:

> The achievements of the peace congress in the controversial area of religious liberty, while not revolutionary, were not insignificant. . . . Complete toleration was not to be expected. The old principle of *cuius regio eius religio* was deeply ingrained in the princely class. Now, however, Calvinists were tolerated and the princes were expressly enjoined not to interfere in the religion of their subjects.

Hans Morgenthau's assertion (1967:299) that, by the end of the Thirty Years' War, "sovereignty as supreme power over a certain territory was a political fact, signifying the victory of the territorial princes over the universal authority of emperor and pope," is similarly exemplary of international relations orthodoxy. Others follow suit. Leo Gross (1968:47) claims that the "Peace of Westphalia consecrated the principle of toleration by establishing the equality between Protestant and Catholic states and by providing safeguards for religious minorities." Terry Nardin (1983:50) described the emergent international society similarly as a system of mutual tolerance and accommodation. Stephen Krasner (1993:242–44; 1999:73–82), though he doubts the claim that Westphalia implemented the *idea* of sovereignty, stresses the attempt of the treaties to contain religious conflict by fixing boundaries in a system of nation-states, by disentangling religion and politics, and by fostering greater religious tolerance. In general, then, and to repeat a point, Westphalia normally is seen as a key marker of the eclipse of the Medieval world by modernity: a movement from the religious to the secular, from the idea of Europe as unified by Christianity to a European system of independent states, and from a web of overlapping and competing authorities to a modern state system based on the demarcation of exclusive territorial jurisdictions.

What is crucial, here, is the intimation that Westphalia and a nascent modernity represent initial but definitive steps towards a solution to the problem of difference. We wish to complicate this reading, challenging the received view because its veneration of Westphalia tends to blind us to: the creative responses to difference that were lost during this period; the persistent, if understandable, evasion of the task of exploring the source of the wounds in the dominant response to difference; and the manner in which the intellectual discourse, originating in the shadow of the Thirty Years' War, reinforced, rather than challenged, the interpretation of difference as a dangerous aberration from the norms of stability, safety, and order. Thus, a richer story necessarily qualifies any effort to establish Westphalia as a clear marker of the transition to a tolerant modernity. We will elaborate these points in two steps.

First, the attempt to contain difference within the state both deferred a deeper exploration and engagement of the problem and forced a diverse set of experiments designed to manage difference. Ronald Asch (1997:193–94) notes that, rather than a solution to the problem of religious difference, Westphalia kept alive the religious conflicts of the previous century, "confirming the existing status, rights, and privileges of the confessional churches," and thereby "perpetuating religious divisions," albeit in a more "muted form." Combined with the recognition of independent sovereigns, the effect was to divide "'Europe' into Catholic and Protestant spaces" and spur "the interstate construction of the continent" (Campbell 1992:51). Thus, despite the treaties' relative embrace of religious liberty, the moral constraints placed on rulers were, as Krasner (1993:244–45) observes, on a collision course with the sovereign right to dictate the faith of the realm as originally acknowledged in the Treaty of Augsburg and as supported by the emerging reality and theory of sovereignty. "[F]rom now on," Toulmin (1990:91) concludes, "established religion was the general rule." This move, by setting difference at a distance, may well have helped to minimize the prospects of religious war on the scale of the Thirty Years' War, but at a price: the problem of difference was simply displaced into the "domestic realm."

However, the consequences for religious liberty were not uniform across the newly sanctified states. Rather, Toulmin (1990:92) describes a situation where each state individually faced "the continuing problem of religious conformity and toleration." Despite the expectation of submission to a national faith, nonconforming minorities remained a troubling issue. The "other," thought to have been placed at a distance, was found within. And, though "[a]fter thirty years of bloodshed, few people still considered the price of imposing religious conformity worth paying," Toulmin (1990:92) reports that "the local pressure for conformity remained strong, and religious minorities were everywhere subject to some degree of discrimination or persecution." But the degree did vary—each national experience representing "a different variation on a common set of tunes." In Austria, the Habsburgs remained as "leaders" of the Counter-Reformation: "continued Lutheranism was seen as disloyalty to the Habsburg dynasty, and the Protestant minority of craftsmen and professionals had to choose between conversion, death, and flight." English papists were targets of discrimination, but the treatment they received paled in comparison to that dealt out to "heretics" in France. Under the rule of Louis XIV, "the Protestant minority was denied the right to work in many professions, and exposed to military attacks that drove them back into their traditional strongholds, deep in the *Massif Central*." Consequently, large numbers of Huguenots exercised the option of "flight," either "across land, or [as] boat people . . . headed for England or America." Calvinist Holland, lacking the constraints of long-standing institutions, was "unusually tolerant" of Catholics. Everywhere, a balance was struck that "stopped short of the horrors of a renewed religious war" (Toulmin 1990:92–93). While this was no mean achievement, it is still clear that the problem was not so much resolved as it was deferred—displaced into the domestic realm where, hopefully, it could be managed and contained. The variety of efforts at management and containment that the Westphalian move sparked, and continues to demand, are important nonetheless.[8] We will return to this theme below.

Second, the received view of Westphalia as a crucial point of transition to a more civilized era ignores the relatively negative impact of the experience of the War on thinking about difference. Rather than supporting openness towards the "other," or fostering a view of difference as a resource, the intellectual legacy of the era is a pervasive suspicion of difference. Disorder and degeneration are thought to result from difference; uniformity or homogeneity is strongly associated with social order and stability. In Toulmin's account (1990:67–69), the Thirty Years' War shook the "cosmopolitical" conception of a hierarchically arranged and integrated natural and social order that undergirded much of late

[8] Nevzat Soguk (1999:62, 67–74) sees the displacement of the Huguenots not only as a key early example of the problem of "refugees," but as a clear marker of the rise of the effort to manage, and often homogenize, populations—an effort central to statecraft in an emergent system of territorial states.

Medieval thinking and practice. Spurred by the resulting anxious and pessimistic mood, the intellectual project to restore such order is best seen as a "defensive counter-revolution"—a closing down of options produced by a frantic search for certainty (Toulmin 1990:16–19, 81; the quoted phrase is on p. 17).

More specifically, the possibility of turning to the pluralism and relative skepticism of Renaissance humanism was discredited as not up to the task of containing religious difference and anchoring social order:

> In this blood-drenched situation, what could good intellectuals do? So long as humane Renaissance values retained their power for Montaigne in the private sphere, or for Henry of Navarre in the public sphere, there was hope that the reasoned discussion of shared experiences among honest individuals might lead to a meeting of minds, or, at least, to a civilized agreement to differ. By 1620, people in positions of political power and theological authority in Europe no longer saw Montaigne's pluralism as a viable intellectual option, any more than Henry's tolerance was for them a practical option. The humanists' readiness to live with uncertainty, ambiguity, and differences of opinion had done nothing (in their view) to prevent religious conflict from getting out of hand: *ergo* (they inferred) it had helped *cause* the worsening state of affairs. If skepticism let one down, certainty was more urgent. It might not be obvious what one was supposed to be certain about, but *un*certainty had become *un*acceptable. (Toulmin 1990:54–55)

And, Toulmin (1990:55) continues, where differences in religious faith had proved so destructive, the appeal of a standpoint beyond question was overwhelming:

> Failing any effective political way of getting the sectarians to stop killing each other, was there no other possible way ahead? Might not philosophers discover, for instance, a new and more rational basis for establishing a framework of concepts and beliefs capable of achieving the agreed certainty that the skeptics had said was impossible? If uncertainty, ambiguity, and the acceptance of pluralism led, in practice, only to an intensification of the religious war, the time had come to discover some *rational method* for demonstrating the essential correctness or incorrectness of philosophical, scientific, or theological doctrines.

Thus, Toulmin (1990:56–62) links the impetus for Descartes' search for a single and certain principle, from which all else would necessarily follow, to this mood and the parallel need to answer Montaigne's epistemological skepticism. Many took hope from Descartes' project and turned to the effort "to construct abstract and timeless intellectual schemes." Certainty became associated with "geometrical proof" or "mathematical structures" (Toulmin 1990:105; see also pp. 20 and 75).[9] And, as Toulmin (1990:76) describes the thought, "if ethics were to join physics and logic on the *rational* side of the fence," humanity could "escape the chaos of diverse and uncertain opinions." This move entailed the gradual privileging of the written, the universal, the general, and the timeless, on the one hand, and the denigration of "practical philosophy," with its reliance on "argumentation" or "case analysis," involving "particular people in specific situations, dealing with concrete cases, where varied things were at stake," on the other (Toulmin 1990:70, 31–35). The former promised certainty and safety; the latter opened the way to disagreement, conflict, and the danger of chaos.

We can trace the parallel and connected consequences of this mood for thinking about politics and political organization. Deborah Baumgold (1993) explains that seventeenth-century thinkers—most prominently Grotius, Hobbes, and Locke in her account—were engaged in a "common intellectual project" of "pacifying politics" in the wake of religious conflict, both international and internal. As in social theory more generally, restoring political order was thought to require a foundation of unchallengeable principles, proofs, and powers (Tuck 1988:29; Toulmin 1990:76–77; Tully 1993:184; Boucher 1998:225). Quite famously, the thinkers of this era sought a foundation for authoritative political organization—a sovereign power—in the idea of a social contract. Because such a contractual arrangement was treated as if it were independent of, or neutral in relation to, religious belief, it was seen as a more certain basis for political authority and, thereby, a solution to the problem of political order (Tuck 1988:29; Baumgold 1993). Not surprisingly, given the primacy assigned to social harmony, the predominant view of the time (Grotius, Pufendorf, Hobbes, and initially Locke) was that the sovereign authority was justified—for practical or political, but not religious, reasons—in subordinating religious liberty whenever necessary to limit conflict and defend social order (Tuck 1998:29–34). Even where religious tolerance was defended (as in Locke's later work), it was often justified on narrow, prudential grounds, not as part of an embrace of pluralism (Waldron 1988).[10] Rather, Locke's extension of tolerance to dissenters is made against the assumption of certain givens: natural law and a Christian Commonwealth. Atheists and Catholics were still beyond the pale, legitimate religiosity was restricted to a distinctly Protestant version of a privatized, individualized faith, and diversity remained a threat to be subjected to community

[9] R. G. Collingwood's discussion (1981: pt. II., Section 1) of this period is remarkably similar. See also Friedrich and Blitzer (1957:1) and Walker (1993:128–130).

[10] Others (Wootton 1993; Creppell 1996) recognize the role of such prudential arguments but suggest that Waldron's reading is much too narrow, ignoring Locke's understanding of religion as intrinsically a voluntary, individual matter and his (albeit inconsistent) embrace of tolerance as a good in itself.

standards and political repression (Tully 1993:53–57; Wootton 1993:38–39, 106–109; Jenkinson 1995; Creppell 1996:202, 217–221). Indeed, as Hinsley (1986:138–150) carefully recounts, the doctrine of sovereign power was necessarily related (by Bodin, Grotius, Hobbes, and Locke) to the conception of a "body politic," bringing together people, state, and territory into a unified, harmonious whole. David Campbell (1992:42) likewise has referred to this emerging notion of citizenship and the state as the "passage from difference to identity." Thus the equation of cultural diversity and political chaos on the one side, and cultural homogeneity and political order on the other, was central to the legacy of political thinking bequeathed to us by this era.[11]

James Tully elaborates this point. The dominant interpretation of the causes of the Thirty Years War was that it stemmed from "conflicts over the locus of sovereignty"—"that the conflicting jurisdictions and authorities of the ancient constitutions were the cause of wars." If ambiguity or uncertainty was the culprit, it was imperative "that authority had to be organized and centralised by the constitution in some sovereign body" (Tully 1995:66–67). For the people to be understood as capable of constituting a sovereign authority, they had to be conceived as "culturally homogenous in the sense that culture is irrelevant, capable of being transcended, or uniform." The idea was embraced, consequently, that the people form "a society"—defined variously as "equal individuals in a state of nature," or as a collective existing "at a 'modern' level of historical development," or as a "community" bound together by a conception of the good—that preexists the "uniform political association" to which they are inevitably (rationally) drawn to construct (Tully 1995:63–64). Unlike the customary and irregular (or "multiform") character of the old regime, that was the source of so much trouble,

> the sovereign people, in modern societies, . . . establish a constitution that is legally and politically uniform: a constitution of equal citizens who are treated identically rather than equitably, of one national system of institutionalised legal and political authority rather than many, and a constitutional nation equal in status to all others. (Tully 1995:64–67; long quotation from p. 66)

---

[11] Despite the distance between Locke's time and the present, including genuine advances in thinking about difference and tolerance in the interim, the presumption that liberalism is an unassailable doctrine that requires a uniform order remains. Toulmin and Tully's assessments, just below, are indicative of the continued power of the thinking of this period and the increasing vibrancy of dissenting views. In fact, liberalism's purported universality (or neutrality) is increasingly rejected as a partisan view, even by its own supporters (Galston 1991: part II; Rawls, 1996: lecture IV). And liberal versions of religious tolerance—secularism, for example—are equally no longer sacrosanct, now challenged as biased and overly restrictive (Nandy 1990; Chatterjee 1995; Connolly, 1999).

Tully (1995:66) sees this "legal and political monism" as "perfectly understandable" given the experience of the years of warfare, but this does not vindicate what he calls an "empire of uniformity." [12] Rather, Tully (1995:1) argues that the modern ideal of uniform constitutionalism serves as an impediment to our capacity to "recognize and accommodate cultural diversity."

Toulmin's assessment is quite close to Tully's. For Toulmin (1990:128), a new "scaffolding of modernity"—constructed on the basis of "principles of *stability* in and among the different sovereign nation-states, and *hierarchy* within the social structure of each individual state"—legitimated a new social and political order. Although this represented a "timely response to the general crisis of seventeenth-century politics"—a suturing of the "wounds" in the Medieval "Cosmopolis"—he is not sanguine about the results. He argues that, though we have found these certainties and legitimations unconvincing ultimately, we have been given inadequate guidance as to how we are to respond to the problem of difference (Toulmin 1990:80, 89, 172–175).

Thus, following Tully and Toulmin, we read Westphalia not only as a deferral of the problem of difference, but also as directing us down a path of theory and practice deeply suspicious of, if not actively hostile, towards diversity. The problem is magnified where our celebration of modernity continues to blind us to the inadequacy of the guidance bequeathed to us by Westphalia. It is to the contemporary resonance of the Westphalian deferral that we now turn.

International Society and the Contemporary Deferral of the Problem of Difference

The society of states, as we have already noted, is strongly associated with the principle of tolerance among different and separate political communities. There is something to this belief, but the association is quite fragile and burdened with numerous complications and discrepancies. We believe it is more accurate to see the theory and practice of international society as largely a deferral of a genuine recognition, exploration, and engagement of difference. This deferral is achieved in several intertwined moves. In international society, the "other" is located outside the state, beyond the boundaries of political community. The idea that the state is a political community suggests that, within the state, a realm of relative "sameness"—a cultural homogeneity and a uniform constitution in Tully's terms—is presumed. To put this set of ideas somewhat differently, the differences constituting each state as a particular political community are kept separate and managed within the boundaries of the state. This demar-

---

[12] The term "empire of uniformity" is in the title of the chapter containing Tully's historical account.

cation and policing of the boundary between the "inside" and "outside" of the political community defines the problem of difference as *between and among* states; difference is marked and contained as *international* difference. This construction of difference allows us to "solve" the problem by negotiating a "modus vivendi" among political communities. A minimal set of rules—revolving around sovereignty and nonintervention—constitutes international society as a world of mutually tolerant political communities. In this account, it is the very minimalism—the impartiality or "neutrality"—of this "sovereignty" solution that stabilizes the system: any and all, regardless of culture or ideology, can find a home in this world. Or so the story the goes.

We suggest a different interpretation of international society in which the problem of difference is pervasive. The bounded political community constructs (and is constructed by) the "other," both beyond its boundaries, lurking as a perpetual threat in the form of other states, foreign groups, imported goods, and alien ideas, and as difference within, vitiating the presumed but rarely, if ever, achieved "sameness." The "other" within the boundaries of the political community is "managed" by some combination of hierarchy, eradication by assimilation or expulsion, and tolerance. The external "other" is left to suffer or prosper according its own means, interdicted at border crossings, and balanced and deterred. Our responses to the "other" seem perpetually drawn towards the equation: difference/inferiority/eradication. Indeed, the "inside/outside" logic performs an act of "splitting"—an exclusion of the overlap of "self" and "other" that works to deflect our responses to difference in the direction of a "purifying hatred." Locating difference beyond the boundaries of "self" impedes our capacity to fully acknowledge and affirm the "other" that always lies within, or to appreciate and claim the "self" that exists as part of the "other" beyond those boundaries. The implication is clear: unless we can respond creatively to this exclusivity of "self" and "other," by exposing and cultivating the points of connection and the spaces of overlap (while still respecting the divergences and incompatibilities), we cannot find our way towards an understanding where equality and difference coexist. In other words, we are still largely hostage to the kinds of impulses towards difference that marked the wake of the Thirty Years' War. We remain bound to a narrow understanding of difference as disorder, perpetuating the "wound" of difference by failing altogether to appreciate the opportunities and resources accompanying an engagement with the "other."

As already asserted, a crucial aspect of the Westphalian impulse—both in theory and practice—is the persistence of "splitting." As Jessica Benjamin (1988:63) explains, the process of "splitting" represents two sides "as opposite and distinct tendencies," available only "as alternatives"—"a polarization in which opposites . . . can no longer be integrated; in which one side is devalued, the other idealized, and each is projected onto different objects." We can see this process at work in the very constitution of the subject matter of international relations (IR). Martin Wight's "Why is there no International Theory?" is paradigmatic in its counterpoising of political theory and IR: political theory—the domain of the "theory of the good life" possible in a state—is contrasted with the moral and political impoverishment of IR theory. Where IR is distinguished as a "realm of recurrence and repetition" or a "precontractual state of nature," there can be no properly international political theory (Wight 1966:17, 20–22, 26, 30–33). It is important to be clear that this is not a simple distinction between disparate elements, but an act of splitting that is mutually constitutive of both the state/political theory and a society of states/IR theory. As Rob Walker (1993: chapter 2) elaborates, IR theory's account of the political and ethical limits and possibilities of modern life turns on this demarcation of "inside/outside": politics and the pursuit of the good life are possible only within sovereign states; the condition of sovereign political community is, however, the ethically limited and tragic interactions of these separate states.

The splitting of "inside/outside" is not only constitutive of the field, but also a precondition of the "solution" to the problem of difference associated with a society of states. This is clear in various accounts of the logic of international society. We limit ourselves to the writings of Hedley Bull and Michael Walzer,[13] a choice dictated in part by the fact that they provide especially richly developed versions of the Westphalian deferral. Also, the very richness of their accounts suggests possibilities that point us beyond the logic of "inside/outside" and the Westphalian deferral.

Hedley Bull, more than any other thinker, is associated with the idea of "international society."[14] By this term, Bull means to focus our attention on the common rules, values, and institutions that both "govern" action within the society of states and shape the self-understandings of states as members of that society (Bull 1977:13–14, 24–26; Watson 1987:147). Though Bull uses the idea of international society, quite helpfully, as a counterpoint to a realist notion of lawless anarchy, he holds strongly to a distinction between the domestic and the international, inside and outside. He (1977:49–51) stresses the difference between the logic of domestic society, with its dependence on government, and "the fact that states form a society without government." This opposition is crucial because the presence of government allows the individual state to act as the "custodian" of the "common good" of a certain segment of humankind in a way that Bull believes is necessarily forbidden to international society. The society of states, by contrast, is a "compact of coexistence," a necessarily thin-

---

[13] Hans Morgenthau, Terry Nardin, and Kenneth Waltz also come immediately to mind as candidates for examination.

[14] For an overview of Bull's importance, see Tim Dunne (1998).

ner set of common values and institutions that affirms the primacy of the individual political community. The relatively thin character of international society must be defended against intrusions that blur the distinction between the opposed logics of the divergent realms. Appeals to more encompassing conceptions of the common good or some idea of cosmopolitan justice are treated thereby as a kind of category mistake, as inconsistent with the logic of the existing basis of international coexistence. That is, inappropriately making claims depending on thicker global purposes and a wider world society potentially threaten the respect for difference embodied in the right and capacity of each political community to pursue its own ways of life and its own forms of governance (Bull 1966; Bull 1977: chapter 4; Bull 1979; Dunne 1995:126–7; Dunne 1998:10–11, 100–102, 146).

At points Bull does appear to open a space for a thickening of international values and purposes. His defense of the very possibility of common values and purposes (1977:94) suggests that some thickening could occur "through processes of consent or consensus." Though resort to such processes can never be fully ruled out, and since failures to address questions of justice may threaten disorder in international society itself, Bull weighs in, until the end of his life and despite the objections of some of his followers, on the side of the view that an order based on mutual accommodation makes resort to such ethical thickening very risky and appropriately rare (Bull 1984a:13).[15]

What needs to be stressed is that this effort to police the "inside/outside" distinction in the name of difference also works to normalize difference as "international," as *between and among* states. The relative homogeneity of the national political community is taken for granted and the "other" is thereby located decisively beyond the boundaries of the state and encompassed within the boundaries of other political communities. With difference normalized and contained in this way, we then can think of international society as legitimated by its unique capacity to provide (in theory at least) an order of relative toleration. As Bull (1977, especially chapter 4) notes, states maintain a commitment to the institutions supporting that order—the principle of sovereignty, the balance of power, international law, diplomacy, war, and the preponderance of the great powers—precisely because these practices (on the whole) preserve the kind of mutual accommodation distinctive of an international society. In all of this, Bull clearly implies what Leo Gross (1968:49, 52) asserts more forcefully: that the preservation of the respect for (international) difference requires that rules be neutral, and thereby acceptable to all states, regardless of religious

---

[15] Various of Bull's followers have taken issue with his stance. See the preface to Vincent (1986), Jackson (1990, especially chapter 5), and Buzan (1991:150–153, 167–173).

view or form of government. In Bull's international society, states are, then, simultaneously the legitimate "containers" of difference and the sole source of the legitimation of the practices that work to police the boundaries containing difference.

This might be thought an ungenerous and one-sided reading of Bull. It is true that, in important sections of his later work, he can be read as characterizing the problem much differently and more usefully, given our concerns. In these writings, Bull (1984b; Bull and Watson 1984) focuses our attention on the challenges faced by a culturally diverse international society, but to somewhat ambiguous effect. On the one hand, Bull's argument might support the line of thinking outlined above. The evolution of international society is the story of increasing inclusiveness, the gradual definition and realization of an order capable of containing the diversity of political communities on the globe. That is, what began as a European society of states came over time to encompass (through both imposition and accession) the entire world, finally achieving the status of a global international society in the twentieth century with the completion of the process of decolonization (Bull, 1977: chapter 2; Bull and Watson, 1984). Even the various forms of resistance by non-Western states may be read as an effort to adapt European-inspired arrangements in a more egalitarian and neutral direction as appropriate to a genuinely tolerant international society (Bull, 1984b). And so we might say that Bull's story allows us to hold onto the idea of international society as a uniquely pluralistic society of states, designed and legitimated by its capacity to accommodate numerous, distinctive, and separate political communities within its bounds. Difference remains contained and the need to face the problem of difference deferred.

On the other hand, Bull seems to be drawn to the idea that the cultural diversity of states and regions provides a substantial challenge to the very idea of international society. He concludes that "the cultural heterogeneity of the global international society of today is evidently a factor making against consensus about its underlying rules and institutions" (Bull and Watson, 1984: 432).[16] We now receive the hint that it is by no means certain that the commonalities of values and institutions definitive of a tolerant international society can be sustained where competing cultural visions pull the peoples and states of the world in different directions. Here, cultural diversity appears more difficult to contain within the confines of an international society; it spills beyond its grasp, exposing international society as a parochial arrangement, associated with a narrow band of (mostly European) states; and it reveals that alternative and incompatible projects of organizing global social and political space emanate

---

[16]This conclusion is influenced by several of the essays in the collection (e.g., Bozeman, 1984; Dore, 1984).

from other states and regions. In a quite dramatic reversal of reasoning (an interpretation that Bull might well have resisted), cultural diversity is no longer contained. Rather, cultural and ethical difference appears as the central problem of international politics. We want to read Bull, then, as recognizing the legitimate concerns of the non-European countries and peoples, treating international society (as well as states and peoples themselves) as unfinished projects, subject to the results of an ongoing negotiation of the problem of difference.[17]

Like Bull, Michael Walzer is relatively reflective about the problem of difference. But instead of exploring the possibilities of difference as a resource for political and ethical life, his reflex is to deploy the Westphalian deferral in a rather radical and encompassing way. Nevertheless, in the end, Walzer's explicit policing of the "inside/outside" boundary continually points to its vitiation in theory and practice and beyond the deferral of the problem of difference.

It is not too far wrong to suggest that Walzer, like Bull, sees international society as a distinct cultural system. Walzer (1997:12–13) himself classifies international society as one of the several "models of a tolerant society," as one of the "regimes" or sets of "social arrangements through which we incorporate difference, coexist with it, allow it a share of social space." In contrast with "multinational empires," as discussed in the introduction, international society ideally achieves a form of toleration among equals[18]—among a society of sovereign states. As Walzer (1997:19–20) describes this regime:

> Sovereignty guarantees that no one on *that* side of the border can interfere with what is done on *this* side. The people over there may be resigned, indifferent, stoical, curious, or enthusiastic with regard to practices over here, and so may be disinclined to interfere. Or perhaps, they accept the reciprocal logic of sovereignty: we won't worry about your practices if you don't worry about ours. Live and let live is a relatively easy maxim when the living is done on opposite sides of a clearly marked line. Or they may be actively hostile, eager to denounce their neighbor's culture and customs, but unprepared to pay the costs of interference.

Though sovereignty has its limits—barbarism is unacceptable—it secures substantial tolerance precisely because it is such a "weak regime." A stronger regime places heavier demands on its members, justifying greater intervention in their "internal" affairs (Walzer 1997:19, 21–22).

---

[17] See the last pages of Bull and Watson (1984) for hints of such a proposal.

[18] Walzer's argument turns mostly on a claim about the formal equality of actors, though he is sensitive to the impact of socioeconomic inequality in his work in general. The issue of material inequality among states in international society is central to earlier work (Inayatullah and Blaney 1995; Blaney and Inayatullah 1996), but mostly bracketed here so as to isolate the issue of difference.

Already we get an indication of the way Walzer's understanding (1994:ix, xi) of international society as a "weak" or "thin" regime capable of toleration informs his version of the splitting of "inside/outside." He elaborates this point elsewhere when he draws a clear distinction between two kinds of "moral argument." At "home"—in the national political community—we speak in terms that are "thick," by which Walzer means "richly referential, culturally resonant, locked into a locally established symbolic system and network of meanings." In discussions across cultures—that is, across political communities—we talk "about the thinner life we have in common." As in Bull's account, Walzer (1994: chapter 4) means that international ethical discourse is circumscribed necessarily as a thin morality, grounded in the principle of self-determination. International society therefore is able to protect the integrity of the "thick" ethical discourse of domestic societies by recognizing "the rights of contemporary men and women to live as members of a historic community and to express their inherited culture through political forms worked out among themselves" (Walzer 1980:210). The move is familiar: difference is circumscribed "inside" the boundaries of political communities so that the relations among political communities "outside" may be mutually accommodating.

To sustain international society as a "regime of toleration," this boundary must be policed. On the one side, this means a constant battle to expose the pretensions of a globalist ethics. Because the idea of a global society is chimerical, the national political community dominates our "bonds of commonality" and is a good in itself (Walzer 1983:29–30). Thus, we are justified in resisting the kind of category mistake that occurs when we speak of humanity or the globe. Walzer (1988:232) suggests we "fight against the propensity of [critics] to think that when they look in the mirror they see the entire world"—a propensity that provides an alibi for imposing such imagined commonalities on others. Walzer's warning is very timely, but we wonder if the choice he poses—either the nation-state or the globe—adequately describes our alternatives. Even Bull doubts that the choice is this simple. We will return to this issue below.

On the other side, a regime of toleration involves controlling the movements of people. For Walzer, questions of justice can only be resolved in relation to the "thick," "culturally resonant" meanings and practices that make up the "bounded world" of the community.[19] This gives a special importance to the community's rules governing "membership," since being a member implies a special communal bond and moral obligation that are not present for those

---

[19] Although we have drawn from a quotation used above, Walzer presents these ideas most clearly in his controversial chapter on "membership" in *Spheres of Justice* (1983). The term "bounded world" is used on p. 31.

beyond the community. To outsiders we owe some weaker obligation of "mutual aid," consistent with the general thinness of international society (Walzer 1983:32–33). The links between national identity and territory and sovereignty and territorial jurisdiction locate the power to control membership and to police boundaries in the hands of the political community. Indeed, Walzer (1983:39) is categorical that a defense of the "distinctiveness of cultures and groups depends on closure." Thus, he grants primacy to the issue of membership:

> The right to choose an admissions policy is more basic than any [other issue], for it is not merely a matter of acting in the world, exercising sovereignty, and pursuing national interests. At stake here is the shape of the community that acts in the world, exercises sovereignty and so on. Admission and exclusion are at the core of communal independence. They suggest the deepest meaning of self-determination. Without them, there could not be communities of character, historically stable, ongoing associations of men and women with some special commitment to one another and some special sense of their common life. (Walzer 1983:61–62).

The policing of boundaries takes on a special urgency here, for not only does coexistence presume the management of difference within boundaries, the very value and justification of international tolerance depends on the maintenance of the purity of the national community. In this set of moves, Walzer, like Bull in much of his work, defers the problem of difference by circumscribing the thickening of international society and defending the national boundaries that contain the "other."

Despite Walzer's unwillingness to directly confront the problem of difference within global space, he is fairly attentive to the various ways that difference is managed within boundaries. There are two facets to this issue in his work. First, Walzer questions that justice and equality are, or ought to be, conceived in terms of the application of a uniform principle. Rather, the kinds of "thick" communities within which we live have their own ways of placing goods into different categories and subjecting each category to a differing principle of distribution (e.g., commodities are distributed differently than offices because of the different meaning and place they have in our society). And so we must recognize that every society should, and does, have heterogeneous institutional arrangements—plural forms of justice and complex modes of equality—reflecting the values and visions of the particular community (Walzer 1983:3–9). Walzer recognizes that this view flies in the face of most current thinking that favors universal rights and uniform procedures; the appeal of uniformity has already been noted in Tully's account of the weight of conventional constitutionalism. It is easy given our concerns to be drawn to Walzer's argument, since it seems to strike a blow at the quest for certainty and universality underlying the Westphalian deferral.

Ronald Dworkin's critique of Walzer's picture pushes us further down that road. Walzer is charged with assuming incorrectly that there is basic agreement within each community on both the categorization of goods and the principle of distribution appropriate to each category. Rather, politics is fueled precisely by such disagreements in meaning and values and the need to strike contingent bargains and compromises (Dworkin 1983:4). If so, Walzer cannot defend a clear distinction between a "thick" community of common concern and a "thin" international society of mutual coexistence. Where this breaks down, the internal complexity of the political community might be thought to mirror the complexity present in global social space, and the heterogeneous institutional arrangements created in domestic society might appear as a model for the reorganization of the global political architecture. Though Walzer disputes that he presumes such unanimity of view within political communities, he still defends the idea that "in a particular case, in a particular culture, there is, in principle, a right decision" (Walzer and Dworkin 1983:43–44). We should note also that Walzer immediately follows his discussion of the complexity of justice and equality with his defense of policing borders in the name of the commonality of national culture.

Second, and despite this conclusion, Walzer admits that cultural homogeneity is a rare condition, so that, when we speak of a nation-state, we can mean no more than "that a single group organizes the common life in a way that reflects its own history and culture." In such a situation, tolerance of minority cultures is difficult. In part, this is because the dominant national group controls the state and, thereby, the means of cultural reproduction. The alternative practices of minority nations appear as an encumbrance, as "suspicious," and subject to, especially linguistic, assimilation. Tolerance can be extended, but normally only to individuals as citizens and not to groups. The status of minority groups therefore is necessarily insecure as they are relegated to the situation of "voluntary associations," lacking the right of cultural reproduction reserved for the dominant national culture (Walzer 1997:25–27).[20]

But alternative organizations of political community are possible and even necessitated by the particular situation. Certain "bi- or trinational" states are arranged as consociations, where national groups, sharing a certain territory, agree to a constitutional arrangement, design institutions and divide offices, and strike a political bargain that protects their divergent interests. Though "heroic" and desirable in Walzer's view (1997:25–27), consociations, because

---

[20]This conclusion is supported by much of the debate about minority rights within liberal societies. See Taylor (1992), Kymlicka (1995), Parkekh (1996), and Spinner (1994).

they parcel out the power of national reproduction among the national groups, are also unstable, subject to sudden disturbances of the trust among the groups.[21] Or, Walzer (1997:29–35) suggests that, in predominantly settler societies, newer immigrants may gradually displace the cultural dominance of the original immigrant group, forcing a more "neutral" constitutional arrangement. In theory at least, all national groups lose the right of cultural reproduction and are transformed into voluntary associations. In this arrangement, cultural practices are (ideally) universally privatized, requiring toleration as an individual performance. Walzer (1997:37) admits that each mode has its limits and, consistent with his notion of complex equality and the heterogeneity of institutions, argues that mixed modes might possibly be more effective. Still, nothing in this account suggests to him the need to rethink the boundary of "inside/outside."

But once again we can see cracks in the edifice he has built; each of the internal arrangements Walzer describes involves a step away from this "splitting" logic and a move towards an overlapping of "self"/"other" and "inside/outside." Consociational forms, for example, are a curious blending of the mutual accommodation of international society and the common life of a political community in that the nations interpenetrate instead of being clearly bounded, and each nation possesses some of the prerogatives of sovereignty but not others (see also Lijphart 1977:9, 49). In this scenario, the cultural reproduction of groups is partly disconnected from the tight linkage of identity and territory. Thus, sovereignty can be divided such that it is exercised by different agents: jointly on some matters governing the entire territory; separately on others that concern only a certain region; or involving overlapping and competing jurisdictions, where the final authority can be negotiated on a case-by-case basis. Here, sovereignty is no longer a homogenous substance; it may be divided and distributed to create complex, if not continually negotiable, jurisdictional arrangements.

If consociational regimes suggest the "thickness" and "complexity" that might accompany the coexistence of nations, the "neutral" arrangements of the settler society move in the opposite direction, thinning domestic society. The purported neutrality of these constitutional arrangements at least partly abandons the "thickness" definitive of the "inside" by treating domestic society as something like a "thin" pact of mutual accommodation among competing groups. What is most striking here is that "thin" coexistence seems no longer to require the containment of difference behind boundaries. "Self" and "other," both within

---

[21] That consociational arrangements are ultimately unsuccessful is disputed by Arend Lijphart (1977). Rather, he suggests that such arrangements should give us some optimism about the possibility of democratic rule in ethnically divided societies.

and beyond political communities, can, in principle at least, negotiate certain commonalities that promote more peaceful interaction.

Thus, in both consociational and settler regimes, and in other mixed modes we could imagine, political arrangements operate in a space where the "other" is no longer securely contained behind a boundary, where difference must be faced, discussed, and negotiated. As perhaps hinted by Bull, this space of negotiation, ruled out by the Westphalian deferral as impossibly dangerous and unstable, now seems open for exploration.

Conclusion: Beyond Splitting and the Westphalian Deferral

Strong habits of mind and deeply rooted impulses counsel and compel us to rule out this space for engaging and negotiating difference. The "purifying hatred" of the Thirty Years' War reminds us just how calamitous unbridled political idealism can be. We are reminded too that such events leave scars—not just on the psyches of survivors, but also on the tone and substance of the social theory produced in their wake. Exploring the events leading up to Westphalia permits us, then, a clearer understanding of the deep anxieties and sense of opportunities that informed the social theory shaping and legitimating a nascent international society. Where difference is understood (and felt) as a source of danger and disorder, an ethical and stable social order demands a homogenous way of life and constitutional uniformity. A system of sovereign states appears, then, as an opportunity to separate and contain difference, to make possible a *modus vivendi* among externalized differences that works to secure internal sameness. Given this legacy, it is little wonder that the warnings and prescriptions of international relations have blinded us to the benefits and opportunities afforded by an engagement with difference.

This overwhelming anxiety and the almost exclusive preoccupation with the threats posed by the "other" direct us to certain clues about the underlying source of this anxiety and preoccupation. It is worth repeating Jessica Benjamin's point that the process of splitting involves breaking down a complex and differentiated whole, parceling out its assumed positive qualities to "self" and the negative qualities to "other." The psychological purpose of splitting, Benjamin (1988:222–23) suggests, is an attempt to escape from uncertainty, ambiguity, and doubt, and thereby evade "the necessity of dealing with the contradictory tendencies within the self."[22] Thus, when the Moravian Hutterites and the Styrian subjects of Ferdinand lament their treatment at the hands of fellow Christians, comparing them unfavorably with Turks and Tartars, per-

---

[22] Compare with Nandy (1983).

haps more is being said than we initially realize. By inverting the polarities of the familiar splitting of Christian and heathen, they achieve a kind of clarity. We would like to read it this way: the real target of a "purifying hatred" within an "empire of uniformity" is not so much the "other" beyond oneself—Turks or Tartars outside "Europe," or Protestants or Catholics within—but a doubt or moment of difference internal to the "self." The tendency is to refuse that doubt—that ambiguity or internal "other"—as our own and to externalize and personify it as a projection onto the "other." The illusion is that we have cleansed ourselves and set doubt to rest.

Herein lays the problem and the hope. Hope may be found in that the "other" is revealed not simply as a "natural" enemy or inevitable antagonist, but as an external representation of a disturbing internal doubt. Facing the uncertainty and ambiguity generated by acknowledging the overlap of "self" and "other" is no less daunting a task in our time, just because (implicitly) identified already by survivors of the Thirty Years' War. As their incisive remarks approach their 400th year, what more can we offer? What tools do we possess that get us beyond the splitting of "inside/outside" and the Westphalian deferral? We will make three brief points.

First, we find in our readings of Bull and Walzer various moments of an argument that take us beyond the splitting of "inside/outside." We draw on Bull and Walzer to suggest that international society is not exhaustive of the possibilities for responding to difference, but is a particular culture or regime that coexists with other conceptions of global social and political space. Our reading of Walzer points more specifically to the competition and mixture of "thin" and "thick" ethical discourses and institutional arrangements available for both domestic and international space, such that we cannot fully distinguish the two spheres of life. Where the problem of difference can no longer be contained by the splitting of "inside/outside," we should come to think of local, national, regional, and global social and political spaces as sites in which difference is explored, negotiated, and perhaps celebrated. It does not follow that we should therefore privilege a discourse of globalist ethics or the human interest. That is, confronting the problem of difference as central to world politics is not to be interpreted as a call for a project of global homogenization. We should continue to heed Bull's and Walzer's warnings about the problem of imposing "global" purposes on an unwilling "humanity." Heeding this warning does not rule out altogether the possibility of genuine global agreement on certain, perhaps many, issues. Nor does the possibility of global agreement guarantee a cosmopolitan outcome. Any genuine conversation presupposes an internal tolerance of the anxiety that results from, and a nurturing of the ambiguity required for, exposing one's views to potential criticism from the "other." Agreement can only be worked out over time in a conversation that engages both "self" and "other" in a process of reflection on the common and divergent values that inform the effort to live both joint and disparate projects (Blaney and Inayatullah 1994; Parekh 1996).

Second, in such a global conversation, the "other" stands not simply as an antagonist, but also as a resource for self-reflecting, learning, and designing arrangements for peaceful coexistence. Clifford Geertz (1986:111–112) calls us to draw "near to other people, engaging them, seeking to grasp them in their immediacy and difference." We should do so partly because difference may offer "alternatives for us," but more because diversity has the power, when engaged, to make it clear to us "at what sort of angle" we and others "stand to the world." However, we cannot be satisfied simply with the self-knowledge made possible by engaging the "other" held at a distance. As our reading of Bull and Walzer indicates, difference cannot be conceived as easily separated by boundaries. Geertz (1986:120–21) himself suggests "that rather than being sorted into framed units, social spaces with definite edges to them, seriously disparate approaches to life are becoming scrambled together in ill-defined expanses, social spaces whose edges are unfixed, irregular, and difficult to locate." The implications are profound: where "those worlds and those alien turns of mind are mostly not elsewhere, but, alternatives for us, hard nearby, . . . a certain readjustment in both our rhetorical habits and our sense of mission would seem to be called for." (Geertz 1986:119)

More precisely, this situation requires that we give up the immediate recourse to invidious comparisons that justify "the application of force to secure conformity to the values of those who possess the force," but that we also refuse to be drawn into a "vacuous tolerance that, engaging nothing, changes nothing" (Geertz 1986:118). Rather, we are called to engage the "other" imaginatively and to "explore the character of the space between" us, as a prelude to living together and separately, better and more peacefully (Geertz 1986:118–19). Designing such arrangements for mutual coexistence may involve drawing on the varied, localized arrangements for negotiating cultural difference as potential models for recognizing, tolerating, and celebrating difference, as our reading of Walzer suggests. This points towards arrangements, both locally and globally, much different from those offered by the Westphalian splitting of "inside/outside." And, as above, we must avoid the temptation to eliminate difference globally by turning too readily to a model of uniform constitutionalism implied by the cosmopolitan political imagination. We can expect the relevance of such a solution to be limited, perhaps only in certain issue areas or across only a limited local or regional spatial domain. We will have to look as much to heterogeneous arrangements, to forms of "accommodation of cultural diversity," in James Tully's terms (1995:184), or "codes of co-survival," in Ashis Nandy (Sheth and Nandy, 1996:20).

Third, given the necessary heterogeneity of such arrangements, our very understanding of sovereignty is stretched, perhaps to the breaking point. As opposed to the hegemony of territorially demarcated jurisdictions, authority might be distributed differently according to task (Onuf 1998:123–24, 134–37)—sometimes territorially in the name of citizenship, sometimes by cultural/identity group dispersed across existing jurisdictions, and sometimes globally in the name of humanity. Any given space may be administered by multiple actors for multiple purposes in such a way that sovereignty appears necessarily divided and overlapping. How is this so? One implication of this heterogeneity of forms is that we can see more clearly that territorial boundaries have always had multiple purposes or been associated with multiple rights that have been bundled together in the name of sovereignty. We can also see that these purposes and rights can be unbundled and assigned different masters or agents in a reformed global social and political architecture (Kratochwil 1986; Ruggie 1993).[23] However, we may have made this sound too easy, implying that each task or purpose can be neatly demarcated from others and that an undisputed authority can be named for each task. Our response to Walzer above suggests that this is not always the case. World politics will revolve around precisely such questions of boundary drawing and the sanctioning of authority. Where agreement is possible, tasks can be performed and areas of action regulated with only minimal controversy. Spirited debate may be required by those involved where there is disagreement about how tasks break down or what kinds of rules are appropriate in an issue area. Where compromise on a standard response is impossible, we may have to accept that different groups (divided by culture, class, gender, religion) will behave differently and work to negotiate the uncertain or even overlapping jurisdictions this creates. We might say that it is never certain who is to be involved in making a "common" decision or how authority might need to be divided in order to respect difference. Such decisions are the stuff of politics in a world facing, rather than deferring, the problem of difference.

References

Asch, Ronald G. (1997) *The Thirty Years' War: The Holy Roman Empire and Europe, 1618–1648.* New York: St. Martin's Press.

---

[23] Another issue that arises concerns the decision about which groups are to be involved and, perhaps more troubling, the possibility that group identities will be frozen in this process of drawing jurisdictions and assigning authority. William Connolly (1995: Introduction) suggests that, though every political settlement inevitably sediments group identities, it also spurs the assertion of alternative identities and demands for new settlements. Since political settlements are inescapable, he recommends the cultivation of an "ethos" of responsiveness to these assertions of new identities. Arend Lijphart (1995) is similarly sensitive to this issue in relation to consociational settlements that may ossify given national or ethnic identities.

Barber, Benjamin. (1995) *Jihad vs. McWorld: How Globalism and Tribalism Are Reshaping the World.* New York: Ballantine.

Baumgold, Deborah. (1993) Pacifying Politics: Resistance, Violence, and Accountability in Seventeenth-Century Contract Theory. *Political Theory* **21**(1):6–27.

Benjamin, Jessica. (1988) *The Bonds of Love: Psychoanalysis, Feminism, and the Problem of Domination.* New York: Pantheon Books.

Blaney, David L., and Naeem Inayatullah. (1994) Prelude to a Conversation of Cultures in International Society? Todorov and Nandy on the Possibility of Dialogue. *Alternatives* **19**(1):23–51.

Blaney, David L., and Naeem Inayatullah. (1996) "The Third World and a Problem with Borders." In *Perspectives on Third World Sovereignty: The Postmodern Paradox*, edited by Mark E. Denham and Mark Owen Lombardi, pp. 83–101. New York: St. Martin's Press.

Boucher, David. (1998) *Political Theories of International Relations.* Oxford: Oxford University Press.

Bozeman, Ada. (1984) "The International Order of a Multicultural World." In *The Expansion of International Society*, edited by Hedley Bull and Adam Watson, pp. 387–406. Oxford: Clarendon.

Brightwell, Peter. (1979) The Spanish Origins of the Thirty Years' War. *European Studies Review* **9**(4):409–431.

Bull, Hedley. (1966) "The Grotian Conception of International Society." In *Diplomatic Investigations: Essays in the Theory of International Politics*, edited by Martin Wight and Herbert Butterfield, pp. 51–73. Cambridge, MA: Harvard University Press.

Bull, Hedley. (1977) *The Anarchical Society: A Study of Order in World Politics.* New York: Columbia University Press.

Bull, Hedley. (1979) "The State's Positive Role in World Affairs." In *The State*, edited by Stephen Graubard, pp. 111–23. New York: W. W. Norton.

Bull, Hedley. (1984a) *Justice in International Relations.* Waterloo, Ontario: University of Waterloo.

Bull, Hedley. (1984b) "The Revolt Against the West." In *The Expansion of International Society*, edited by Hedley Bull and Adam Watson, pp. 217-228. Oxford: Clarendon.

Bull, Hedley, and Adam Watson. (1984) "Conclusion." In *The Expansion of International Society*, edited by Hedley Bull and Adam Watson, pp. 425–435. Oxford: Clarendon.

BURZAN, BARRY. (1991) *Peoples, States, and Fear: An Agenda for International Security Studies in a Post–Cold War Era*. Boulder and London: Lynne Rienner.

CAMPBELL, DAVID. (1992) *Writing Security: United States Foreign Policy and the Politics of Identity*. Minneapolis, MN: University of Minnesota Press.

CHATTERJEE, PARTHA. (1995) Religious Minorities and the Secular State: Reflections on an Indian Impasse. *Public Culture* **8**(1):11–39.

COLLINGWOOD, R. G. (1981 [1945]) *The Idea of Nature*. Oxford: Oxford University Press.

CONNOLLY, WILLIAM E. (1995) *The Ethos of Pluralization*. Minneapolis, MN: University of Minnesota Press.

CONNOLLY, WILLIAM E. (1999) *Why I Am Not a Secularist*. Minneapolis, MN: University of Minnesota Press.

CREPPELL, INGRID. (1996) "Locke on Toleration: The Transformation of Constraint." *Political Theory* **24**(2):200–240.

DORE, RONALD. (1984) "Unity and Diversity in Contemporary World Culture." In *The Expansion of International Society*, edited by Hedley Bull and Adam Watson, pp. 407–424. Oxford: Clarendon.

DUNNE, TIM. (1995) "International Society: Theoretical Promise Fulfilled?" *Cooperation and Conflict* **30**(2):125–154.

DUNNE, TIM. (1998) *Inventing International Society: A History of the English School*. New York: St. Martin's Press.

DWORKIN, RONALD. (1983) To Each His Own. *New York Review of Books* (April 14):4–6.

FALK, RICHARD A. (1995) *On Humane Governance: Towards a New Global Politics*. Cambridge, U.K.: Polity Press.

FERGUSON, YALE H., AND RICHARD W. MANSBACH. (1996) Political Space and Westphalian States in a World of "Polities": Beyond Inside/Outside. *Global Governance* **2**(2):261–287.

FRASER, NANCY. (1997) *Justice Interruptus: Critical Reflections on the "Postsocialist" Condition*. New York and London: Routledge.

FRIEDMAN, THOMAS. (1999) *The Lexus and the Olive Tree*. New York: Farrar, Straus, and Giroux.

FRIEDRICH, CARL, AND CHARLES BLITZER. (1957) *The Age of Power*. Ithaca: Cornell University Press.

GALSTON, WILLIAM A. (1991) *Liberal Purposes: Goods, Virtues, and Diversity in the Liberal State*. Cambridge, U.K.: Cambridge University Press.

GEERTZ, CLIFFORD. (1986) The Uses of Diversity. *Michigan Quarterly Review* **21**(1):105–123.

GREIDER, WILLIAM. (1997) *One World, Ready or Not: The Manic Logic of Global Capitalism.* New York: Simon and Schuster.

GROSS, LEO. (1968) "The Peace of Westphalia, 1648–1948." In *International Law and Organization*, edited by Richard A. Falk and W. Hanreider. New York: J. B. Lippincott.

GUTMANN, MYRON P. (1988) The Origins of the Thirty Years' War. *Journal of Interdisciplinary History* **18**(4):749–770.

HERZ, JOHN. (1959) *International Politics in the Atomic Age.* New York: Columbia University Press.

HINSLEY, F. H. (1986) *Sovereignty*, 2d. ed. Cambridge, U.K.: Cambridge University Press.

INAYATULLAH, NAEEM, AND DAVID L. BLANEY. (1995) Realizing Sovereignty. *Review of International Studies* **21**(1):3–20.

INAYATULLAH, NAEEM, AND DAVID L. BLANEY. (1996) "Knowing Encounters: Beyond Parochialism in International Relations Theory." In *The Return of Culture and Identity in IR Theory*, edited by Yosef Lapid and Friedrich Kratochwil, pp. 65–84. Bounder and London: Lynne Rienner.

JACKSON, ROBERT H. (1990) *Quasi-States: Sovereignty, International Relations, and the Third World.* Cambridge: Cambridge University Press.

JENKINSON, SALLY J. (1995) Bayle on Hobbes, Locke, and Fundamentalism: A Critique within the Liberal Ethical Tradition. Manuscript.

KRASNER, STEPHEN D. (1993) "Westphalia and All That." In *Ideas and Foreign Policy: Beliefs, Institutions, and Political Change*, edited by Judith Goldstein and Robert O. Keohane. Ithaca and London: Cornell University Press.

KRASNER, STEPHEN D. (1999) *Sovereignty: Organized Hypocrisy.* Princeton: Princeton University Press.

KRATOCHWIL, FRIEDRICH. (1986) Of Systems, Boundaries, and Territoriality: An Inquiry into the Formation of the State System. *World Politics* **39**(1):27–52.

KYMLICKA, WILL. (1995) *Multicultural Citizenship.* Oxford: Oxford University Press.

LANGER, HERBERT. (1980) *Thirty Years' War.* New York: Hippocrene Books.

LIJPHART, AREND. (1977) *Democracy in Plural Societies: A Comparative Exploration.* New Haven and London: Yale University Press.

LIJPHART, AREND. (1995) "Self-Determination versus Pre-Determination of Ethnic Minorities in Power-Sharing Systems." In *The Rights of Minority Cultures*, edited by Will Kymlicka, pp. 275–287. Oxford: Oxford University Press.

LINKLATER, ANDREW. (1998) *The Transformation of Political Community*. University of South Carolina Press.

LIPSCHUTZ, RONNIE J., WITH J. MAYER. (1996) *Global Civil Society and Global Environmental Governance*. Albany, NY: SUNY Press.

LOCKHART, PAUL DOUGLAS. (1995) Religion and Princely Properties: Denmark's Intervention in the Thirty Years' War, 1618–1625. *International History Review* **17**(1):1–22.

LYNN, JOHN. (1991) Soldiers on the Rampage. *MHQ: The Quarterly Journal of Military History* **3**(2):92–101.

LYONS, GENE M., AND MICHAEL MASTANDUNO, EDS. (1995) *Beyond Westphalia: State Sovereignty and International Intervention*. Baltimore and London: Johns Hopkins.

MACMILLAN, JOHN, AND ANDREW LINKLATER. (1995) *Boundaries in Question: New Directions in International Relations*. London: Pinter.

MORGENTHAU, HANS. (1967) *Politics among Nations: The Struggle for Power and Peace*, 4th ed. New York: Alfred Knopf.

MORSE, EDWARD L. (1976) *Modernization and the Transformation of International Relations*. New York: Free Press.

NANDY, ASHIS. (1983) *The Intimate Enemy: Loss and Recovery of Self under Colonialism*. Delhi: Oxford University.

NANDY, ASHIS. (1990) "The Politics of Secularism and the Recovery of Religious Tolerance." In *Contending Sovereignties: Redefining Political Community*, edited by R. B. J. Walker and Saul H. Mendlovitz, pp. 125–144. Boulder and London: Lynne Rienner.

NARDIN, TERRY. (1983) *Law, Morality, and the Relations of States*. Princeton: Princeton University Press.

NICHOLS, GARY. (1989) The Economic Impact of the Thirty Years' War in Habsburg Austria. *East European Quarterly* **23**(3):257–268.

ONUF, NICHOLAS GREENWOOD. (1998) *The Republican Legacy in International Thought*. Cambridge, U.K.: Cambridge University Press.

PAGES, GEORGE. (1970 [1939]) *The Thirty Years' War*, trans. by David Maland and John Hooper. New York: Harper and Row.

PAREKH, BHIKHU. (1996) "Minority Practices and Principles of Toleration." *International Migration Review* **30**(1):251–284.

PARKER, GEOFFREY, ED. (1997) *The Thirty Years' War*, 2d ed. New York: Routledge.

RAWLS, JOHN. (1996) *Political Liberalism.* New York: Columbia University Press.

RUGGIE, JOHN GERARD. (1993) Territoriality and Beyond: Problematizing Modernity in International Relations. *International Organization* **47**(1):139–174.

RUGGIE, JOHN GERARD. (1998) *Constructing the World Polity: Essays on International Institutionalization.* London and New York: Routledge.

SHAPIRO, MICHAEL J., AND HAYWARD ALKER, EDS. (1996) *Challenging Boundaries: Global Flows, Territorial Identities.* Minneapolis, MN: University of Minnesota Press.

SHETH, D. L., AND ASHIS NANDY. (1996) "Introduction." In *The Multiverse of Democracy: Essays in Honour of Rajni Kothari*, edited by D. L. Sheth and Ashis Nandy, pp. 9–23. New Delhi: Sage.

SOGUK, NEVZAT. (1999) *States and Strangers: Refugees and Displacements of Statecraft.* Minneapolis, MN: University of Minnesota Press.

SPINNER, JEFF. (1994) *The Boundaries of Citizenship: Race, Ethnicity, and Nationality in a Liberal State.* Baltimore and London: Johns Hopkins University Press.

SPRUYT, HENDRIK. (1994) *The Sovereign State and Its Competitors.* Princeton: Princeton University Press.

STRANG, DAVID. (1996) "Contested Sovereignty: The Social Construction of Colonial Imperialism." In *State Sovereignty as Social Construct*, edited by Cynthia Weber and Thomas J. Biersteker, pp. 22–49. Cambridge, U.K.: Cambridge University Press.

TAYLOR, CHARLES. (1992) "The Politics of Recognition." In *Multiculturalism and the "Politics of Recognition,"* by Charles Taylor and Amy Gutmann, pp. 25–73. Princeton: Princeton University Press.

THEIBAULT, JOHN. (1995) *German Villages in Crisis: Rural Life in Hesse-Kassel and the Thirty Years' War, 1580–1720.* Atlantic Heights, NJ: Humanities Press.

THOMSON, S. HARRISON. (1963) *Europe in Renaissance and Reformation.* New York: Harcourt, Brace, and World.

TODOROV, TZVETAN. (1986) *The Conquest of America: The Question of the Other.* New York: Harper and Row.

TOULMIN, STEPHEN. (1990) *Cosmopolis: The Hidden Agenda of Modernity.* Chicago: University of Chicago Press.

TREVOR-ROPER, H. R. (1962) Why Do Wars Begin? *Horizon* **5**(2):32–41.

Tuck, Richard. (1988) "Scepticism and Tolerance in the Seventeenth Century." In *Justifying Toleration: Conceptual and Historical Perspectives*, edited by Susan Mendus, pp. 21–35. Cambridge, U.K.: Cambridge University Press.

Tully, James. (1993) *An Approach to Political Philosophy: Locke in Contexts*. Cambridge, U.K.: Cambridge University Press.

Tully, James. (1995) *Strange Multiplicity: Constitutionalism in an Age of Diversity*. Cambridge, U.K.: Cambridge University Press.

Van Creveld, Martin. (1999) *The Rise and Decline of the State*. Cambridge, U.K.: Cambridge University Press.

Vincent, John. (1986) *Human Rights and International Relations*. Cambridge, U.K.: Cambridge University Press.

Waldron, Jeremy. (1988) "Locke: Toleration and the Rationality of Persecution." In *Justifying Toleration*, edited by Susan Mendus, pp. 61–86. Cambridge: Cambridge University Press.

Walker, R. B. J. (1993) *Inside/Outside: International Relations As Political Theory*. Cambridge, U.K.: Cambridge University Press.

Walzer, Michael. (1980) "The Moral Standing of States: A Response to Four Critics." *Philosophy and Public Affairs* **9**(3):209–229.

Walzer, Michael. (1983) *Spheres of Justice: A Defense of Pluralism and Equality*. New York: Basic Books.

Walzer, Michael. (1988) *The Company of Critics: Social Criticism and Political Commitment in the Twentieth Century*. New York: Basic Books.

Walzer, Michael. (1994) *Thick and Thin: Moral Argument at Home and Abroad*. Notre Dame, IN: Notre Dame University Press.

Walzer, Michael. (1997) *On Toleration*. New Haven and London: Yale University Press.

Walzer, Michael, and Ronald Dworkin. (1983) Spheres of Justice: An Exchange. *New York Review of Books* (July 21):43–44.

Watson, Adam. (1987) "Hedley Bull, States Systems, and International Societies." *Review of International Studies* **13**(2):147–153.

Weber, Cynthia, and Thomas J. Biersteker, Eds. (1996) *State Sovereignty As Social Construct*. Cambridge, U.K.: Cambridge University Press.

Wedel, K. A. (1991) History as Truth: The Hutterian (Habansky) Experience in Moravia During the Thirty Years' War. *Studia Comeniania Et Historica* **21**(43):41–60.

Weeks, Charles Adrian. (1991) Jacob Boheme and the Thirty Years' War. *Central European History* **24**(2–3):213–221.

WEISS, THOMAS G,. AND LEON GORDENKER, EDS. (1996) *NGOs, the UN, and Global Governance.* Boulder and London: Lynne Rienner.

WIGHT, MARTIN. (1966) "Why is there no International Theory?" In *Diplomatic Investigations: Essays in the Theory of International Politics*, edited by Martin Wight and Herbert Butterfield, pp. 17–35. Cambridge, MA: Harvard University Press.

WOOTTON, DAVID. (1993) "Introduction." In *Political Writings of John Locke*, edited by David Wootton, pp. 7–122.

The End of Empire and the Extension of the Westphalian System: The Normative Basis of the Modern State Order

Hendrik Spruyt

Department of Political Science, Arizona State University

The Case for the Impact of Norms on Decolonization

Winston Churchill confidently remarked in 1942 how he had not "become the King's minister in order to preside over the liquidation of the British Empire."[1] The French government similarly ruled out African independence for many years to come at the Brazzaville conference of 1944. The Dutch governor-general proclaimed proudly in 1937 that he expected Dutch rule over the East Indies to last another three hundred years.[2] Nevertheless, within two decades all their vast imperial holdings had dwindled to a few scattered territories. Those that remained had been granted considerable autonomy—and ultimately became fully independent as well. The sun had set on the empires that once held sway over the world.

The speed and ubiquitousness of the decolonization process demonstrates that this was not an isolated process relating only to the fortunes of individual powers. Small states such as the Netherlands and Belgium were ousted within fifteen years of the war. But more powerful Britain and France similarly lost vast territories in the span of only a few years. Only Portugal fought a rearguard action but eventually had to yield by 1974. The similarity across outcomes and synchronicity of events suggests that a broad systemic process was at work.

[1] Betts (1985:182).

[2] Van den Doel (1996:244).

Published by Blackwell Publishers, 350 Main Street, Malden, MA 02148, USA, and 108 Cowley Road, Oxford OX4 1JF, UK.

Despite domestic differences within the various metropoles all West European countries (save Portugal) decolonized in the span of less than two decades.

Changes in the material conditions in the postwar period had something to do with it. Shifts in the relative balance of power between center and periphery made empire more costly. The economic benefits of empire also declined. Moreover, with a hegemonic United States opposing imperial preference schemes in favor of a liberal trading system, the West European powers could no longer claim their empires as their exclusive markets.

This essay, however, does not address such materialist accounts, even though they may be important elements of a theory of decolonization. I do not offer an explanation of decolonization per se. Instead I consider a rival explanation that stresses how normative changes within the imperial metropoles were the key causal variable. Can the decisiveness and pace of decolonization be explained by normative changes in the metropoles?[3] This seems at least intuitively plausible. The historical record suggests that the metropoles had started to modify their justification for holding on to these territories well before the post–World War II era. Dutch colonial policy, once officially denoted as the "Policy of the Positive Balance Sheet," had been reclassified as "The Ethical Policy" at the turn of the century.[4] The British and French, in the interwar period, held some areas as "mandates" and later "trustee territories" rather than outright colonies. Other peripheries were reclassified as "overseas provinces." The rhetoric had thus most certainly changed. Nineteenth-century jingoism and "white man's burden" had become slogans of a bygone era.

Contrary to this literature, however, I argue that norms played a far more important role in the periphery than in the metropoles. Imperial capitals and populations were relatively untroubled with the moral rectitude of empire.

Moreover, much of the discussion on the impact of norms fails to distinguish between the different types of normative discourse, and does not clarify how they might have causal significance. Yes, norms mattered, but how did they matter, and what kinds of norms were invoked? I, therefore, link a discussion of the various types of normative discourse to an explanation of why normative concerns about empire played only a minor role in the imperial centers, but emerged as key mobilizing forces in the colonial periphery. Three factors determine the relative impact of norms: the internal consistency of a particular normative framework, the incentives for political entrepreneurs to champion

---

[3] I use Doyle's terminology. "Empire . . . is a system of interaction, between two political entities, one of which, the dominant metropole, exerts political control over the internal and external policy—the effective sovereignty—of the other, the subordinate periphery." Doyle (1986:12). In this essay I interchange "metropole" and "center," as well as "periphery" and "colony."

[4] Van den Doel (1996:153).

certain norms over others, and the feedback from the broader environment. In tracing the causal impact of norms on the retreat from empire and the extension of the Westphalian system, I hope to illuminate the dynamics behind decolonization and hope to contribute to a growing body of literature on the impact of norms.[5]

A Typology of Normative Arguments

While there is a large and growing body of literature that stresses the role of norms, this literature often interchanges different understandings of norms. I advocate distinguishing among three types: norms that delineate moral rules, norms that are part of taken-for-granted scripts, and norms that serve as guidelines for utilitarian purposes. In this section I further discuss how each of these types of discourse pertains to decolonization.

Norms as Moral Rules

Norms in this understanding refer to rules that distinguish moral from immoral actions and behaviors.[6] They are internalized guidelines that substantively inform preferences. Norms are not derivative of exogenously postulated (material) interests but are independent determinants of preferences and behaviors.

This view of the causal impact of norms informs the claim that metropolitan democracies ultimately deemed democracy inconsistent with empire. At its core, argue the proponents of this view, democracy implies equal access to office, the right to choose one's political officials, and equality before the law. Contractual elements in democratic theory stress the reciprocal exchange between government and its citizens. Such contractual aspects are absent in the subjugation of colonial subjects to the imperial metropole. The former was expected to recognize rule, but did not receive the rights of metropolitan citizens. Hence, imperial rule was morally reprehensible.

This tension between the inequality of the colonial relation and the equality proffered by metropolitan democratic principles ultimately led to dissension within the metropole and delegitimation of the unequal and coercive imperial relation. Robert Jackson is certainly one of the most articulate advocates of this view:

---

[5] See Finnemore (1993, 1996); Price (1995, 1998); Tannenwald (1999).

[6] Finnemore similarly distinguishes between norms as rule-like prescriptions and as moral statements (1993:566). Goldstein and Keohane (1993:9) use the term "principled beliefs" for the latter category.

> Underlying all these causes . . . was a fundamental shift of normative ideas and a corresponding change of mind on the part of most sovereign governments and the public opinion influencing them concerning the right to sovereign statehood.[7]

Adam Watson similarly claims that

> "within ten years [of WW II] it had become clear to political leaders and to the majority of informed opinion in the democratic countries of the west that colonialism had by then become as unacceptable as slavery a century before."[8]

Norms thus had independent causal force. They were not derivative of other (imputed) preferences but indeed formed metropolitan preferences.

It is worth pointing out that these norms were not endogenous elements of the Westphalian system. Recognizing territorial sovereignty as the constitutive principle of the international system does not imply that states must have democratic regimes, nor does it speak about the relations of the sovereign authority and the regions that make up the polity. If there were moral tensions, they were between empire and other principles that emerged within the West European states.

Norms as Taken-for-Granted Scripts

Norms can also be understood as a matrix of constitutive principles that govern the behaviors of members of a given social group. Group members accept and play certain roles that lend predictability to their behaviors and credibility to their statements. Entrants have little choice but to accept these existing rules and principles. Socialization into the script forms a *sine qua non* condition for entry and recognition.[9]

As with the previous understanding of norms (as moral precepts), this meaning gives norms considerable independent explanatory power. If actors take particular principles as a given, then such normative frameworks determine choices and preferences. Norms are not derivative of other presumed "real" interests and preferences, nor are they merely invoked to explain the residual variation of behavior that is not fully explained by more materialist accounts.

In this spirit, one might argue that the current script in the international system legitimates only sovereign territorial states as actors of that society.

---

[7] Jackson (1993:129). See also Jackson (1990: chapter 4).

[8] Watson (1992:295).

[9] See the discussion of the concepts of taken-for-grantedness and social scripts in DiMaggio and Powell (1983); Abercrombie (1986); and Finnemore (1996).

Other actors are excluded.[10] Hence, political elites do well to take the sovereign state system for granted, and structure their polities according to expectations and principles that govern the behavior of others.

Robert Jackson argues not only that empire is morally suspect but also that empire violates the sovereignty script.[11] Empire might be at odds with the constitutive principle of sovereign territoriality in two ways. First, it denies some actors legal equality, the premise contained in the sovereignty principle.[12] Subjugation of others to a colonial position, mandate status, or a euphemistic overseas territory, violates that equality. Second, sovereign statehood entails territorial delimitation of jurisdiction. Empire and commensurate expansionist policies suggest that the actor seeks to expand its sphere of hierarchical governance, and hence encroach on the sovereignty of others. The quest for world empire is the starkest representation of such behavior.

In a long process of maturation, sovereign territoriality has emerged as a key principle of international relations—often associated with the Peace of Westphalia but arguably emerging well before that, and only entrenched well after 1648. Hence, it has now acquired a taken-for-granted quality in that it informs individual actors' calculations and behaviors. The reinforcement of this script over many decades has made empire obsolete and illegitimate. Miles Kahler thus argues that empires have become less viable forms of organization as sovereignty has become more entrenched.[13]

The taken-for-grantedness has not only been reinforced by diplomatic practice and the repetitive interaction of states on the basis of territorial sovereignty, but also by international agreements and organizations. The United Nations charter thus delegitimizes imperialism—a trend that commenced with the League of Nations.

Norms as Utilitarian Conventions

A third approach stresses norms in the utilitarian sense. Norms serve functional purposes: They regulate behavior, reduce uncertainty by institutionalizing conventions, signal expectations, and reveal information.[14] For example, the norm "cooperate with another, and punish transgression, but be forgiving," might emerge as the consequence of iterative behavior over time.[15]

---

[10] See Spruyt (1994); Thomson (1990).

[11] Jackson (1993:114).

[12] For discussions see Hinsley (1969); James (1986); and Benn (1967).

[13] Kahler (1997).

[14] For a similar understanding, see Garrett and Weingast (1993).

[15] Axelrod (1981, 1984, 1986).

Contrary to the first two approaches, norms do not inform preferences. Instead preferences are postulated exogenously and norms emerge in response to those preferences. Norms are thus derivative of those preferences and the explanation of why they emerge must center on their efficacy and efficiency in meeting actors' interests.

This understanding of norms could very well acknowledge that normative discourse about the legitimacy of empire had shifted, as the two previous interpretations of the causal impact of norms on decolonization suggest. However, it would add that such norms must be explained by the preferences of actors and their changed calculations about the usefulness of empire. Moral appropriateness and taken-for-grantedness in this view are derivatives of established patterns of behavior over time. Because empires were once held to be useful (for security or economic purposes), they were subsequently legitimated as the general norm. Changing material conditions will thus lead to changes in preference structures and norm erosion, and to delegitimation of empire. Examining the change in discourse coterminously requires the analysis of material conditions surrounding the pursuit of empire.

An Examination of the Historical Record

I examine the impact of each of these three types of normative arguments—the claim that colonialism was incompatible with democracy (and hence morally reprehensible); the argument that the state system constituted a taken-for-granted script that contradicted empire; and the view that utilitarian norms suggested alternative logics of organization. I do so by examining two cases of decolonization: the Netherlands' retreat from the Dutch East Indies, and French decolonization.

These cases allow us to run a variety of tests and comparisons. Robert Jackson argues, largely by examining the British case, that democracy was antithetical to empire and colonies.[16] If so, then the democratic regimes in both the Netherlands and France should demonstrate a change in attitudes in the government and the general population about the moral rectitude of holding on to their subject territories.

He also suggests that sovereignty imposed a dominant script that challenged imperial rule. Again, both France and the Netherlands should have been subject to such rules. Both were members of key international organizations, such as the UN, that enshrined principles of sovereign self-determination. Indeed

[16] To be fair, Jackson acknowledges the strength of anticolonial sentiments in the East Indies and Indochina (Jackson 1990:82). However, this still does not clarify why moral sentiments in the Netherlands and France did not change. In fact it puts the question of why they did not change in even starker relief.

the Dutch had traditionally been ardent supporters of international organizations and international law. The French, of course, were one of the permanent members of the Security Council. One might thus have expected that these countries would accept the principles of self-determination that had been expounded at the dismantling of the German, Ottoman, and Austrian empires, and that had gained momentum in the interwar period. Did they indeed take the sovereignty/self-determination script for granted?

Finally, one might contend that instrumental calculations of declining benefits and rising costs of empire in general would change the previous justifications for empire. Such an argument should also apply to these two cases. Both countries had traditionally validated empire on utilitarian principles. Empire was morally justifiable because it improved the welfare and security of the home country. For France, the empire had been deemed essential for home defense and great power standing. The Dutch required that all policies in the East Indies be self-supporting and yield a positive benefit over costs for the mother country. Empire was considered legitimate and moral, and profitable to boot. The utilitarian perspective of norms should thus demonstrate a close fit between the changes in political discourse about the legitimacy and usefulness of empire, and a recalculation of the drawbacks and advantages of empire.

Jackson's view, and I do not take this as a straw-man perspective but as an insightful and potentially very powerful argument, presents the strong case for norms. He emphasizes the independent causal effect of moral sentiments and normative scripts. They inform individuals' preferences. The utilitarian perspective conveys norms' less independent explanatory power. Instead, the norms that individuals adopt show an elective affinity with material interests. (The latter are exogenously derived). France and the Netherlands pose "easy cases" for all of the three types of normative arguments—they were democracies, they ascribed to the sovereignty script, and they justified empire on functional grounds. Hence, they form good test cases.[17]

The Absence of Normative Concerns in the Metropole

Empire as a moral burden. There is little evidence to suggest that governments and societies in the Netherlands or France were particularly troubled with their subjection of distant territories. Quite the contrary: Despite the fact that both cherished fundamental democratic principles, democracy was not considered inherently antithetical to having overseas provinces (Algeria's status) or seeing distant territories as an integral part of the realm (as the East Indies). Among

[17] For discussions of the logic of case selection, see Eckstein (1975); Lijphart (1971); Van Evera (1996).

the parties in both countries only the far left favored outright independence for the colonies. The left, however, was not propelled by liberal democratic principles of equality and self-determination but by Marxist views that imperialism was a logical consequence of capitalism. Opposing the latter implied opposition to the former. Moreover, liberal political rights were simply epiphenomena of more fundamental economic rights. The far left's opposition to colonialism was thus not a consequence of democracy but of anticapitalist sentiments.

The positions of the socialist parties were more ambiguous. Less inspired by Marxist doctrine, they entertained liberal democratic notions of equality and self-determination. Labor solidarity should also extend to those subject to employer exploitation in the periphery. Such principles, however, were constantly weighed against the apparent benefits of empire for the metropolitan labor force. Rapid decolonization seemed to clash with protecting the economic welfare of domestic constituents. The Dutch Labor Party thus favored decolonization in principle but they believed there was no need to rush to decolonization given the serious consequences for Dutch labor.[18] Economic estimates (later proven to be incorrect) suggested that 14 percent of Dutch national income depended on control over Indonesia, and hence decolonization would impose considerable hardship on the socialist worker.[19] It is true that socialist workers became more ardent supporters of decolonization after the war, but even then they were willing to compromise their position in exchange for participation in the metropolitan governments.

To their right, the Christian-democratic parties, the liberals, and more extreme factions, proved even less bothered by normative concerns. The Catholics and Protestants in the Netherlands opted for hard-line policies and police actions against the newly proclaimed Indonesian republic.[20]

Similarly, the French centrist parties, the Socialists, and the Gaullists were more than willing to quell nationalist demands by force, most notably in Algeria and Indochina. Miles Kahler thus notes how parties outbid each other on the colonial issue, arguing not about the moral justifications of empire, but about who was responsible for the loss of the colonies. Ian Lustick reinforces this perspective of the French political situation in the 1950s when describing how politicians strove to create an image of "Greater France" encapsulating Algeria. Tony Smith notes "the stubborn colonial consensus that reigned from the Social-

---

[18] Van Doorn (1995a:22, 23; 1995b).

[19] Van den Doel (1996:248); Maddison (1990).

[20] Less well known than the French efforts to quell demands for independence, the Dutch deployed more than 150,000 troops in 1947 and 1948 to combat nationalist insurgents (Van Doorn 1995b).

ists to the Right."[21] Here too the Communists were the only ones who opposed empire outright.

The general electorate as well seemed relatively untroubled with maintaining its colonial presence. When the Dutch government launched the Second Police Action in December of 1948, it met concerted criticism from its western allies (England and the United States) and the United Nations. Nevertheless, surveys reveal that fully two-thirds favored the military actions despite international opposition.

French public opinion similarly seemed to suggest that opinion swung against those defeatists who spoke of retreat. De Gaulle acceded to power, not because people thought he would lead the country out of Africa, but because they believed he could resolve the impasse in domestic politics, and resolve the Algerian question.

In short, there was no dramatic shift in public opinion on colonial issues in either of these two democratic metropoles. If Jackson's argument perhaps holds for the British case, the West European democracies, by contrast, did not question the normative validity of maintaining their subject territories by whatever means deemed necessary. Stronger even, the political discussions suggested a moral burden on the metropole to remain rather than pull out.[22] The Dutch settlers (more than 200,000), business interests, and the pro-Dutch Indonesians, demanded Dutch presence. In France, the discussion centered around the obligation to the Pieds Noirs (about a million), and French sympathizers in the colonies. Abandonment was normatively unacceptable.[23]

The not so taken-for-granted script. Nor did metropolitan governments surrender their colonies because they recognized that they violated the principle of sovereign territorial rule. They freely acknowledged that the principle of sovereign territoriality formed a constitutive rule of international relations. However, they denied that this implied decolonization.

As said, sovereignty entails that governments be supreme within recognized borders and have no claims to authority beyond such borders. Sovereignty is thus based on mutual recognition and juridical equivalence among states. Alternative governance structures might claim internal hierarchy but not territorial delimitation (e.g., theocratic authorities); or they might be neither hierarchical nor territorially exclusive (feudal organization). Indeed some political organizations need not be territorially fixed (nomadic institutions). Such

---

[21] Smith (1981:106). See also Kahler (1984, 1997); Lustick (1993).

[22] Betts (1985: chapter 2).

[23] Betts (1985:207)

political entities would thus violate the sovereignty principle. Older empires, similarly, would be incompatible with sovereignty. Pre-modern empires were largely universalist in their claims to rule. They recognized no limits to their authority and recognized no other authority as equivalent.[24]

Modern colonial empires made no such claims. They recognized fixed territorial limits to their claims of jurisdiction. Subject territories were internally hierarchical (the metropolitan government ruled) and were externally represented by that same authority. They posed therefore no challenge to the sovereignty of recognized independent states. There was no contradiction between the sovereignty principle and control over the colonies—the latter were simply territories within the realm, even if they were not fully integrated.

Metropolitan policies, however, did contradict the principle of national self-determination.[25] If sovereignty meant that nations should be independent, as Woodrow Wilson claimed with particular regard to the remnants of Austria-Hungary and the Turkish Empire, then clearly modern empires violated that principle. But that principle was hardly taken for granted. Indeed, it is untenable in practice unless one argues that the roughly 3000 to 5000 ethnic groups that exist today should all constitute independent states.[26] Even apparently homogeneous nation-states are often recent amalgamations of different ethnic and racial groups.

One could, therefore, recognize and enshrine the principle of sovereign territoriality through a plethora of treaties and organizations to which both France and the Netherlands subscribed, while denying the principle of national self-determination. Sovereign territoriality constituted part of a taken-for-granted script; national self-determination did not.

This is not to say that there had not been any changes at all. We already noticed how the terms of political discourse regarding the colonies had changed. Indeed, the very term "colonies" had become suspect. They were relabeled as overseas territories or overseas provinces. Some of this was no doubt a semantic ploy to avoid violating international charters. Subjection of territories was passed off as an internal matter and hence falling under domestic jurisdiction rather than the de facto exercise of power of one state in the international system over another potentially independent entity. It was, however, not just semantics. Few metropoles espoused blatant exploitation, as in the nineteenth century. Instead, rational management of colonized peoples was the avowed aim. But, and this is key, the colonies were as of yet deemed unfit to be independent.

---

[24] Kratochwil (1986).

[25] Sovereignty can thus be contested in interpretations other than legal sovereignty. See also Barkin and Cronin (1994).

[26] Gellner (1983) and Hobsbawn (1990) mention those numbers.

To conclude, there is truth to the argument that the international system had moved towards further entrenchment of the sovereignty principle. Those areas controlled by the losing imperial powers of World War I, while not being granted independence, gained greater measures of self-governance as mandates. They were thus not simply incorporated as part of the victorious powers' other colonies. The international script, that determined what type of metropolitan rule was permissible, was thus changing. But here lay the rub: It left unanswered which territories were to be considered potentially sovereign entities. The modern sovereignty rule territorializes authority, it does not imply that such authority must be egalitarian or democratic.

Metropolitan powers thus regarded demands for secession as cases of civil, not international, conflict. Any attempt to suppress such sentiments did not constitute a violation of the sovereignty principle, since that principle only applied to the relation of internationally recognized independent entities. The taken-for-granted script was thus accepted, but considered inapplicable to these specific cases. Thus, metropoles could, with perfect logical consistency, repress nationalist sentiments *and* expect the international community to be on their side.

Utilitarian arguments for shifting norms. If neither France nor the Netherlands was swayed by moral quandaries of having overseas territories, and if neither thought that the principle of sovereignty precluded them from having colonies, is it nevertheless possible to argue that they changed their minds about the use-value and, concomitantly, the legitimacy of empires? Did they indeed change their views about the appropriateness of empire as an efficacious means of pursuing their states' interests, and did this lead to a shift in attitudes about the justifiability of empire?

At face value, given the changes in the postwar international conditions, one might have expected this indeed to be the case. England has since long calibrated the costs of empire against the costs of maintaining an imperial presence.[27] France, like England, had consistently derived military benefits from its overseas territories. Not only did its vast territorial holdings lend credence to the French claim of being a great power in the first place (the empire of prestige argument), but the colonies contributed in a very direct sense to the security of the metropole. Hundreds of thousands of colonial subjects had fought for France in World War I.[28] And going into World War II, French strategy still called for a stalling action on the European continent that would allow the metropole to mobilize thousands of Africans for home defense.[29]

---

[27] Friedberg (1988).

[28] See Betts (1985: chapter 1).

[29] Kupchan (1994:222).

Given the failure of the imperial strategy in World War II, and given the advent of nuclear weapons as a key benchmark for great power status, one might expect that Paris would have developed a different understanding of the appropriateness of empire for military purposes. Changes in material benefits would thus correlate with a reevaluation of the premise that France needed to maintain such territories for sake of prestige, moral obligation, or whatever terms had previously been employed to justify France's imperial pursuits.

Nothing of the kind emerged. Instead, the metropole reemphasized the notion that France needed the empire to retain its great power standing. Counter to realist expectations it even drew down its home defenses to maintain its subject areas while a greater danger loomed on the European continent. A more sober-minded realist perspective would have expected that utilitarian calculi would have generated a different understanding of the need for empire, but such a change in attitudes and discourse did not occur.[30]

Economic shifts might similarly suggest that empires might not be an efficient form of organization as well. If imperial preference schemes still seemed a viable alternative in the interwar period, particularly after the American Hawley-Smoot tariffs, the strategy had been made obsolete by Bretton Woods and American free trade. English domestic politics reflected such debates, between the imperial preference and Commonwealth advocates on one side and the liberal traders on the other.[31]

Moreover, the economic use-value of the colonies could be questioned regardless of the American success in spearheading a liberal trading regime with Bretton Woods and GATT. With growing economic interdependence in the decades before the war, some of the peripheral metropolitan commerce had started to shift to other participants. Indonesian trade, for example, had in the two decades prior to World War II switched decisively to Japan and the United States. In 1913 the Netherlands still accounted for 34 percent of the East Indies' exports and for 36 percent of its imports. By 1939 both these figures had dropped to 15 percent, while the United States had become the Indies' most important export market (21 percent of its total) with most imports (30 percent) coming from Japan.[32]

Such factors could potentially have led to a reevaluation of the economic advantages of empire; neither one did. French economic interests were more concerned with rebuilding their domestic economy, and with the appropriate

---

[30] For the Dutch the empire had never been a military resource, since it, as a small power, depended on alliances with greater powers (or neutrality) to maintain its defense. So for them not much had changed.

[31] Mansergh (1969:242–246).

[32] Maddison (1989, 1990); Van den Doel (1996:234).

degree of government interventionism. The profitability of overseas investments and holdings figured only in the background, although French economic interest groups were more protectionist and colonial than the British.[33] The mythology of "Greater France" did not help. The French "cartieriste" position, the rational calculation of the costs and benefits of empire, was a minority position at best.[34]

Rather than worry to what extent imperial preferences were antithetical to the principles of free trade and fair field, French policy aimed to incorporate special arrangements in the international agreements of which Paris was a part. French colonies thus had to have preferential access to the nascent European Economic Community.

The Dutch hard-nosed business sense would seem to make rational calculations more likely. After all, they had at one time labeled their own policy as one of the "Positive Balance Sheet." But they continued to argue that losing the Indies would lead to economic catastrophe, with job losses mounting into the hundreds of thousands. These figures proved later inaccurate, and of course none of the calculations presented the opportunity cost argument (whether investments at home would be more profitable). But the figures provided a rationale for the Dutch presence.

Interestingly, Robert Jackson argues that "the military and economic relations between European states and their colonies from 1955 to 1959 were not very different from what they had been from 1935 to 1939."[35] Hence, he suggests that normative changes in the metropole (that is, not in the sense of utilitarian guidelines) must have caused decolonization. Given the advent of the two superpowers and the Cold War, the occupation of many colonies by foreign powers during the World War II, and the emerging international trade regime after 1945, his starting proposition cannot hold. The international environment looked decidedly different. Two conclusions follow: first, material explanations for the withdrawal from empire might have considerable explanatory power, and hence the strong view of norms determining material interests does not hold in this case; second, at the very least, one would have expected changing instrumental calculations to lead to different justifications.

The Impact of Norms in the Periphery

Contrary to claims that the contradictions between democratic principles and the reality of colonialism challenged the West European colonial powers, these

[33] Smith (1981:109).

[34] Lustick (1993:151).

[35] Jackson (1993:130).

metropoles did not change their stance on the issues of colonialism and self-determination. Indeed, the very fact that the metropoles engaged in violent repression of nationalist movements—the Dutch in two Police Actions in the East Indies, the French particularly in Indochina and Algeria—already contradicts such an assessment. Thus, normative arguments go wrong in locating the impetus for imperial retreat within the metropole. Instead, the center of gravity lay in the nationalist capitals. Neither Paris nor the Hague was overcome by moral self-doubt. It was the periphery that reared up and used normative arguments against those very metropoles whence, at one time, such ideas as equality and self-determination had emerged.

The moral indignation with colonialism. If the metropoles were slow to see contradictions between democratic principles and colonialism, peripheral elites were far more aware of the hypocrisies of Western rule. Modernization of the periphery and the need to train local elites in Western governance exposed such elites to Western ideals of democratic equality, state building, and national self-determination. The indigenous cadres, some of which had been educated in the West, proved to be the primary suppliers of incipient nationalist leaders.[36]

Gandhi in England, Ho-Chi Minh in Paris, Hatta in Rotterdam, all had first-hand knowledge of democratic politics at work. And they were painfully aware that such principles had not been extended to the colonies. For example, the Dutch utilized three different legal systems based on the ethnic origins of the individuals. (They recognized a European legal system; an Indonesian one; and an Asian, non-Indonesian framework.) Equality before the law applied only within the operative legal code.

The metropolitans did not only deny indigenes political rights. Locals also continuously confronted limits to their career paths. Even the English, more progressive than the French and the Dutch in this regard, only belatedly opened up their civil service in India. Education, and thus career opportunities, were restricted.[37] As Benedict Anderson notes, these artificial ceilings created a motivation for elite resistance.[38]

Sovereignty as the taken-for-granted script. Nationalist leaders adopted the system of sovereign territorial rule from the West. Rather than resort to the pre-colonial forms of rule (such as clanship, patrimony, kingship), which either did not claim to be the sole locus of authority or which did not base their authority on territorial parameters, they adopted modern forms of public office and gov-

[36] For a discussion of the origins of nationalist leaders, see Emerson (1967).

[37] See Yasunaka (1970); Betts (1985:68f).

[38] Anderson (1991).

ernance. The nationalists demanded juridical equivalence with the "advanced" metropolitan countries. Moreover, adopting western notions of sovereign territoriality enhanced their acceptance among the already existing states. As David Strang points out, new polities that received such classification had greater chances at survival than those not so defined.[39]

But while adopting sovereign territoriality as the dominant script, they were far more cautious in accepting the principle of self-determination for all nationalist claims. While claiming the right of national self-determination as a rhetorical tool in the struggle with the metropolitan powers, they simultaneously denied those claims to indigenous groups within the territorial state that the nationalist leaders envisioned.[40] The Dutch were not incorrect in asserting that the nationalist (Javanese) claim for Indonesian independence subverted the possible independence of many areas and ethnic groups within the East Indies. Sukarno himself of course recognized that "the Dutch had invented Indonesia" given that it had never been a coherent political entity before. He was eager to lay claim to the entire territory as a unified state on the principle of sovereign equality with other states, disregarding local demands for true national self-determination.

French colonies as well built their new political institutions on the territorial parameters laid down by the metropole. National self-determination meant independence for the territorial unit constructed by the former imperial master, not self-determination for ethnic groups within that territorial unit. In short, the appropriation of the Western script was selective.

Moreover, international organizations provided fora for newly independent states to be heard.[41] No surprise, therefore, that erstwhile colonies, such as Australia and India, became strong proponents of decolonization in East Asia. As their numbers grew so did their voting power, which in turn emboldened yet other quests for independence. The non-Western powers thus became the strongest proponents of the sovereignty script.

Norms as correlates of instrumental choices. As suggested by the two previous sections, utilitarian calculations influenced how political elites packaged certain norms or how they chose to disseminate particular interpretations. Such elites selectively used norms to rise to power.[42] If they had been local inter-

---

[39] Strang (1991).

[40] Mayall (1990:120f).

[41] Between 1945 and 1970 one-third of the ninety-eight cases brought before the UN involved decolonization issues (Jacobson 1979:212).

[42] Snyder and Ballentine (1996) similarly suggest that political entrepreneurs may inflame particular nationalist discourses in newly democratizing states for strategic purposes.

mediaries who had been hampered by the glass ceiling in their careers, and who never could rise above the metropolitan representative, independence meant an end to artificial limits to their authority.

Independence not only entailed a rise in the domestic political hierarchy, but also conveyed international recognition of their status as leaders. Such legitimation enhanced their ability to retain office within their countries. Nationalist leaders were keenly aware of the dual status of sovereign authority. Not only does it limit other domestic claims to authority, but the international system—through mutual recognition of that sovereign—validates the sovereign as sole locus of authority in negotiating with the external environment.

This utilitarian use of norms does raise questions about the explanatory power of norms. Can one suffice with demonstrating that norms exogenously determine preferences or need one ascertain as well how they are related to the incentives and ability of elites to accept and "market" those norms? The argument presented here lends credence to the latter position. This does not reduce norms to mere epiphenomena. What may start as utilitarian calculi by individual actors to champion certain norms can, over time, take on the form of a given script. It does suggest that the impact of norms as moral guidelines or as taken-for-granted scripts cannot be devoid from accounts of the particular role they play in political agendas.

To sum up: the periphery rather than the metropoles invoked the normative arguments for decolonization, and they did so by turning Western principles against their rulers. Democratic ideals shaped how political leaders justified their resistance against the metropole. The existing constitutive rule of sovereign territoriality defined the range of international behaviors that nationalists could adopt, and entailed particular domestic strategies to simultaneously deny local ethnic and subnational claims. The international order empowered those individual political elites who were willing to play according to existing rules, while denying such status to others. Consequently, strategically motivated indigenes had incentives to adopt those behaviors rewarded by the system.

The Causal Dynamic of Normative Concerns in Metropole and Periphery

Some of the scholarly analysis has concentrated on demonstrating the independent impact of norms, rather than clarifying their causal origins. Nina Tannenwald, for example, demonstrates how normative concerns influenced behavior in directions that are not well understood by the realist paradigm.[43] Richard

[43] Tannenwald (1999).

Price argues for a genealogical method and distinguishes this from causal explanation.[44]

This essay supports the view that norms play an important independent role—they are not mere epiphenomena of exogenously postulated material interests. However, I argue that the acceptance of particular norms and their use correlate with utilitarian incentives to insert them into broad political platforms. Not content with merely tracing the relative impact of normative arguments in imperial metropoles and colonial peripheries, I suggest a general framework for studying how norms emerge as a causal factor influencing policies and preferences. The impact of particular norms will depend on three conditions. First, norms become politically salient when the relevant normative universe appears uniform. This makes it difficult to mobilize rival normative frameworks. Second, political entrepreneurs need to have strategic incentives to support and champion particular norms. This does not mean that the general population only adopts these norms on instrumental grounds. People might very well believe that certain principles constitute categorical imperatives and are just in and of themselves. However, the provision of such norms involves advocacy and the challenging of nonadherents, and thus constitutes in effect a public good. Individuals at large will thus free ride. The good will be underprovided unless there are individuals who are willing to bear the costs (in this case potential imprisonment or death for nationalist leaders) to advocate such norms. I hypothesize that without side payments (i.e., instrumental benefits) few leaders will champion such norms on ulterior motives alone.[45] Third, norms will spread when the international environment is permissive. Domestic normative frameworks require positive reinforcement from the environment in which they are placed. The domestic reinforcement in turn has a catalytic effect on other normative patterns.[46]

I illustrate this causal dynamic by clarifying how conditions in the metropole worked against continuation of empire becoming an important normative concern, whereas peripheral conditions facilitated the use of normative discourse against the center.

Metropolitan Dynamics

Contradictions in the substantive content of ideas. If normative concerns played a role in British decolonization (the example of Gandhi's appeal to the British public comes to mind) such similar dynamics were not at work in other West

---

[44] Price (1995:84).

[45] For the general exposition of collective action problems, see Olson (1965).

[46] The logic is similar to Axelrod's explanation (1981, 1984, 1986).

European democracies. Instead they opted for repression of nationalist demands even after World War II. Why did normative concerns play such a minor role in the decolonization processes of these democracies?

The first reason lies in the moral ambiguities of territorial retreat. Was colonialism antithetical to democracy? Was empire at odds with the principle of sovereign territoriality? Was empire becoming less useful and on those grounds less justifiable? Such queries sparked other questions rather than provide for easy benchmarks to delineate inappropriate policies from others. For example, even if colonialism was at odds with democracy, it left unanswered what specific type of metropolitan governance was odious. The Dutch recognized the more egregious exploitation of the mid-nineteenth century and had overhauled their imperial administration. Paternalistic arguments and policies became more prominent. Similarly, the French mixed colonialism with its much vaunted "mission civilisatrice."[47] So if all could agree that the nineteenth-century norms that justified blatant exploitation had changed, there was far less clarity on whether colonialism constituted such exploitation in the twentieth century. Indeed, independence in principle was not the issue. The question was rather whether the local elites were deemed capable of self-rule. Even if repressive and exploitive colonialism had become odious, the classification of what constituted colonialism in the pejorative sense was contested and hence open to multiple interpretations.

Normative arguments also played a relatively minor role in the metropole because arguments for decolonization conflicted with other moral concerns.[48] Paternalistic arguments were not merely instrumental calculations. They were in some respects perhaps even well intentioned concerns with the capacity of local indigenes for effective self-rule. There was also concern about the self-interested motives inspiring some nationalist leaders. (For example, the Dutch concern with Javanese dominance over the other islands influenced their decision-making, and indeed at least some of the non-Javanese shared those concerns.) Moreover, the nationalists had associated themselves with enemies of the metropole (Japan in particular during World War II, and the USSR thereafter). Combating nationalist demands thus justified fighting those who had made common cause with Imperial Japan during the war (in the Dutch case) or with communist powers (in the Indo-Chinese and Algerian cases).[49] Furthermore, loyalty to

---

[47] Betts (1985:190).

[48] Kathryn Sikkink somewhat similarly argues that human rights concerns only came to the forefront when other "more powerful clusters of ideas/interests had subsided" (Sikkink 1993:162). But note that this observation still requires one to explain why certain clusters become salient and others do not.

[49] Goto (1996).

the brethren abroad dictated that metropolitan powers maintain their presence. Abandoning kin to unscrupulous, self-serving, and nondemocratic nationalists would jeopardize their properties, indeed their very lives. If there were norms pushing for decolonization, there were also norms that suggested continuation of the imperial hold. Indeed, the correct course of action might be construed as the responsibility to stay in.

Finally, the impact of norms depends on their position within larger webs of significance.[50] The argument that normative shifts precipitated debates on decolonization presupposes that the metropole recognizes the other actor as distinct from itself. Hence, I have used the terms "core" and "periphery." But as Ian Lustick points out, this very terminology is at stake.[51] All states at some points in their history of state-building may be deemed "imperial" in how they incorporate distinct ethnic groups and local governance structures. Modern France, often used as an exemplar of a nation-state, only really constituted itself as such in the course of the nineteenth century. And while few Americans would see contemporary Arizona, California, or Hawaii as distinct and subject polities (and hence perhaps deserving independence) they were, of course, not part of the original federation. Successful state building requires the transgression of a Gramscian threshold. Polities that can successfully transgress such a threshold will integrate into a coherent entity. Core and periphery fade to become one entity. History covers the tracks of diversity.

Whether this was true for the French with regard to Algeria is a matter of debate. But to the extent that some Frenchmen and settlers saw Algeria as an integral part of France proper, the issue no longer was one of independence for a subject area, but one of secession from the home country. Algeria could not be regarded as a decolonization question in the same vein as sub-Saharan Africa could. The latter had not been considered part of the home country and, hence, could be incorporated in the normative discourse within the metropole and periphery about decolonization because both core and periphery recognized each other as such. If such recognition is not present, the very vocabulary of "decolonization" is considered inappropriate and nonsensical.

A comparison with the British in India might be illustrative. Why did normative concerns in the metropole perhaps play a greater role there? First, English paternalism contrasted with the French push for cultural assimilation.[52] The

---

[50] The term is Clifford Geertz's (1973).

[51] Lustick (1993). While I agree with Lustick that part of the Gramscian move is to get metropolitans to identify the erstwhile periphery as part of the home country, I would argue that the Gramscian hegemony is only complete when the periphery comes to see itself as an integral part of the former core.

[52] Smith (1981:98).

overall cognitive framework differed. Second, the nationalists in India had not exploited the Japanese war efforts to the same extent as some nationalists in Southeast Asia (as did Sukarno and Hatta in Indonesia). Third, British settlement in India was marginal. Dutch settlement in Indonesia, by contrast, was twice as high in absolute terms as British presence in India, despite having a much smaller metropolitan population base. The million or so "pieds noirs" in Algeria could similarly argue that they were entitled to continued metropolitan governance. In other words, alternative norms to the nationalist arguments were more difficult to deploy in the British case.

Few benefits for moral entrepreneurs. The contradicting strands within metropolitan discourse made it possible for political entrepreneurs to stress competing visions of appropriate behavior.[53] Given that the norms were substantively diverse, politicians could pick and choose among those that gave the greater political payoff. Those advocating decolonization and sovereignty for the colonies essentially catered to a constituency (supporters of nationalist demands in the colonies) that could yield them no benefit.

Political entrepreneurs that catered to metropolitan interests conversely had strong instrumental reasons to do so. Given that the military, economic groups with direct investments, and settlers were well-entrenched interest groups, claiming that continued metropolitan presence was necessary yielded political benefits. Moreover, these groups could easily overcome collective action problems because of their narrow interests and long-standing history of influencing metropolitan decision-making. The anticolonialists, by contrast, had far more diffuse benefits from decolonization, and far less experience in influencing policy, and were thus weakly organized. In other words, entrepreneurs had incentives to select normative claims to bolster their electoral success. The moral high ground was thus constituted as maintaining metropolitan presence until the overseas territories were deemed ripe for independence, meaning decolonization on the terms of the imperial power.

The international environment. It might be argued that the overall environment had shifted against the proponents of colonialism. After all, the United States and the USSR had both come out in favor of decolonization. The United Nations,

[53] One might phrase this in the terminology employed by Snyder and Ballentine (1996) who argue for the concept of a marketplace of ideas. Competing political entrepreneurs supply certain ideas, and the populace "purchases" these through its support for the preferred entrepreneur. In this context, imperialists had "brand loyalty" among their consumers, while their rivals faced diffuse, new, and thus undependable consumers.

moreover, apparently embodied similar sentiments. Consequently, international pressure should have gradually required the imperial powers to retreat and be forced to stop legitimizing their colonial practices.

To the proponents of empire, though, the situation was not that clear. First, they still saw viable means of resisting outside pressure. Britain was not convinced that the United States was guided by ulterior motives but believed instead that the United States planned to fill the void left by retreating European powers. The alternative was to join with others (France and intermediate states) to oppose American encroachment.[54] What held true for England, held *a fortiori* for France. In order for France to play the role of a great power it required an empire. Consequently, all American efforts to diminish the French presence had to be interpreted as attempts to elevate American standing at France's expense.[55]

Second, American anticolonialism was tempered by its reluctance to see communist nationalists replace colonial governments. The United States thus supported French efforts in Indochina and later the Portuguese colonial wars. The Indonesian nationalists astutely disavowed such communist connections, and gradually gained American support against the Dutch. The Hague, however, continuously misread the British and American position, and believed that the latter two would support its efforts to maintain a presence in Indonesia.

International organizations, such as the United Nations, did act as conduits for opposing points of view. But as was the case with the Dutch misreading of their allies' position, the Netherlands thought that the UN (influenced by Britain and the United States—permanent members of the Security Council) would not actively confront its aims in Indonesia. France, more comfortable with its permanent seat, and convinced that its allies would not tolerate a loss to communist supported nationalists, correctly ascertained that international organizations would only exert limited pressure on Paris to retreat.[56]

To sum up, for the metropolitans colonialism was not as tainted as one might believe. Multiple interpretations competed with each other. Political entrepreneurs had little motivation to oppose well-entrenched single-issue interest groups, and the pressure of the international environment to adhere to certain norms seemed modest.

---

[54] Fry (1997).

[55] Kimball (1991: chapter 7) discusses the tension between the Roosevelt Administration and de Gaulle on French colonialism. (Cordell Hull noted how Roosevelt's dislike of de Gaulle was visceral. Smith [1981:101].)

[56] Only by 1960 did the UN rule, through General Assembly Resolution 1514, against delay in granting independence on the basis of insufficient competence (James 1986:183; Mayall 1990:48).

The Impact of Norms in the Periphery

The internal coherence of norms in the periphery. Unlike metropolitan discourse, few consistent indigenous arguments could be made in support of continued colonial status. Indeed, local elites that did profit from metropolitan control weakened their position if openly acknowledging their debt to their colonial masters. Given local nationalist demands, the more local elites identified with colonial discourse, the weaker their position vis-à-vis their indigenous populations. If there was an independent indigenous discourse, it favored the traditional modes of governance—as for example, with the aristocratic elites in Indonesia. But given their association with the Dutch, the arguments to return to such modes of governance if the Dutch should retreat were hardly persuasive.[57] Moreover, traditional modes of legitimating authority were sometimes difficult to reconcile with state-centric, territorially based, forms of authority.

Finally, the colonies themselves did not accept the idea that they formed part of the metropolitan home country. Given their secondary legal status, and their lack of access to higher office, it was clear that they were not part of the metropole. Indeed, it was the differentiation between European and non-European which created the very identities that opposed European rule. Whatever ethnic background one had or whatever language one spoke, in being treated uniformly as different from Europeans, the indigenous peoples developed a unified identity. Racial categorization, status differentiation, etiquette, sexual mores, all served to distinguish European from non-European. All locals were "the other."[58]

Strategic benefits of independence. In view of the unambiguous nature of dominant norms in the periphery, that is, there was a clear preference for independence, political entrepreneurs did well to cater to this local constituency. There were unmistakable rewards for favoring arguments opposed to decolonization and stressing the right to independence.

Independence would mean the rise to power of previously disempowered local nationalists. The reward for successful propagation of such norms would be political office. Moreover, competing on a nationalist agenda provided entrepreneurs leverage against rival local elites who were leftovers from precolonial times, or power brokers pushed forward by the imperial power. Nationalists could thus easily outbid the traditional ruling elites. Additionally, running on a

---

[57] Van Doorn (1995:166).

[58] Given makes a general argument in analyzing European state-building. English repression of the various Welsh clans and their treatment as a coherent group (i.e., non-English) gave rise to a Welsh national consciousness where previously there had been none (Given 1990).

sovereign, territorial program, allowed leaders to create coherent identities and imagined political communities that previously had been disjoint. Consequently, they denied radical self-determination to ethnic groups in favor of an artificial notion of the nation, which happened to be coterminous with the borders drawn by the colonial powers. Claims to independence, as Mayall points out, were coterminous with nation-building.[59]

Moral entrepreneurs thus had strategic incentives to favor particular interpretations derived from Western political discourse. The incentive structure even dictated outbidding and competing on nationalist ideas in order to best advance their position.

The permissiveness of the international environment. The postwar environment greatly facilitated the advancement of norms of self-determination and sovereignty. Both superpowers sought the support of nationalists, and hence indigenous elites could play one off against the other, depending on whose support was more forthcoming. Thus Indonesian nationalists, more convinced of American leverage over the Dutch than other nationalists were of American intentions, cracked down on communist elements within their ranks (in repressing the Madiun Revolt of 1948) and gained unambiguous American and British support.[60]

While international organizations lacked the means to exert direct influence on the metropoles they did provide a forum to vent anticolonial sentiments. The superpowers, reluctant to counter such sentiments in international organizations, thereby provided voice to those states that had experienced colonialism themselves. At the very least such international fora worked as coordinating devices for the aspiring nationalists.

In short, the unambiguous nature of norms for decolonization; the strategic incentives for political entrepreneurs to take up specific interpretations of self-determination; and the permissive international environment, explain why the articulation of ideas championing sovereignty was far more influential in the colonies than in the metropoles. Not fundamental changes in normative stances in the metropoles but new claims from the periphery pushed the decolonization process.

Conclusion

This essay has addressed two main issues. First, it examined whether changes in normative stances in the imperial metropoles were a key causal variable of

[59] Mayall (1990:123).

[60] Reid (1974:143).

decolonization. My conclusion is that they only played a limited role in the metropoles, but worked as mobilizing devices for the periphery.

Second, not content with tracing the effect of norms on behaviors, I have advanced a general argument about the origin of norms as causal forces in political change. Careful analysis of the origin of norms need not reduce norms to epiphenomena—as mere reflections of instrumental calculations or exogenously postulated interests—nor should it engage in the impossible task of seeking the ultimate origins of ideas and moral standards. Instead, one should trace how, among the various sets of norms and ideas available, certain sets become key conceptualizations for mobilizing individuals and for providing a context through which individuals interpret and signify their own actions.

Certain configurations of norms become salient if they form part of a coherent whole and do not conflict with other strongly held normative frameworks. In order for such normative beliefs to become salient they, furthermore, need to be championed by political elites. Political leaders must perceive some individual gains in order to provide such public goods. In this respect my argument resembles that of Ikenberry and Kupchan (1990), who suggest that elite receptivity to norms is key to those norms becoming institutionalized as political practices. Finally, a permissive international environment will enhance the probability that such normative positions will take root.

The creation of the modern state system at the second millennium's end contains more than a bit of irony. The inventors of the principle of sovereign, territorial rule denied that same principle to the non-European subject territories. These former subjects, however, turned the principle against their colonial masters to obtain their independence. But in so doing they also participated in the final completion (and perhaps the high water mark) of the West European project: the full extension of the Westphalian order across the globe.

References

Abercrombie, Nicholas. (1986) "Knowledge, Order, and Human Autonomy." In *Making Sense of Modern Times*, edited by James Hunter and Stephen Ainlay, pp. 11–30. London: Routledge and Kegan Paul.

Anderson, Benedict. (1991) *Imagined Communities*. New York: Verso.

Axelrod, Robert. (1981) The Emergence of Cooperation among Egoists. *American Political Science Review* **75**(2):306–318.

Axelrod, Robert. (1984) *The Evolution of Cooperation*. New York: Basic Books.

Axelrod, Robert. (1986) An Evolutionary Approach to Norms. *American Political Science Review* **80**(4):1095–1112.

BARKIN, J. SAMUEL, AND CRONIN, BRUCE. (1994) The State and the Nation: Changing Norms and the Rules of Sovereignty in International Relations. *International Organization* **48**(1):107–130.

BENN, STANLEY. (1967) "Sovereignty," Volume 7/8 of *The Encyclopedia of Philosophy*, pp. 501–505. New York: MacMillan.

BETTS, RAYMOND. (1985). *Uncertain Dimensions*. Minneapolis: University of Minnesota Press.

DIMAGGIO, PAUL, AND WALTER POWELL. (1983) The Iron Cage Revisited: Institutional Isomorphism and Collective Rationality in Organizational Fields. *American Sociological Review* **48**:147–160.

DOYLE, MICHAEL. (1986) *Empires*. Ithaca: Cornell University Press.

ECKSTEIN, HARRY. (1975) "Case Study and Theory in Political Science." In *Handbook of Political Science* (Vol. 7), edited by Fred Greenstein and Nelson Polsby, pp. 79–138. Reading, MA: Addison-Wesley.

EMERSON, RUPERT. (1967) *From Empire to Nation*. Cambridge: Harvard University Press.

FINNEMORE, MARTHA. (1993) International Organizations as Teachers of Norms: The United Nations Educational, Scientific, and Cultural Organization and Science Policy. *International Organization* **47**(4):565–597.

FINNEMORE, MARTHA. (1996). Norms, Culture and World Politics: Insights from Sociology's Institutionalism. *International Organization* **50**(2):325–347.

FRIEDBERG, AARON. (1988). *The Weary Titan*. Princeton: Princeton University Press.

FRY, MICHAEL. (1997) "Decolonization: Britain, France, and the Cold War." In *The End of Empire?*, edited by Karen Dawisha and Bruce Parrott, pp. 121–154. Armonk, NY: M. E. Sharpe.

GARRETT, GEOFFREY, AND BARRY WEINGAST. (1993) "Ideas, Interests, and Institutions: Constructing the European Community's Internal Market." In *Ideas and Foreign Policy*, edited by Judith Goldstein and Robert Keohane, pp. 173–206. Ithaca: Cornell University Press.

GEERTZ, CLIFFORD. (1973) *The Interpretation of Cultures*. New York: Basic Books.

GELLNER, ERNEST. (1983) *Nations and Nationalism*. Ithaca: Cornell University Press.

GEORGE, ALEXANDER. (1979) "Case Studies and Theory Development: The Method of Structured, Focused Comparison." In *Diplomacy: New Approaches in History, Theory, and Policy*, edited by Paul Lauren. New York: The Free Press.

GIVEN, JAMES. (1990) *State and Society in Medieval Europe*. Ithaca: Cornell University Press.

GOLDSTEIN, JUDITH, AND ROBERT KEOHANE, EDS. (1993) *Ideas and Foreign Policy*. Ithaca: Cornell University Press.

GOTO, KEN'ICHI. (1996) "Cooperation, Submission, and Resistance of Indigenous Elites of Southeast Asia in the Wartime Empires." In *The Japanese Wartime Empire*, edited by Peter Duus, Ramon Myers, and Mark Peattie, pp. 274–301. Princeton: Princeton University Press.

HINSLEY, F. H. (1969) "The Concept of Sovereignty and the Relations Between States." In *In Defense of Sovereignty*, edited by W. Stankiewicz. New York: Oxford University Press.

HINSLEY, F. H. (1986) *Sovereignty*. Cambridge, U.K.: Cambridge University Press.

HOBSBAWN, E. J. (1990) *Nations and Nationalism Since 1780*. New York: Cambridge University Press.

IKENBERRY, JOHN, AND CHARLES KUPCHAN. (1990) Socialization and Hegemonic Power. *International Organization* **44**(3):283–315.

JACKSON, ROBERT. (1990) *Quasi-States: Sovereignty, International Relations, and the Third World*. New York: Cambridge University Press.

JACKSON, ROBERT. (1993) "The Weight of Ideas in Decolonization: Normative Change in International Relations." In *Ideas and Foreign Policy*, edited by Judith Goldstein and Robert Keohane, pp. 111–138. Ithaca: Cornell University Press.

JACOBSON, HAROLD. (1979) *Networks of Independence*. New York: Alfred Knopf.

JAMES, ALAN. (1986) *Sovereign Statehood*. London: Allen and Unwin.

KAHLER, MILES. (1984) *Decolonization in Britain and France*. Princeton: Princeton University Press.

KAHLER, MILES. (1997). "Empires, Neo-empires, and Political Change: The British and French Experience." In *The End of Empire?*, edited by Karen Dawisha and Bruce Parrott, pp. 286–312. Armonk, NY: M. E. Sharpe.

KIMBALL, WARREN. (1991) *The Juggler*. Princeton: Princeton University Press.

KRATOCHWIL, FRIEDRICH. (1986) Of Systems, Boundaries, and Territoriality: An Inquiry into the Formation of the State System. *World Politics* **39**(1):27–52.

KUPCHAN, CHARLES. (1994) *The Vulnerability of Empire*. Ithaca: Cornell University Press.

LIJPHART, AREND. (1971) Comparative Politics and the Comparative Method. *American Political Science Review* **65**(3):682–693.

LUSTICK, IAN. (1993) *Unsettled States, Disputed Lands*. Ithaca: Cornell University Press.

MADDISON, ANGUS. (1989) Dutch Income in and from Indonesia, 1700–1938. *Modern Asian Studies* **23**(4):645–670.

MADDISON, ANGUS. (1990). "Dutch Colonialism in Indonesia: A Comparative Perspective." In *Indonesian Economic History in the Dutch Colonial Era*, edited by Anne Booth, W. J. O'Malley, and Anna Weidemann. New Haven: Yale University.

MANSERGH, NICHOLAS. (1969) *The Commonwealth Experience*. New York: Praeger.

MAYALL, JAMES. (1990) *Nationalism and International Society*. New York: Cambridge University Press.

OLSON, MANCUR. (1965) *The Logic of Collective Action*. Cambridge: Harvard University Press.

PRICE, RICHARD. (1995) A Genealogy of the Chemical Weapons Taboo. *International Organization* **49**(1):73–103.

PRICE, RICHARD. (1998) Reversing the Gun Sights: Transnational Civil Society Targets Land Mines. *International Organization* **52**(3):613–644.

REID, ANTHONY. (1974) *The Indonesian National Revolution 1945–1950*. Westport, CT: Greenwood Press.

SIKKINK, KATHRYN. (1993) "The Power of Principled Ideas: Human Rights Policies in the United States and Western Europe." In *Ideas and Foreign Policy*, edited by Judith Goldstein and Robert Keohane, pp. 139–170. Ithaca: Cornell University Press.

SMITH, TONY. (1981) *The Pattern of Imperialism*. New York: Cambridge University Press.

SNYDER, JACK. (1991) *Myths of Empire*. Ithaca: Cornell University Press.

SNYDER, JACK, AND BALLENTINE, KAREN. (1996) Nationalism and the Marketplace of Ideas. *International Security* **21**(2):5–40.

SPRUYT, HENDRIK. (1994) *The Sovereign State and Its Competitors*. Princeton: Princeton University Press.

STRANG, DAVID. (1991) Anomaly and Commonplace in European Political Expansion: Realist and Institutional Accounts. *International Organization* **45**(2):143–162.

TANNENWALD, NINA. (1999) The Nuclear Taboo: The United States and the Normative Basis of Nuclear Non-use. *International Organization* **53**(3):433–468.

THOMSON, JANICE. (1990) State Practices, International Norms, and the Decline of Mercenarism. *International Studies Quarterly* **34**(1):23–48.

VAN DEN DOEL, H. W. (1996) *Het Rijk van Insulinde*. Amsterdam: Prometheus.

VAN DOORN, J. A. (1995a) *Indische lessen*. Amsterdam: Uitgeverij Bert Bakker.

VAN DOORN, J. A. A. (1995b) The Dutch-Indonesian Conflict and the Persistence of the Colonial Pattern. *The Netherlands Journal of Social Sciences* **31**(2):153–171.

VAN EVERA, STEPHEN. (1996) *Guide to Methodology for Students of Political Science*. Cambridge: The MIT Press.

WATSON, ADAM. (1992) *The Evolution of International Society*. Routledge: New York.

YASUNAKA, AKIO. (1970) Basic Data on Indonesian Political Leaders. *Indonesia* **10**:107–142. Translated by Kenichi Goto.

Popes, Kings, and Endogenous Institutions: The Concordat of Worms and the Origins of Sovereignty

Bruce Bueno de Mesquita[1]

Hoover Institution, Stanford University

The modern state-centric international system is generally thought to have originated with the Treaty of Westphalia. International politics prior to 1648 are believed to have been less territorially focused, with feudal ties taking precedence over considerations of state. Here I set out a modest theory of competition between the Catholic Church and European kings, especially the Holy Roman Emperor and the kings of France and England, from 1122 onward. I propose that the modern territorial state has its origins in the Concordat of Worms, which was established five hundred years earlier than the Treaty of Westphalia. The theory offered here suggests that the development of important institutions of the modern sovereign state are partially an endogenous product of strategic maneuvering between the Catholic Church and European kings over political control within their domains. The theory further implies that the Concordat of Worms created incentives for the pope to stifle economic growth. This views stands in contrast to the general accounts of economic growth or of institution building found in the sociological literature beginning with Weber, or in the historical and much of the political economy literature (Kantorowicz 1957; Weber 1958, 1968; Wesson 1978; Tuchman 1984; Baldwin 1986; Rosenberg and L. E. Birdzell, Jr. 1986; Greif 1998).

---

[1] I am grateful for helpful suggestions given to me by Kenneth Arrow, James Caporaso, John Ferejohn, Steven Haber, Edward Lazear, James Morrow, Heiner Schulz, Guido Organski, Kenneth Organski, and Barry Weingast based on earlier drafts of this study. I thank the Hoover Institution for its generous support. All errors are, of course, my own.

Published by Blackwell Publishers, 350 Main Street, Malden, MA 02148, USA, and 108 Cowley Road, Oxford OX4 1JF, UK.

I begin by reviewing the essential features of Westphalia that posit fundamental elements of sovereignty. Then I investigate how these elements are tied to church–king competition over the appointment of bishops. I show that the resolution of the Investiture Struggle established a property right that adhered to sovereign territory, placed the king in a new fiduciary role regarding that territory, and that this property right fostered competition that influenced economic growth in Europe for centuries and was an important element moving kings and popes to erect new political institutions. The property right established at Worms in 1122—the right of kings to the income from the territory defined by the domain of each bishop—gave impetus to the end of feudalism and was essential to the rise of the modern, territorially based state system. In this view, Westphalia marks a critical point along the way, but the modern state system was set in motion five centuries earlier.

A Brief Review of Westphalia

The Treaty of Westphalia contains more than one hundred specific articles laying out the terms and conditions under which the Thirty Years' War ended. Most of these articles deal with matters of allocating valuable resources among aristocrats or restoring valuables lost by some aristocrats to others during the War. But a few articles pertain directly to the establishment of territorial sovereignty. Some central examples of these articles highlight this important feature of Westphalia:[2]

Article LXIV.

> And to prevent for the future any Differences arising in the Politick State, all and every one of the Electors, Princes and States of the Roman Empire, are so establish'd and confirm'd in their antient, Prerogatives, Libertys, Privileges, free exercise of Territorial Right, as well Ecclesiastick, as Politick Lordships, Regales, by virtue of this present Transaction: that they never can or ought to be molested therein by any whomsoever upon any manner of pretence.

Article LXV.

> They shall enjoy without contradiction, the Right of Suffrage in all Deliberations touching the Affairs of the Empire; but above all, when the Business in hand shall be the making or interpreting of Laws, the declaring of Wars, imposing of Taxes, levying or quartering of Soldiers, erecting new Fortifications in the Territorys of the States, or

---

[2] The full text of the Treaty of Westphalia can be found at http://www.tufts.edu/departments/fletcher/multi/texts/historical/westphalia.txt

> reinforcing the old Garisons; as also when a Peace of Alliance is to be concluded, and treated about, or the like, none of these, or the like things shall be acted for the future, without the Suffrage and Consent of the Free Assembly of all the States of the Empire: Above all, it shall be free perpetually to each of the States of the Empire, to make Alliances with Strangers for their Preservation and Safety; provided, nevertheless, such Alliances be not against the Emperor, and the Empire, nor against the Publick Peace, and this Treaty, and without prejudice to the Oath by which every one is bound to the Emperor and the Empire.
>
> Article LXVII.
>
> That as well as general as particular Diets, the free Towns, and other States of the Empire, shall have decisive Votes; they shall, without molestation, keep their Regales, Customs, annual Revenues, Libertys, Privileges to confiscate, to raise Taxes, and other Rights, lawfully obtain'd from the Emperor and Empire, or enjoy'd long before these Commotions, with a full Jurisdiction within the inclosure of their Walls, and their Territorys: making void at the same time, annulling and for the future prohibiting all Things, which by Reprisals, Arrests, stopping of Passages, and other prejudicial Acts, either during the War, under what pretext soever they have been done and attempted hitherto by private Authority, or may hereafter without any preceding formality of Right be enterpris'd. As for the rest, all laudable Customs of the sacred Roman Empire, the fundamental Constitutions and Laws, shall for the future be strictly observ'd, all the Confusions which time of War have, or could introduce, being remov'd and laid aside.

Article 64 establishes territoriality and the right of the state to choose its own religion, as well as the right to noninterference by other states in any of these matters. Under Article 65 sovereign authority is further spelled out, especially with regard to foreign policy. This article establishes that no supernational authority (i.e., the Catholic Church or the Holy Roman Empire) can make or negate alliances made between sovereigns for the purpose of protecting their respective nation's security. In a similar manner, Article 67 establishes that sovereign states can determine their own domestic policies, free from external pressures and "with full Jurisdiction within the inclosure of their Walls and their Territorys."

A review of the major innovations of the treaty makes clear that the new system emphasized territoriality. Borders, rather than fealty, became a critical institutional feature that defines where sovereign authority is exercised. Feudalism, by contrast, defined authority in terms of a hierarchy of personal relations, with only loose reference to territorial rights.

Borders are a natural source of conflict in international relations (Siverson and Starr 1991; Vasquez 1993, 1995; Senese 1995, 1997; Huth 1996) because shifts in their location expand or contract sovereign authority. One way rulers can expand their authority is to usurp the sovereign claims of another ruler by snatching some territory and redefining the location of the state's perimeter. Because each state's territorial borders defines a domain within which its rulers have sovereign authority over the use of force (Spruyt 1994; Krasner 1999), acting in a fiduciary role for their citizen-subjects, international law has come to view all states as legally equivalent entities. This understanding of the role of the state is traced here to the property right granted by the Concordat of Worms to kings as fiduciaries in vacant territorially defined bishoprics.

The Power of the Pope

The power and authority of the pope reached its high point roughly from the papacy of Innocent III (1198–1216) to that of Boniface VIII (1295–1303). During the preceding three centuries the pope's influence was dramatically transformed. Where once he was no more than the bishop of Rome, by the period discussed here he had expanded the authority associated with his title as the Vicar of Christ, the presumptive living embodiment of Christ's will. Having once been subservient to secular rulers, serving largely at their pleasure, the pope had become essential to the coronation and legitimation of the Catholic kings of Europe (Kantorowicz 1957; Schimmelpfennig 1992, pp. 170–197). The pope was elevated to such a degree that the bishop of Rome now claimed the authority to excommunicate or depose kings.[3] Indeed, some, like the king of England, explicitly owed fealty to the pope. The infallibility doctrine that had originally constrained popes' following of precedence was, sometime between 1316 and 1334, converted into something closer to its modern interpretation in which the pope can overturn precedence by invoking infallibility. It was a time when the pope was arguably the most powerful leader in the world and when the Roman Church was Europe's hegemon. After the early thirteen hundreds, the pope's influence went into a slow decline as the authority of sovereign kings rose to replace the church as the dominant political factor in Europe. The Thirty Years' War marked the culmination of that process. After the War, Catholicism no longer could claim successfully to be the one true faith among European monarchs.

My central contention is that the institutional arrangements that elevated the pope and church to such an exalted position during the twelfth and thirteenth centuries also planted the seeds of the church's slow demise as a secular European or world power and created the nascent modern territorial state, gradually shifting political control from the pope to heads of state. Here I focus on

---

[3] See the epistle, *Unam Sanctum* (http://www.shrine.com/unam.htm) issued by Boniface VIII, and the commentary by John of Paris (1971).

one small part of this thesis. I examine the appointment of bishops in France during the reign of Philip Augustus (1179–1223). In the course of my analysis I hope to establish that the modern international system has its origins in the Investiture Struggle and in the Concordat of Worms (1122) as well as in earlier, similar agreements with the kings of France and England. This stands in contrast to the conventional view among students of international affairs (Waltz 1979; Krasner 1999). Furthermore, I hope to lay the foundation for an argument that shows that the survival of the Catholic Church's secular power depended, in part, on its adopting policies designed to retard economic growth outside areas that were under its direct control. And I hope to establish that growth-oriented economic, social, and political policies were critical for secular rulers to elevate themselves above the authority of the papacy.

To summarize, the standard view is that:

1. The church promoted growth;
2. Institutions, both secular and ecclesiastic, developed without a strategic link to the relationship between the church and the monarchies of the day; and
3. The appointment of bishops reflected the decision by monarchs, like Philip Augustus in France, to cooperate with the pope, rather than a decision by the pope to cooperate with monarchs.

This standard perspective is clearly reflected in the following statements by distinguished historians examining these very questions:

John Gilchrist (1969:38), for instance, writes, "During the vital period of growth the church did not impede but fostered economic progress."

Ernst Kantorowicz (1957:197), observing the emergence of new institutions, claims, "When in the twelfth century the church, including the clerical bureaucracy, established itself as the 'mystical body of Christ,' the secular world sector proclaimed itself as the 'holy Empire.' This does not imply causation, either in the one way or the other. It merely indicates the activity of indeed interrelated impulses and ambitions . . . [that] happened to emerge simultaneously—around the middle of the twelfth century."

John Baldwin (1986:68) maintains that "Louis VII's policy of uncoerced cooperation [with the pope] worked still more advantageously for his son."

By contrast, I argue that the church did try to impede growth in the secular sector as a strategic maneuver to sustain the pope's political power. Kings developed new administrative and judicial institutions as a strategic response designed to increase their power and to counteract the efforts by the church to enhance the authority of the pope. One consequence of these strategic efforts was that where monarchs were successful in the promotion of economic growth, they were able to compel the pope to appoint bishops that satisfied their interests above the church's, thereby enhancing their political power and the independent, sovereign authority they exercised over the territory defined by the bishoprics within their domain.

I begin by setting out a game theory model for the appointment of bishops. Through comparative static analysis, I examine the appointment process in the light of different levels of economic development. I show that the pope, as leader of the church, had incentives to retard those aspects of economic growth that disproportionately advantaged secular rulers relative to the advantages conferred on the church. I contend that the pope promoted new institutions designed to thwart growth and that kings, responding to the shifting strategic environment, invented new political institutions to promote their authority over the Catholic Church. Following the theory, I offer empirical evidence and indicate how the evidence contradicts previous historical accounts. The evidence is presented in two forms. First, I offer a narrative discussion of some of the important institutions that emerged within the church and in France and England after the Concordat of Worms and show how they were associated with the concessions each side made at Worms. Then I offer statistical evidence drawn from data on the appointment of bishops in France between 1179 and 1223. The statistical evidence, in conjunction with the narrative account, points consistently to a shift in influence between the pope and kings in a manner consistent with the notion that Worms undermined the feudal order and set the sovereign, territorial state into motion.

Brief Historical Review

From approximately the tenth century until the black death in the fourteenth century, the economies of Europe experienced remarkable expansion. Though agricultural pursuits remained dominant, still an extraordinary commercial and technological revolution took place (De Roover 1948; Ladurie 1971; Lopez 1976; Duby 1991; Gies and Gies 1994; Miller and Hatcher 1995). During this period a money economy flourished and the foundations were laid for modern banking practices. Contracts became more sophisticated and more standardized, setting the stage for the ascent of merchants and lawyers as influential community leaders. Indeed, even popes became increasingly likely to have been trained in law, rising to the papacy through the church's law offices.

Technology was harnessed to improve productivity to a degree unprecedented in the preceding millennium. Mills powered by water and wind became commonplace, and mining on a large scale occurred in much of Europe as this period's industrial awakening called for new sources of metal, fuel, and other industrial materials. The technology of textile production, Europe's most important industry, made great leaps forward as did international trade in textiles. Fuels for industrial production were diversified as coal and coke assumed an increasing role alongside wood.

The growth in wealth did not bypass the Catholic Church. As the owner of about one-third of Europe's land, and as a voracious source of demand for new construction, the church was an intimate beneficiary of and agent for economic expansion during the high middle ages. Indeed, many technological innovations were first applied on church lands, especially the lands of the newer monastic orders, most notably the Cistercians and the Crusading Orders, like the Hospitalers and the Knights Templar. These new orders, unlike their predecessors that eschewed money-making labor (e.g., the Benedictines), became wealthy through leadership in industry and banking. It is worth noting that these entrepreneurial orders, which refused to engage in such churchly activities as performing burials or hearing confession, came into existence beginning around 1100 and grew to great influence, wealth, and prominence over the next two centuries. I will return to them later as they are an instance of the new institutions promoted by the papacy to prevent the erosion of church influence by kings.

The growing wealth of the church contributed to the rising stature and influence of the pope. By the twelfth century, the pope had diligently pursued elevation to the status of first among equals. He had risen above all other bishops, especially after the break with the eastern orthodox church, and now strove also to rise above the kings of Europe and even above the Holy Roman Emperor. This can be seen in the adoption of the purple robe for the pope as of 1075 and by the secondary position accorded the Holy Roman Emperor at papal coronations after 1122 (Robinson 1990). The pope succeeded over a span of a few generations to rise to such a level that the kings of Catholic Europe were subservient to him. English kings, from the Conqueror on, pledged fealty to the pope.

In France, Philip Augustus is said to have "promised royal bishoprics and abbeys freedom to elect their leaders as long as the canons and monks chose men who were both 'pleasing to God' and 'useful to the kingdom.' Cooperation, with both parties respecting mutual interests, was Philip's guiding principle" (Baldwin 1986:176–77). That is, Philip Augustus ostensibly would not interfere in the pope's prerogative under the Concordat of Worms and the specific agreements with France when it came to selecting nominees as bishops. The sentiment that called for supporting the interests of the church, even when they opposed those of the king, are cogently stated by Louis IX (Saint Louis) in his letter of advice to his son, who became King Philip III (Philip the Bold, 1270–1285) of France:

> I wish here to tell you what is related concerning King Philip [Augustus], my ancestor, as one of his council, who said he heard it, told it to me. The king, one day, was with his privy council, and he was there who told me these words. And one of the king's councillors said to him how much wrong and loss he suffered from those of Holy Church, in that they took away his rights and

> lessened the jurisdiction of his court; and they marveled greatly how he endured it. And the good king answered: 'I am quite certain that they do me much wrong, but when I consider the goodness and kindness which God has done me, I had rather that my rights should go, than have a contention or awaken a quarrel with Holy Church.'[4]

These observations naturally encourage the conclusion that the pope was the hegemon in Europe and that, therefore, the economic expansion probably occurred with the church's participation and blessings. Indeed, as the earlier quotation from Gilchrist indicates, historians of this period argue that the church favored growth. Yet I show that the pope had strong incentives, created by the Concordat of Worms, to retard secular growth and he acted on those incentives. The pope erected new institutions to protect his power against the threat of secular rulers. In response, monarchs created new institutions of their own to enhance their power relative to the pope and, in doing so, launched the modern state system.

The Model

I assume that Catholic kings found papal opposition to their policies costly and, likewise, that the king's opposition to church views was costly for the pope. That is why it was customary for nominees for high church office to be individuals both pleasing to God and useful to the kingdom (*qui Deo placeat et utilis sit regno*). One important arena in which the pope and kings hoped to coordinate their behavior was in the appointment of bishops. Naturally, the pope and each king had their own preferences among prospective candidates.

Why should the pope and monarchs have cared to coordinate the appointment of bishops? There are several reasons. Bishops were important emissaries between the pope and secular rulers who possessed specialized information. Depending on personal loyalties, they might more faithfully reflect the interests of the king or the pope. They also were major tax collectors who could be used to help advance royal or papal interests. Under the terms of the Concordat of Worms, bishops owed allegiance to both pope and king. Bishops were obligated to guarantee the king's right to call upon them for military service. For both the king and the church, loyal bishops were potential sources of armed knights, major sources of tax collection, and large-scale property owners and ecclesiastical landlords with the power to turn the population in the bishopric in favor of or against a monarch or pope. They were a central source of informa-

[4] King Louis's letter of advice is available from the Medieval Sourcebook at www.fordham.edu/halsall/source/stlouis1.html.

tion, capable of swaying policy debate to favor the interests of the king or the church within the territory of their See.

Under the Concordat of Worms, the pope gained the right to nominate bishops and the king the right to approve the nominees. To protect the interests of the king, the Concordat required that each bishop swear fealty to the king upon installation; that is, in exchange for the return of the bishop's regalia by the king to the new bishop, the bishop promised military assistance and loyalty to the king as sovereign of the territory occupied by the bishopric.[5] In this way, the king transferred back to the church and the bishop as its agent the right to the tax revenues from the Sees. During the vacancy between the death of the old bishop and the consecration of the new bishop, the revenue from the bishopric went to the king under the terms of the Concordat of Worms and associated treaties. This revenue was substantial. It represented a property right that adhered to the king as sovereign over the territory of the See and not to the king as an individual. The king could not sell the future right to control the regalia, nor could it be inherited except by ascent to the throne. The right belonged to the king's successor, who might be his child or might be from an entirely new line. The king held the right to this income, then, as a fiduciary for the kingdom and not as his personal, private property. This is a significant departure from typical feudal practice. It establishes the sovereign claims of the king on behalf of his citizen-subjects within the territory of each bishopric in his domain. It is the beginnings of the state.

There was competition between each Catholic king and the pope to ensure that a newly appointed bishop was likely to view the pope or the king respectively as his primary master. The king could use delay in accepting the pope's nominee as a lever to encourage the pope to select a candidate to the king's liking. The pope could use the threat of excommunication or interdiction (and both were used) to encourage the king to accept the church's candidate. Excommunication, for believers, placed their souls at eternal risk of damnation. Inter-

---

[5] The regalia, consisting of the ring and staff, were the symbols of the bishop's office and authority. In exchange for the return of these regalia to the bishop, that is, the return of authority over the bishopric to the Church, the bishop promised to defend the king. As the Concordat stipulates, "The one elected, moreover, without any exaction may receive the regalia from thee [the Holy Roman Emperor] through the lance, and shall do unto thee for these what he rightfully should." The Emperor's promise at Worms includes the critical passage, "I . . . do remit to God, and to the holy apostles of God, Peter and Paul, and to the holy catholic church, all investiture through ring and staff [that is, the regalia], and do grant that in all the churches that are in my kingdom or empire there may be canonical election and free consecration. All the possessions and regalia of St. Peter . . . which I hold: I restore to the same holy Roman church." The full text of the Concordat of Worms can be found in the Medieval Sourcebook at http://www.fordham.edu/halsall/source/worms.html.

diction, which prevented residents in the interdicted area from receiving the sacraments, placed their souls at risk because of actions taken by the pope against the king. Excommunication and interdiction called for people to shun the excommunicated or interdicted king. This had the effect, even among non-believers, of making normal activities difficult and costly. Furthermore, interdiction raised the specter of civil unrest against the king by subjects deprived of the sacraments. These were powerful weapons in the hands of the pope.

Because of the privileged access to revenue and information enjoyed by bishops, they could tilt important policy choices and negotiations in favor of the pope or a king. Consequently, their loyalty was a valuable resource.[6] Indeed, if this were not so there would have been no basis for the Investiture Struggle or for the Concordat of Worms and associated agreements. Under the terms of these agreements, the pope nominated bishops whose election required the king's consent. There was a general understanding, though certainly not a binding commitment, that the king would approve the pope's nominee. Indeed, with a few exceptions French kings routinely accepted the pope's nominee for bishop. In the early years of his reign, Louis VII contested three elections, but did not intervene again directly in the election of bishops from 1149 until his death in 1179. Philip Augustus appears to have followed his father's lead by rarely intervening, though he too contested some elections.

It is evident that the king stood to benefit financially from vacancies in bishoprics just as the pope stood to benefit from minimizing the length of interregna. The significance of vacant regalian Sees can be inferred from their duration, which the king could manipulate, and by the income they generated. The pope had, at least from 1139 onward, called for vacancies to last no more than three months. Of the eighteen vacancies during Philip's reign that can be measured in months, thirteen lasted more than three months with only five falling within the time sought by the pope. Of Philip's total income in 1202/1203, one of the few periods for which the data exist, 5 percent came from regalia. This was about 17 percent of his discretionary income (Baldwin 1986:156).

The period of vacancy, and therefore the monarch's control over income, could be extended by a failure of the king to accept the church's nominee. Accepting nominees, then, calls for an explanation since it was costly. Of course, we must keep in mind that repeated rejection of the pope's nominees would

---

[6] That policy was influenced by the loyalties of bishops is evident from Philip Augustus's experience. Pope Innocent III interdicted Philip, depriving the king's subjects of access to the sacraments. The interdiction was faithfully observed by virtually every bishop whose background indicated close personal ties to the pope. Almost every bishop who was a blood relative of the king, by contrast, ignored the interdiction and continued to provide the king's subjects in their domain with the sacraments (Baldwin 1986: Appendix).

also have been costly. It would have been tantamount to rejection of agreements like the Concordat of Worms, leaving the struggle over investiture to loom over church–king relations and to jeopardize the eternal soul of the king, not to mention his ability to conduct business as usual within his realm and between his realm and the church. The pope, after all, as noted earlier, had powerful means to retaliate against recalcitrant kings. Interdiction and excommunication were not mere idle threats, but were measures invoked by the pope to have his way not only on theological questions, but also on decidedly secular matters, as in the cases of France's Philip Augustus and England's Henry II (Robinson 1990).

The competition between the church and the French king over the appointment of bishops was indicative of a broader issue of sovereignty. Control over bishoprics was a central theme of the reform movement in the church since before the revolutionary papacy of Gregory VII. The practice of simony not only harmed the religious mission of the church, but also represented a potential threat to church revenues and the church's political discretion. By putting bishoprics up for bids, secular authorities deprived the church of important control over the flow of tax revenues and alms given to the church through bishops and their underlings. The church also lost control over a key source of information and a key agent for policy implementation. As John Gilchrist has aptly noted, "although some of the opposition to church reform may have been genuinely religious, a large part derived from concern over the implied threat to lay, and individual clerical, control of church property and income" (1969:22). It is evident that a delicate balance existed in which kings and the church had mutual incentives to reach agreement on the selection of bishops, but each also had private incentives to shift the selection towards a candidate of his own choosing. It is also evident that the Concordat of Worms and the associated agreements established a property right that adhered to the king as head of state rather than adhering to the monarch as an individual. Thus, this revenue source represented an early element in the establishment of modern state sovereignty, including the right to tax within a well-defined territory, one of the central sources of sovereignty pointed to later in the Treaty of Westphalia. From the resolution of the Investiture Struggle, then, there emerged a bargain between church and state.

The decision over nominations and election of bishops can be characterized as a simple game. The game in Figure 1 is a close approximation of the nomination and election procedure, and the payoffs fairly reflect the terms established at Worms.

Assume a two-player game consisting of the pope and a king. Each is charged with joint responsibility for selecting bishops in accordance with the agreement at Worms. The pope, moving first, nominates a candidate. He prefers candidates who are expected to be loyal to him, while the king prefers candidates,

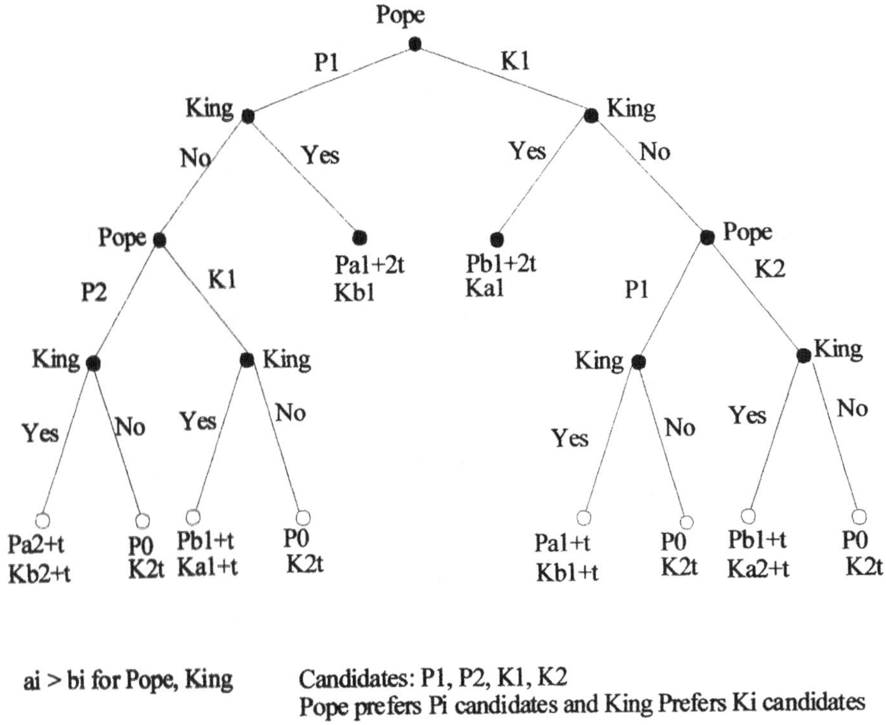

FIGURE 1. Selection of Bishops: The Game Created at Worms

such as relatives or members of his court, expected to be loyal to the royal family. The pope's first nominee is designated as P1 or K1, with the pope preferring candidates who are identified in the game as P1 or P2 to any candidates designated with the letter K. The king prefers candidates designated as K1 or K2 to any candidate identified with the letter P. After the pope nominates a candidate, the king decides whether to accept the candidate. If the king accepts the candidate, the pope receives the payoff associated with that candidate (a1 if P1 is chosen and b1 if K1 was nominated and approved) plus 2t, where t represents the one-period income from the bishopric. The add-on to the payoff is 2t to denote that in this two-stage game, the pope gets this income from the bishopric during both periods. The king's payoff is b1 if P1 was approved and is a1 if K1 was approved. For both the king and the pope, a1 > b1. All of the king's utilities are prefaced with the letter K and all of the pope's are prefaced with the letter P.

If the king rejects the pope's nominee, then the pope offers a new candidate. If P1 was offered first, the pope nominates either P2 or K1. If K1 was nominated originally by the pope, then the pope nominates P1 or K2. If the king approves the new nominee, the pope receives a2 (if the approved nominee is P2), b1 (if the nominee is K1), a1 if the nominee is P1, and b2 if the nominee is

K2. With approval, the pope also receives the income from the regalian See for the one remaining period and so gets an additional payoff of t. The king is rewarded comparably and also receives t because, by rejecting the first nominee, he received the income for one period. Finally, if the king again rejects the pope's nominee, the pope receives a payoff of zero and the king receives 2t. Of course, in reality the king could reject the pope's nominee an indefinite number of times. Two stages, however, are sufficient to elaborate on the central themes I explore.

Let us examine the cases that point to alternative equilibrium outcomes of the game in Figure 1. The first case of interest arises when t, the regalian revenue, is sufficiently small that the king in the final round strictly prefers to approve the pope's nominee rather than take the income. In this case the pope will never give the king either of the two prospective candidates (K1 or K2) most desired by the king. On the left side of the tree, the king's choice reduces to approving P1 immediately or collecting some of the regalian income and approving P2 later. The pope presumably can find a candidate P1 whom the king likes sufficiently more than P2 that the king will forego the regalian income by making the interregnum as short as possible. This outcome mirrors the general account offered by historians.

If the pope likes P2 better than P1 as bishop so sufficiently that he is willing to forego some regalian income to get P2, and the pope anticipates that the king will reject P2 if he is not compensated with some regalian revenue, then the pope can nominate as P1 someone sufficiently unattractive to the king that the king will prolong the interregnum a bit and let the pope have his more preferred bishop in the end. On the right side of the tree, assuming t is small enough, the king would choose to accept K1 in the first instance because he is better for the king than P1 who is the choice by the pope if the king rejects K1. Naturally, facing a choice between K1 or either P1 or P2, the pope nominates P1 and not K1 at the outset, ensuring that a candidate more desirable for the pope is elected. If t is small enough, the pope gets his preferred choice as bishop.

Suppose now that t is not so small that the king will always prefer to approve a papal nominee rather than take the regalian income at the end of the game. If t, the regalian income, is large enough that the king prefers to take the income rather than cooperate with the pope by approving either P1 or P2, but is not large enough for the king to prefer the income to K1 or K2, then the pope's hands are tied. The pope can avoid losing any of the regalian income by nominating as K1 someone the king prefers by enough to K2 that the king will approve K1 right away, foregoing any regalian income. If the pope prefers K2 over K1 enough to give up some income and if the king prefers K2 (a2 + t) to K1 (a1) without an interregnum, then the pope can ensure his third most preferred candidate is selected over his least preferred candidate. But, in any event, the pope must give the king one of his two preferred candidates. This scenario contradicts the standard historical accounts.

Should the value of the regalian income rise still further, it becomes easier for the pope to avoid his least preferred candidate and it becomes harder for the pope to keep the interregnum short. Indeed, if the income becomes sufficiently valuable, the pope loses all ability to obtain the king's approval, the agreement at Worms breaks down, and the king monopolizes the taxes raised from the bishop's territory. This, in essence, marks the end of the pope's prospects of being a European hegemon and is, essentially, what happened by the end of the Thirty Years' War and the rise of Protestantism as a rival to Catholicism.

Implications for Pope and King

The game leads to several hypotheses about relations between popes and kings as well as about the incentives popes and monarchs had regarding the creation of wealth in the secular domain. So long as regalian Sees remained poor enough, the pope could ensure that the elected bishops would be men loyal to the church, ensuring the pope's political control. In fairly wealthy regalian Sees, political control shifts from the pope to the king. In sufficiently wealthy bishoprics, the king values the income from a vacant See more than the value he derives from cooperating with the pope. In such a circumstance, the pope had no choice but to nominate as bishop a man expected to be more loyal to the king than to the pope, thereby yielding significant political influence to the king. If the wealth became really large, the king would prefer, in essence, a perpetual vacancy so that he gained the tax benefits in perpetuity. Under such a circumstance, the church could no longer vie with the monarch for political control and so would be reduced to the role of the modern church as a major religious body but not as a major political-military entity. Because in wealthy Sees the pope would choose candidates especially pleasing to the king, it is evident that we cannot properly infer whether the king was obedient and deferential to the pope or whether the pope was deferential to the king without examining the wealth of the bishopric and the anticipated loyalties of the bishop-nominee. In other words, the observation by historians that Philip Augustus accepted all papal nominations for bishop after the beginning of his reign cannot, by itself, be taken as evidence for his cooperation with or subservience to the pope.

What could the pope or the king do to influence whether this competition ended in the selection of bishops preferred by the pope or preferred by the king? The value of t can be taken as endogenous. The value of the income from a See depended on the wealth of the area. Since the revenues extracted from the Sees were generally proportionate to the wealth, the pope had incentives to keep any wealth accessible to secular authorities at a low enough level that the king would accept as bishop a candidate preferred by the pope. The pope could facilitate the prospects of getting bishops loyal to him by retarding economic growth in the secular portion of the economy. Naturally, the king had incentives to promote growth for many reasons, one of which was that it gave him a general advantage vis-à-vis the powerful Catholic Church. In a period already experiencing marked economic expansion, the pope's recently acquired hegemony was certainly at risk. In fact, the conflict between the pope and the French king erupted in virtually open warfare by the time of Philip IV (the Fair, 1285–1314) and Boniface VIII (1294–1303).

Narrative Account of Evidence

The church's hegemony benefitted from policies that hindered economic expansion, prolonging the time before the game shifted to yield bishops loyal to the king or, in the extreme case, made bishops largely irrelevant from the perspective of the king (as occurred by the time of the Treaty of Westphalia). By holding down the value of t, the pope could ensure that more bishops would be of type P and fewer of type K. Unfettered economic expansion in the secular realm meant that the expected value of t would rise, making it increasingly likely that the revenues earned by the king during interregna exceeded the value the king attached to agreement with the pope. Such a shift would have marked the decline of papal influence, at least in bishoprics with sufficient wealth.

The popes of this period introduced policies whose consequences include retarding secular economic growth relative to what one would have expected in their absence. In the first Lateran Council (1123), at which hundreds of bishops confirmed the agreement at Worms, celibacy was elevated and reinforced by prohibiting the clergy from marriage or having concubines. This insured that the property of the clergy would devolve to the church rather than to heirs. At the second Lateran Council (1139) more serious changes were instituted that must have limited secular economic growth. The council dealt with questions of inheritance and usury. On the inheritance of the private property of deceased bishops, now more fully elaborating on the consequences of the celibacy arguments at Lateran I, the church raised the stakes and insured that it, and not any secular venue, would be the beneficiary:[7]

> the goods of deceased bishops are not to be seized by anyone at all, but are to remain freely at the disposal of the treasurer and the clergy for the needs of the church and the succeeding incumbent. . . . Furthermore, if anyone dares to attempt this behaviour henceforth, he is to be excommunicated. And those who despoil the goods of dying priests or clerics are to be subject to the same sentence.

[7] The text of Lateran II is found at http://www.netins.net/showcase/dewa/catholic/ecum10.html.

By imposing excommunication on violators, the church raised the risks families or monarchs ran in trying to seize the "personal" property of deceased clerics.

The Council ruled regarding usury that:

> we condemn that practice accounted despicable and blameworthy by divine and human laws, denounced by Scripture in the old and new Testaments, namely the ferocious greed of usurers; and we sever them from every comfort of the church, forbidding any archbishop or bishop, or an abbot of any order whatever or anyone in clerical orders, to dare to receive usurers, unless they do so with extreme caution; but let them be held infamous throughout their whole lives and, unless they repent, be deprived of a Christian burial.

In Lateran II the church also erected other barriers to lay or secular authority that might jeopardize church interests. For instance, the church forbade lay people to receive tithes from churches, even if given by the bishop or the king, and subjected any who took such financial benefits to excommunication. It further decreed that "lay people, no matter how devout they may be, have no power of disposal over ecclesiastical property," thereby attempting to deprive nobles of the right to dispose even of their private, proprietary churches and chapels.

Prior to 1139, usury was forbidden the clergy, but was not elevated to a mortal sin for lay people, nor was a ban on usury by lay people long discussed and debated at the highest levels in the church. The effect of banning usury was to raise the price of money and to create a potential shortage of would-be lenders. Just as modern-day central banks increase interests rates to slow growth (and inflation), so the twelfth-century church raised interest rates by denying heaven to those who leant money for profit. Though the church used scripture to justify its action, there was a widely held view among church canonists that there was no doctrinal ban on usury in early Catholic teachings or scripture. And, of course, the church had not used scripture to ban such usury in the preceding thousand years.

Enforcement was a problem. The church recognized the difficulty inherent in determining whether a lender *intended* to commit usury; that is, to derive any profit from allowing the use of one's money. To deal with intent, the church wisely shifted enforcement from the canonists to the theologians. They reasoned that while human law might fail to recognize a usurious loan, God knew whether a lender intended to make a profit no matter what subterfuge was used to mask the return. Therefore, anyone having made such a profit and failing to make restitution or to show sufficient contrition before death was condemned eternally. This was the consequence of being denied a Christian burial.

To facilitate restitution for usury and to heighten the threat of damnation associated with lending, the church established new institutions. The fourth

Lateran Council (1215), for instance, made annual oral confession mandatory. This period also saw the spread of confessors manuals with specific instructions for dealing with merchants and others likely to have engaged in usury (Le Goff 1980). Through the confessional the church provided a means by which those otherwise damned for usury could save their souls. The path to forgiveness, however, generally was strewn with a combination of making financial restitution to the church and cessation of the sinful behavior. While the threat of eternal damnation was powerful indeed in the twelfth century, still, money lending continued. Merchants and others devised clever schemes of their own (including misleading contracts, exchange rate manipulation, and false stock companies) to hide their true financial arrangements, but the risks (including eternal damnation) had been raised and so, naturally, the expected rate of return had to rise commensurately (De Roover 1974). The upshot was to make loans costlier and, thereby, to diminish growth relative to what it otherwise would have been.

During the twelfth century the church's rhetoric also shifted in ways that may have dampened economic growth. At the same time that the Cistercians built and operated mills and other labor-saving devices to improve efficiency, the church began to promote the view that idle hands are the work of the devil. The church discouraged the spread of machines and other technology in the secular realm, ostensibly fearing that labor-saving devices would lead to idleness and that idleness, in turn would lead to sin. Certainly by discouraging the spread of labor-saving technology, the church was reducing productivity and, therefore, economic growth in the lay sector. By the thirteenth century, with the rising wealth and influence of merchants, the church gradually abandoned its arguments against improvements in technology, but this shift coincides with the diminution in church authority hypothesized to be associated with growth in secular wealth.

The church erected or strengthened other institutions as well in this period to bolster the pope's political position. The election of the pope had previously been the responsibility of the electors of the Holy Roman Empire. The College of Cardinals, introduced in the eleventh century, grew steadily in importance after Worms. Before the twelfth century, the College did not have authority to elect the pope. Beginning in that century, a two-thirds vote in the College became a necessary condition for papal election, though approval by secular authority, especially the Holy Roman Emperor, also remained necessary. By the beginning of the thirteenth century, the College of Cardinals became the dominant body for selecting the pope, wresting control over that fundamental process from the secular realm.

It is also noteworthy that entrepreneurial monastic orders, like the Cistercians, Templars, and Hospitalers, came into existence at the end of the eleventh century. This is the exact time when the pope was driven out of Rome and when the Holy Roman Emperor had created a schism by selecting an anti-pope, itself a clever secular institutional maneuver to strengthen the emperor in competition with the pope. By being driven out of the papal states, the "real" pope was cut off from financial support. That the new, entrepreneurial orders were organized and recognized by the exiled pope in this period seems hardly coincidental. Quite the contrary. Pope Paschal II (1099–1118) and Innocent II (1130–1143), for instance, exempted monks from tithes. The Cistercians, founded in 1098, took advantage of this exemption to obtain a virtual monopoly on the highly valuable wool trade. Not until the late-thirteenth century, as kings rose in prominence relative to the pope, were the Cistercians subjugated to the interests of the king. By the end of the thirteenth century they were driven into bankruptcy by the heavy taxes of the French crown (Gilchrist 1969).

In the late eleventh and early twelfth centuries, these new monastic orders looked to the pope for protection from taxation by kings and their local bishops. The new orders were freed from all secular authority, including secular taxation, and put directly under the supervision of the pope. In exchange for his protection, the pope derived a significant portion of his income from the new entrepreneurial orders during the long periods he was driven out of the papal states by the anti-pope and the Holy Roman Emperor. So, the new orders served to finance the pope against the secular authorities who, in exchange, were given a free hand to generate great wealth for themselves (and the papacy), an activity that had been anathema for earlier monastic orders.

Kings were no less innovative than the pope in erecting institutions to wrest political control and to increase their wealth and enhance their competition with the pope. The decades immediately after the Concordat of Worms saw a dramatic flowering of political institutions in England and France. Whether intentionally or not, many of these had the effect of weakening the pope's influence and securing a higher growth rate for the king's subjects and, therefore, higher tax revenues for the king. Consider, for instance, the series of legal reforms introduced by Henry II in England during the mid-twelfth century. These reforms became the foundation of English common law. Most noteworthy for the issues raised here are the writs of *novel disseisin, mort d'ancestor, utrum*, and *darrein presentment*.

The first protects property rights and the second rights of inheritance. These two writs provided an important improvement in a person's ability to predict whether he will maintain access to and the benefits from the land he worked. These writs greatly shortened the judicial process for determining rights of access to the land and enhanced a smoother operating agricultural system. They proved highly popular and effective in securing the property rights that are essential to economic growth and they enhanced the king's credibility as the person to turn to who would insure order and justice in matters of property (Van Caenegem 1988; Barzel 1989; North and Weingast 1989; Eggertsson 1990; Przeworski 1991).

The third and fourth writs deal with restrictions on ecclesiastical rights. *Utrum* established the king's primacy in determining whether a dispute belonged in his secular courts or in the church's ecclesiastical courts. Prior to Henry there was a presumption in favor of the jurisdiction of the ecclesiastical courts. *Utrum* reversed this presumption among litigants in England, and the period of which I write was a litigious age. *Darrein presentment* addressed Henry's interest in protecting the tradition of patronage that gave landowners the benefit of presenting or selecting clerics for appointment in their proprietary churches. This ran directly counter to the efforts of the church to take all such influence away from the secular domain, as is evident from the rulings in Lateran II (1139) and III (1179), some of which are quoted above. In *darrein presentment*, as in *utrum*, Henry challenged church authority and, as in the first two writs, he sought to protect a property right that, in this case, the church was trying to usurp for itself (Van Caenegem 1988).

The four major writs of Henry II were also accompanied by the introduction and spread of the jury system to replace trial by ordeal.[8] Henry sought to insure "victory of a reasoned, rational mode of proof over the old irrational appeals to God or the obscure forces of nature" (Van Caenegem 1988:63). This effort is also found at the same time in France and elsewhere on the continent. Probably not coincidentally, the shift to a jury system from trial by ordeal also weakened church institutions and income. Trials by ordeal were supervised by the clergy who were well compensated for their participation. For instance, two priests are known to have been paid 10s for blessing the ordeal pits near St. Edmund's Bury in 1166. At the time, a worker's daily wage was about one penny and a villein, and his entire family could be purchased for 22s (Van Caenegem 1988:64).

The administrative structure of the modern state likewise began to emerge in the twelfth and thirteenth century. The king's right to levy taxes for reasons other than necessity gradually developed in exchange for political concessions to his subjects, most notably in 1297 when Edward I accepted *Confirmatio Cartarum*. These tax revenues gave the king the ability to muster an army without having to rely on the intricate rights and restrictions implied by the feudal order. Consequently, the bishop's military guarantee to the king "through the lance," granted at Worms, diminished in importance. The pope, in contrast, continued to rely on feudal commitments to raise an army.

King's courts at a fixed location in England and in France replaced the itinerant justice of an earlier time, thereby centralizing judicial control in the hands of the king, further diminishing the role of the church as an adjudicator of disputes and further emphasizing the king's territorial sovereignty. Additionally, kings began to claim that they ruled by divine right, thereby challenging

---

[8] Trial by ordeal was the process by which innocence or guilt was determined through the presumed intervention of God. Two common ordeals, both supervised by the church, involved submersion of the accused in deep water and forcing the accused to hold a red-hot piece of iron. Failure to stay submerged for a prescribed period of time was taken as proof of guilt, as was the inability to hold a red-hot iron for a specified period.

the pope's special position as allegedly chosen by God. In the jockeying back and forth for control, both kings and church evolved new institutions and methods to foster or stymie economic growth and wrest political control.

The Selection of Bishops: An Empirical Assessment

The narrative account suggests a period rife with institutional innovation, much of which influenced the relative autonomy of the pope and monarchs. Whether these institutional changes and the level of political influence shifted with growth, as suggested by the game, can now be examined with available statistical evidence.

The reign of Philip Augustus was a period of economic expansion in France. This implies that later in Philip's reign more bishoprics would have had large enough revenues to tie the pope's hands in nominating bishops than was true earlier in his reign. In fact, we can make a pretty good estimate of the time when economic growth would have pushed many regalian Sees over the threshold to insure that the king would get the bishops he wanted. Philip renounced his regalian rights in 1203; that is, he ostensibly gave up his right to the income from bishoprics during inter-regna. While some interpret this gesture by Philip as an act of contrition towards the church (Baldwin 1986), it might be that Philip knew that he now had a winning strategy in most dioceses that would lead to the selection of his preferred candidates for bishop. In that case, Philip could afford to appear magnanimous by renouncing the rights hard-earned in the resolution of the investiture controversy. After all, Philip's declaration itself was not binding. In fact, Philip later reneged in some Sees. If the theory presented here is correct, the pope should have recognized the increased need to select bishop candidates who were acceptable to the king. The game had changed from one of domination by the pope to one of domination by Philip.

If the game structure proposed here is correct, we should observe an increase in the proportion of new bishops who were Philip's candidates after 1203 relative to what we observe before. If the standard historical account is right—that Philip learned to cooperate with the church—then we should observe a decrease in the nomination (and selection) of candidates believed to be preferred by the king.

Table 1 shows the distribution of bishops appointed during Philip's reign based on whether they were more likely to be loyal to the king or to the pope.[9] The historical record is clear. After 1203 Philip increasingly got bishops who

[9] Judgments about expectations of loyalty are from the appendix of regalian Sees in Baldwin (1986). Newly appointed bishops are identified as blood relatives of Philip or known at the time to be under his influence or as relatives of the pope or within his circle. The judgments are all Baldwin's who, recall, contends that Philip learned contrition towards the pope.

TABLE 1. Selection of the King's Man for Bishop (before and after renouncing regalian income)

Bishop	Before 1203	After 1203
Pro-King	11	17
Pro-Pope	36	18

$\chi^2 = 5.65$; $P < .01$ One-tailed.

were loyal to him. This is consistent with the explanation associated with my argument.

Less than one-fourth of all new appointees in Philip's first twenty-four years in office were expected to be favorable to the king rather than the pope. In his last twenty years, after 1203, despite renouncing his regalian rights, 50 percent of those appointed were relatives and close associates expected to be his supporters. If, as the standard historical accounts suggest, Philip had learned to comply with the wishes of the church, then we must wonder why the pope switched to appointing the king's relatives late in his term rather than earlier when Philip was seemingly less contrite towards the church?

Other measures of the relationship between economic growth and the appointment of bishops are available for Philip Augustus's France. Since the general thesis is that where there was sufficient wealth, the pope would nominate, and Philip would approve, bishops loyal to the king rather than the pope, we can test the proposition spatially as well as temporally. Maps of twelfth- and thirteenth-century France identify towns with significant textile industries, towns in touch with the Champagne fairs, or towns located on major water or land-based trade routes (Lopez 1966). The Sees in these areas presumably generated more wealth than the Sees not on any of these trade routes or involved in the merchant and export markets. These wealthier communities can be matched against the locations of the regalian Sees to ascertain whether a pattern exists between the expected loyalties of newly appointed bishops and the wealth of the bishopric.

Table 2 portrays papal nominees and whether the bishopric is located on a major trade route or not. Table 3 shows the same relationship, but this time the independent variable is an index categorized as 1 if any of the three wealth-criteria (trade route, cloth manufacturing, or contact with the Champagne fairs) are satisfied. Neither cloth manufacturing nor being in touch with the Champagne fairs, as a single factor, is statistically significantly associated with the bishop-nominee's type, though each is in the predicted direction. Unfortunately, the wealth data other than with regard to location on a major trade route are spotty, with missing information for many regalian Sees. Finally, Table 4 shows the interaction effect of both wealth and being post-1203 on the likelihood that the nominee was expected to be loyal to Philip or to the pope.

TABLE 2. Selection of the King's Man for Bishop (See is on or not on a major trade route)

Bishop	Trade Route	Not a Trade Route
Pro-King	20	8
Pro-Pope	27	27

$\chi^2 = 3.46$; $P < .03$ One-tailed.

Tables 2, 3, and 4 point to a substantial proclivity for the pope to nominate bishop candidates who were relatives or close associates of Philip's in those bishoprics that were wealthy, and to nominate papal loyalists more often in poorer Sees. This is consistent with the expectations from the game.

The tables tell a story that reinforces the view that the struggle over growth was also a struggle over political control and that, gradually, the king was winning against the efforts of the church. The French king was 2.5 times more likely to have a relative or close associate nominated as bishop by the pope in regalian Sees on important trade routes than he was elsewhere. In wealthy dioceses, as measured by satisfying any one of the three economic indicators, the king was more than three times more likely to get a loyal bishop than in less wealthy dioceses. After 1203—when according to standard historical accounts Philip conceded control to the pope—61 percent of new appointments in wealthy Sees went to Philip's loyalists, whereas elsewhere and before, only 24 percent of appointees were expected to be loyal to Philip.

The standard historical account is difficult to sustain in light of the evidence. Papal appointments varied systematically with the wealth of each bishopric. Where wealth was minimal, the pope and church, rather than the king, controlled the appointment of bishops. As the loyalty of bishops was a major factor in the exertion of political control, the church had a strong incentive to minimize growth in wealth and, therefore, the influence of the king over the appointment of key political figures. Church policies aimed at reducing growth helped prolong papal hegemony, but the new secular institutions invented in the

TABLE 3. Selection of the King's Man for Bishop (See is wealthy or not wealthy)

Bishop	Wealthy	Not Wealthy
Pro-King	22	6
Pro-Pope	30	24

$\chi^2 = 4.21$; $P < .02$ One-tailed.

TABLE 4. Selection of the King's Man for Bishop (interaction of wealth and year >1203)

Bishop	Wealthy and Year > 1203	Not Wealthy
Pro-King	14	14
Pro-Pope	9	45

$\chi^2 = 10.15$; $P < .01$ One-tailed.

twelfth and thirteenth centuries gradually insured the demise of papal influence. In the process, these new institutions, many being outgrowths of the competition over economic expansion fostered by the property right granted by the Concordat of Worms, gave rise to the modern sovereign state system. By the end of the Thirty Years' War, the wealth and influence garnered by kings became so great that the game against the pope entered its final stage. With the Protestant Reformation and the defeat of the church, the Treaty of Westphalia made the appointment of bishops irrelevant to kings and so ended the pope's role as a central political figure in Europe. From that time forward, the state, rather than the church, was the primary seat of political authority.

CONCLUSION

The Concordat of Worms created a property right over territory (specifically, bishoprics) that adhered to the sovereign as a fiduciary rather than to the sovereign as an individual. This fiduciary role was new. The property right created competition between kings and the pope over political control. The contest for control manifested itself, in part, through the erection of new political institutions. Some of these institutions on the side of the church appear to have been designed to slow economic growth, thereby prolonging the ascendancy of the papacy. The institutions erected by monarchs appear to have stimulated growth and hastened the day when they would be politically ascendant over the church. The struggle for political control gave advantage to the church in the first century or two after the Investiture Struggle, and a gradual decline in papal authority after that culminated in the rise of Protestantism and the modern state at the end of the Thirty Years' War.

The competition that was institutionalized at Worms fomented the construction of new executive, judicial, taxing, and legislative apparatus that eventually emerged as the state as we know it. Worms set in motion the evolution of many of those institutions, insuring that the territorial property right it created would form the foundation for a new political structure. Over the span of about five hundred years, the agreement at Worms served to preserve and protect papal authority. It also served to insure the development of new means to produce growth, including much of the administrative apparatus of sovereign states, so that kings could escape the powerful grip of the pope. Those new means ultimately resulted in the demise of the Catholic Church as Europe's hegemon and the emergence of the terms at Westphalia that codified the sovereign authority of the territorial state.

References

Baldwin, J. W. (1986) *The Government of Philip Augustus*. Berkeley: University of California Press.

Barzel, Y. (1989) *The Economic Analysis of Property Rights*. New York: Cambridge University Press.

De Roover, R. A. (1948) *Money, Banking, and Credit in Mediaeval Bruges*. Cambridge, MA: Mediaeval Academy of America.

De Roover, R. A. (1974) *Business, Banking, and Economic Thought in Late Medieval and Early Modern Europe*. Edited by J. Kirshner. Chicago: University of Chicago Press.

Duby, G. (1991) *France in the Middle Ages: 987–1460*. Translated by Juliet Vale. Oxford: Blackwell.

Eggertsson, T. (1990) *Economic Behavior and Institutions*. New York: Cambridge University Press.

Gies, F., and J. Gies (1994) *Cathedral, Forge, and Waterwheel: Technology and Invention in the Middle Ages*. New York: Harper Collins.

Gilchrist, J. (1969) *The Church and Economic Activity in the Middle Ages*. New York: Macmillan.

Greif, A. (1998) "Cultural Beliefs and the Organization of Society." In *The New Institutionalism in Sociology*, edited by Mary C. Brinton and Victor Nee. New York: Russell Sage Foundation.

Huth, P. K. (1996) *Standing Your Ground: Territorial Disputes and International Conflict*. Ann Arbor: University of Michigan Press.

John of Paris ([1302], 1971) *De Potestate Regia et Papali*, translated by J. A. Watt as *On Royal and Papal Power*. Toronto: The Pontifical Institute of Mediaeval Studies.

Kantorowicz, E. (1957) *The King's Two Bodies*. Princeton: Princeton University Press.

Krasner, S. (1999) *Sovereignty: Organized Hypocrisy*. Princeton: Princeton University Press.

LADURIE, E. L. R. (1971) *Times of Feast, Times of Famine*, translated by Barbara Bray. New York: Farrar, Straus and Giroux.

LE GOFF, J. (1980) *Time, Work, and Culture in the Middle Ages*, translated by Arthur Goldhammer. Chicago: University of Chicago Press.

LOPEZ, R. S. (1966) *The Birth of Europe*. J. M. Dent and Sons.

LOPEZ, R. S. (1976) *The Commercial Revolution of the Middle Ages, 950-1350*. Cambridge: Cambridge University Press.

MILLER, E., AND J. HATCHER. (1995) *Medieval England: Towns, Commerce, and Crafts, 1086–1348*. London: Longman.

NORTH, D. C., AND B. R. WEINGAST. (1989) Constitutions and Commitment: The Institutions Governing Public Choice in Seventeenth Century England. *Journal of Economic History* **44**: 803–832.

PRZEWORSKI, A. (1991) *Democracy and the Market*. New York: Cambridge University Press.

ROBINSON, I. S. (1990) *The Papacy 1073–1198: Continuity and Innovation*. Cambridge: Cambridge University Press.

ROSENBERG, N., AND L. E. BIRDZELL, JR. (1986) *How the West Grew Rich: The Economic Transformation of the Industrial World*. New York: Basic Books.

SCHIMMELPFENNIG, B. (1992) *The Papacy*. New York: Columbia University Press.

SENESE, P. D. (1995) "Militarized Interstate Dispute Escalation: The Effects of Geographical Proximity and Issue Salience." Paper presented at the meetings of the Peace Science Society, October 13–15, Ohio State University, Columbus, Ohio.

SENESE, P. D. (1997) "Contiguity, Territory, and Their Interaction." Presented at the Annual Meetings of the International Studies Association, March 18–22, Toronto.

SIVERSON, R. M., AND H. STARR. (1991) *The Diffusion of War*. Ann Arbor, MI: University of Michigan Press.

SPRUYT, H. (1994) *The Sovereign State and Its Competitors*. Princeton: Princeton University Press.

TUCHMAN, B. (1984) *The March of Folly*. New York: Alfred A. Knopf.

VAN CAENEGEM, R. C. (1988) *The Birth of the English Common Law*, 2d. ed. Cambridge, U.K.: Cambridge University Press.

VASQUEZ, J. A. (1993) *The War Puzzle*. New York: Cambridge University Press.

VASQUEZ, J. (1995) Why Do Neighbors Fight?—Territoriality, Proximity, or Interactions. *Journal of Peace Research* **32**:277–93.

WALTZ, K. (1979) *Theory of International Politics*. Reading, MA: Addison-Wesley.

WEBER, M. (1958) *The Protestant Ethic and the Spirit of Capitalism*. Translated by Talcott Parsons. New York: Scribner.

WEBER, M. (1968) *Economy and Society*, edited by Guenther Roth and Claus Wittich. Translated by Ephraim Fischoff. New York: Bedminster Press.

WESSON, R. (1978) *State Systems*. New York: Simon and Schuster.

Environment, Wealth, and Authority: Global Climate Change and Emerging Modes of Legitimation

Karen T. Litfin[1]

University of Washington

A central feature of modernity is that state authority has been conceived as resting on the consent of the governed, which in turn depends upon governments' ability to promote economic prosperity. The performance criteria upon which political authority has been judged in large part are positively correlated with the exponential growth in the use of fossil fuels. An international scientific consensus has emerged: the burning of fossil fuels will cause global climate change sometime in this century. This suggests that the authority of science presents a challenge to a key source of the state's political authority: its role as guarantor of wealth production. Moreover, since the real impact of global climate change will not be felt for several decades, the notion of intergenerational responsibility is implicit in contemporary efforts to reduce greenhouse gas (GHG) emissions. Given that the liberal notion of political authority entails consent of currently living self-interested citizens, efforts to promote intergenerational responsibility suggest that the basis of political authority is being revised by efforts to cope with global environmental degradation.

[1] I am grateful to Matthew Auer, James Caporaso, and Ronald Mitchell for their helpful comments on earlier drafts of this paper.

Published by Blackwell Publishers, 350 Main Street, Malden, MA 02148, USA, and 108 Cowley Road, Oxford OX4 1JF, UK.

The Argument

With the manmade patchwork of territorial states standing in apparent contradistinction to the web of nature, efforts to cope with transnational and global environmental degradation are generally construed as posing a challenge to state sovereignty. Yet the popular "erosion-of-sovereignty" thesis fails to disaggregate a complex and variegated set of domestic and international pressures on states to engage in environmental protection (Conca 1994). Sovereignty may be understood as comprising three interrelated yet conceptually distinct elements: autonomy, control, and authority (Litfin 1997). Control, like power, is the ability to produce an effect. Autonomy, or independence, is closely related to control since genuine independence requires some degree of power. Changes in authority, or the legitimate exercise of power, are the most difficult to measure because of the intersubjective nature of legitimacy. Of the three, autonomy is most obviously reduced by ecological interdependence and international environmental cooperation. Problems such as acid rain, marine pollution, ozone depletion, and climate change, in a sense representing nontraditional forms of foreign intervention, also undercut states' ability to control events within their own territorial jurisdiction. On the other hand, efforts to cope with environmental degradation may require enhanced state capacity, or control. Thus, rather than diminishing some monolithic principle of sovereignty, international environmental responses typically involve trade-offs among autonomy, control, and authority (Litfin 1997).

The "erosion-of-sovereignty" thesis is most commonly articulated with respect to the dimensions of control and autonomy, rarely taking into consideration questions of authority. Political authority is generally conceived as the recognized right to make rules or to wield power legitimately (Weber 1947:153). As such, it contains a strong normative component, albeit one that is reinforced by control and autonomy. Domestically, a state's authority depends upon its citizens *believing* in the legitimacy of its institutions; internationally, it rests substantially on *recognition* by other states. Authority, whether granted internally or externally, entails a perception of rightfulness, although what counts as "rightful" could include superior virtues or expertise, historical pedigree or practice, consent or a fiduciary relationship. This paper examines the impact of scientific authority on political authority for one global environmental problem: climate change.

Of the three dimensions of sovereignty, authority is the most problematic for international relations (IR) theorists both because of its intersubjective character and because of its close association with state–society relations. Conventional models of the state as a rational unitary actor preclude a focus on either of these factors. Consequently, IR theorists have tended either to rely on overly juridical notions of authority linked to states' standing in international law or else collapse authority into power or control. One could certainly argue that these approaches have never been adequate, that the international arena has always been ordered according to consensually legitimated norms (Wendt 1992; Katzenstein 1996) and that states' authority with respect to their international behavior has always required some degree of consent from their citizens. Even putting these claims aside, conventional approaches to authority in IR are utterly deficient in the face of both transnational societal pressures and efforts to address global environmental problems. The politics of global climate change, perhaps more so than any other international issue, highlight the emergence of new patterns of authority rooted in scientific legitimation and Earth stewardship.

A central feature of modernity, and one that has been neglected by IR scholars, is that state authority has been conceived as resting on the consent of the governed. While the Westphalian order legitimated the power of monarchs within territorially delineated jurisdictions, and to that extent gave birth to the modern notion of sovereignty, its authoritative basis was conceived more in terms of "divine right" than any notion of popular consent. The Treaty of Westphalia may have established the territorial state,[2] but it did not establish the modern state as we know it. The whole meaning of democracy in the modern era is that state authority is grounded upon the consent of the governed, which in turn is institutionalized through fair and open elections. Modernity, especially in the second half of the twentieth century, has been substantially about the spread of democracy, or the notion that rightful political authority depends upon consent of the governed (Huntington 1991; Shin 1994).

Political authority based upon consent takes two forms: an acceptance of the deep constitutional principles of a polity, and popular support for (or at least acquiescence to) the governmental policies, a distinction that grows out of the distinction between state and government. Were we to reduce legitimacy to its constitutional foundations, democratic elections would lose their significance as the key mechanism through which consent is granted or revoked. Although it is true that modern states rarely undergo full-scale revolutions, we should not therefore assume that all matters of political authority have been settled. Indeed, some have argued that globalization in its various guises is precipitating an authority crisis for the state—not just for specific governments (Rosenau 1990; Strange 1996). While that argument is beyond the scope of this paper, the key point is that modern political authority rests upon consent of the governed, and consent refers not only to the deep constitutional principles of the state but also to the actual performance of governments. More concretely, the performance criteria according to which the modern state is judged derive from its dual role as guarantor of territorial integrity and wealth production. In the absence of

---

[2] Although even this is debatable. See Buena de Mesquita's article in this volume.

major threats from foreign aggressors, elections tend to be decided on the basis of key economic performance criteria: jobs and economic growth. Moreover, rule based upon consent of the governed is increasingly an international norm (Franck 1992).

Throughout the industrial era, economic performance has been positively correlated with exponential growth in fossil fuel production—first from coal and later from petroleum and natural gas. Besides generating local and regional pollution, the burning of fossil fuels emits large quantities of carbon dioxide, which scientists believe is the primary greenhouse gas responsible for global climate change. Aside from a small handful of dissenters, the scientific community has urged governments to take action to reduce greenhouse gas (GHG) emissions. Barring a major technological shift in the direction of alternative energy resources or a dramatic commitment to energy efficiency, the authority of science can therefore be interpreted as being deployed to challenge a key source of the state's political authority: its role as guarantor of wealth production. Thus, while the 1997 Kyoto Protocol requiring industrialized countries to reduce greenhouse gas emissions by seven to eight percent by 2012 may be relatively meaningless in terms of ameliorating climate change, it is nonetheless remarkable as evidence of a tangible commitment of political leaders to the authority of climate science.

This interplay between scientific and political authority is of great interest not only because of its policy relevance to the future ecological health of the planet, but also because of the theoretical issues raised by the juxtaposition of these two rather different forms of authority. The authority of science rests on its claim to objective, disinterested, and verifiable knowledge, whereas political authority rests on the consent of the governed and is exercised on the basis of power. Because of its unrivaled status as universal legitimator in the modern era, science may facilitate international cooperation. Yet, for the same reason, political actors on all sides have an incentive to deploy it on behalf of their policy goals, with the ironic outcome that the demand for legitimation results in a process of delegitimation (Litfin 1994). Once science enters the political fray, especially for a high-stakes issue like global climate change, it risks being perceived as contaminated and thereby losing its authority. The Intergovernmental Panel on Climate Change (IPCC), the scientific body charged with producing periodic international assessments on global climate change, has continually faced these dilemmas since its inception in 1988. Yet it has managed, for the most part, to maintain its authority. If the international agenda of the twenty-first century is increasingly concerned with science-driven questions, as we have good reason to assume that it will be, then the experiences of the IPCC offer an important precedent for understanding the evolution of authority.

The climate change issue also highlights an anomaly with respect to prevailing accounts of political authority rooted in liberal notions of consent. Even if scientists have detected "a discernible human influence on climate" (IPCC 1996:5), the brunt of that influence will not be felt until sometime in the next fifty to one hundred years. The modern notion of consent refers to the sanction of *contemporary* self-interested citizens who not only accept the deep constitutional principles of the polity but also evaluate their government's performance in fostering security and prosperity. Claims about intergenerational responsibility are foreign to liberal notions of consent and political authority, yet efforts to address climate change hinge, either explicitly or tacitly, upon such claims. In their efforts to induce governments to adopt meaningful reductions in greenhouse gas emissions, both scientists and nongovernmental organizations are in effect revising the basis of political authority to include obligations to future generations. To the extent that these efforts are successful, the performance criteria according to which governments are evaluated entail safeguarding the welfare of those who cannot voice their consent: the unborn. If political authority in the modern era has rested on the consent of the governed, such a shift would represent a meaningful reorientation of the basis of state authority.

In the following section, I argue that IR theorists, with their focus on interstate relations, have traditionally ignored the consensual dimension of authority. They have generally evaded the troublesome question of legitimacy either by adopting a juridical conception of authority or by conflating authority with power and control. While external factors (e.g., recognition by other states or the ability to exercise legitimate leadership in the international arena) are significant sources of authority, the internal bases of authority are equally important, perhaps even more so. Indeed, if democratic governance is becoming a normative rule in the international system, as some have argued it is (Franck 1992), then IR scholars will be compelled to include public consent in their notions of authority, legitimacy, and sovereignty. Under a pluralist system, a government that fails to protect the state's territorial integrity or enhance the production of wealth will likely find itself out of office, a fact that is no less true in the international arena than in domestic politics. Thus, authority should be grasped in internal and popular terms as well as external and statist terms.

Authority in IR Theory

Authority should not be confused with power or control; they may facilitate authority, they do not supply legitimacy. Authority in the Western tradition of political thought is construed as the *rightful* governance of human action by means other than coercion or persuasion (Arendt 1968:92; Friedman 1990:63). Hannah Arendt offers a colorful illustration: "Its hallmark is unquestioning recognition by those who are asked to obey; neither coercion nor persuasion is needed. (A father can lose authority either by beating his child or by starting to argue with him, that is, either by behaving like a tyrant or by treating him as an equal)" (1970:45). The core question is: What constitutes rightfulness? Increasingly in the modern era, that question has been answered in terms of consent of the governed and institutionalized through democratic elections.

Authority is a vexing concept for international relations theorists because of its intersubjective character and its close association with state-society relations. Legitimacy, which is key to the modern notion of authority, depends upon the extent to which those addressed by a rule understand themselves as being obliged by it, rather than merely coerced by whatever power created and supported the rule (Stokke 1997:48; Franck 1990). Legitimacy therefore requires a reflective subject capable of judging whether an action, rule, or proposal is in accordance either with its interests or else with established rules, principles, or standards. That requirement, which is not particularly problematic in the domestic context of pluralist democracies, becomes much more so in the international arena. Citizens, unlike states, are reflective subjects.

IR theorists have generally sidestepped the thorny question of legitimacy by either embracing a juridical model of authority or by conflating authority with power. For those taking the former approach, legitimacy is externally derived from gaining recognition from other states or by having standing in international law (Bull and Watson 1982; James 1986). While this conception at least recognizes the normative character of legitimacy, it ultimately rests on interstate rather than state-society relations; the latter are effectively black-boxed. This juridical conception of authority reduces legitimacy to "the collective judgement of international society about rightful membership in the family of nations" (Wight 1977:153). Even if they fail to incorporate citizens into their conceptions of authority, with the attendant risk that international relations appears as a set of practices devoid of people, these theorists at least recognize that authority (and thus sovereignty) rests ultimately on normative grounds.

The other tack, most commonly taken by realists, is to conflate authority with power or autonomy. Even Thomson (1995), who emphasizes the analytical distinction between authority ("the claim to the exclusive right to make rules") and control ("the capability of enforcing that claim"), leaves the normative basis of the state's "exclusive right" indeterminate. Consequently, the distinction she attempts to articulate becomes blurred as authority slides over into control. A kind of solipsism emerges here, such that a state's authority is legitimated by the behavior or perceptions of other sovereign states, rendering citizens invisible.

Properly speaking, the state is a reification that neither acts nor judges. Governments, individual leaders, and policymakers are the real actors in international politics and, at least in modern democracies, their political fate is intimately tied to the consent of the governed. There is no reason to presume that they forget this fact when they turn their attention to the international arena. Indeed, the pervasive background presence of electorates in international negotiations can be profoundly influential. Proponents of two-level game approaches recognize that negotiators are constrained simultaneously by domestic and international factors (Putnam 1988). Ultimately, political leaders depend upon the consent of their citizens in order to retain their positions of power. In the modern era, the mechanism for granting that consent has been elections.

While "consent" entails a number of thorny practical and philosophical problems, it has nonetheless enjoyed considerable staying power in political thought, even serving as the principal basis for international political obligation.[3] Yet problems abound. Philosophical anarchists argue that consent, which entails autonomy, conflicts with the abdication of autonomy implicit in accepting authority, thereby concluding that no authority can be morally legitimate (Wolff 1990).[4] Social contract theorists and their critics have wrestled with the practical question of how consent is granted (Pateman 1980; Greenwalt 1990; Lincoln 1991). Critical theorists contend that "the notion of consent tends to equalize the positions of subjects and obscures the asymmetry of power relations between the governed and the governed" (Cutler 1999:65). Feminist theorists have challenged the notion of the atomistic individual and highlighted the invisibility of women in notions of authority based upon consent (Pateman 1988; Jones 1993).

Other than the anarchist challenge, which would abolish political authority altogether, the full range of critique paradoxically serves to reinforce the sense that consent remains central to legitimate political authority. Consent may require more than an originary covenant; we may have trouble measuring it; the disempowered members of society may not have truly given it. Nonetheless, it remains a touchstone for discerning legitimate political authority, for the aim of theorists and critics alike is "to develop a doctrine of political authority which makes its legitimacy conditional on the existence of a population which regards the government as its representative" (Raz 1990:17).

The notion of popular sovereignty, so critical to domestic politics, is nonexistent in traditional approaches to international relations. Yet the dramatic increase in transnational citizen activity over the past two decades suggests that the field must begin to consider the impact of popular participation on international patterns of authority (Keck and Sikkink 1998). There is no *a priori* rationale for confining democratic practices to the territorial container of the state (Connolly 1993). That they were so restricted in the past was a result of

---

[3] International law explicitly depends upon the consent, in the form of signing and ratification, of sovereign states. See Linklater 1982.

[4] For a response to the anarchist dilemma based upon the similarities between political authority and the authority of experts, see Raz 1990. For communitarian responses, see Green 1990 and Dworkin 1990.

specific historical conditions that are now changing under the dynamic processes variously referred to as globalization (Held 1995). This is one of the implications of the literature on global civil society (Peterson 1992; Lipschutz 1996) and world civic politics (Wapner 1996). Transnational environmental activism is not merely about the growing importance of nonstate actors, but it is also about the emergence of new modes of legitimation and the recognition of new authorities.

Transnational environmental activism may be understood as an attempt to modify existing authority relations by erecting alternative criteria for legitimation (McCormick 1989). At its most fundamental level, the politics of environmental accountability seeks to inculcate a sense of intergenerational responsibility at all levels of social organization, a norm that would significantly reconfigure state sovereignty. As Edith Brown Weiss (1989) argues, only areas beyond any national jurisdiction have been considered global commons. But from the intergenerational perspective, the planet is a global commons shared by all generations, such that those of us living today are bound by a "planetary trust" that entails certain rights and obligations. At least implicitly and even though it is not monolithic, transnational environmentalism aims to transform the modern conception of authority to include not only popular legitimacy, which has emerged in tandem with the spread of democracy, but also intergenerational and even interspecies criteria of accountability.

Before turning to an analysis of political and scientific authority and a subsequent examination of the politics of global climate change, the following section looks briefly at the historical origins of sovereignty and the territorial state. While the Treaty of Westphalia did promote the emergence of the territorial state, the modern notion of sovereignty developed later. Rather, the foundations of modern political authority were laid by thinkers and activists in Restoration England who conceptualized it in terms of consent of the governed. The twin principles of territoriality and consensual authority, both central to the modern conception of sovereignty, have important yet neglected implications for an era in which the human species has become a geophysical force.

Westphalia and the Modern State in Ecological Perspective

In innumerable international relations courses, the signing of the Treaty of Westphalia in 1648 is cited as the birth of the nation-state and the origin of the modern conception of sovereignty. Yet this account is only partially correct. The Thirty Years' War, which devastated central Europe, began as a civil war between Protestants and Catholics and devolved into a continent-wide scramble for political power and territory. The Treaty's primary objectives were to rectify debts incurred during the war; to reestablish lineages of heirs; and to reconcile religious practice with political authority, with the latter having the greatest significance for the development of the modern nation-state." "To prevent for the future any Difference arising in the Politick State," rulers were granted "free exercise of Territorial Right, as well as Ecclesiastick" (Article LXIV). The rights of monarchs and princes included making and interpreting laws, declaring war, imposing taxes, and forging alliances (International Law Database). Thus, the norm of territorial exclusivity, which is central to the modern notion of sovereignty and had been blocked by the continental predominance of the Holy Roman Emperor, was advanced at Westphalia. Yet only a handful of the political entities sanctioned by the Treaty were recognizable as nation-states. For two centuries after Westphalia, Europe remained a hodgepodge of states, city-states, and other principalities (Spruyt 1994).

The carving up of Europe, and eventually the entire planet, into a patchwork of mutually exclusive territorial states is modernity's political rendering of nature. Nature is not inherently constituted so as to become subject to state sovereignty, but rather must first be mapped and constructed as territory (Kuehls 1998). Maps are powerful political documents, yet they have little or no relation to ecosystems and geophysical processes. Territoriality presumes that political authorities can address, if not solve, problems that arise within their specific jurisdictions, a presumption rendered problematic under conditions of global ecological interdependence. Territorial exclusivity stands in sharp contrast to the outlook of global ecology, based on holism and the mutual dependence of Earth's ecosystems (Ruggie 1993).

By itself, the territorial state did not articulate a fully modern conception of sovereignty. Rather, Westphalia signified the Age of Absolutism (Anderson 1974). While the Westphalian order enshrined the political and religious authority of princes within their own jurisdictions, and to that extent gave birth to the modern system of mutually exclusive territorial states, the basis of that right was conceived more in terms of "divine right" than any notion of popular consent. That basis was being laid in England, which was isolated from the bloody war on the continent but experienced its own civil war between the constitutionalists and monarchalists from 1642 to 1646. Despite being an absolutist, Thomas Hobbes, whose *Leviathan* was published in 1651, is widely considered the father of modern political thought. Rather than founding his theory of political authority on any considerations of religion, tradition, or even brute force, Hobbes deduced the political rights and obligations from the interests of atomistic individuals. Individuals in the state of nature, conceived by Hobbes as bundles of matter in motion driven by their desire for power yet also capable of authoring their own actions, experience life as "nasty, short, and brutish." Thus, they enter into a "covenant," or a transfer of authority from individuals to an all-powerful sovereign who becomes the "author" of their actions (Hobbes 1976

[1651]:217, 222). In Restoration England, even the monarchicalist Hobbes found it necessary to root his conception of authority in the consent of the individual. Moreover, in contrast to the organic worldview linking the individual to God in a "great chain of being," Hobbes conceived of both the state and the individual as machines, and may thus be considered a founder of modern thinking on the basis of his contribution to a mechanistic worldview (Merchant 1990).

While Hobbes may deserve the title of "father of modern political thought" on the basis of his radical individualism and his secular materialism, the constitutionalists' understanding of the basis of political authority has been far more influential in the modern era. For them, consent was not a once-and-for-all occurrence; rather, it could be revoked. In his *Two Treatises of Government*, published in 1690, John Locke argued that the purpose of the state is to protect men's fundamental rights, most importantly the right to property. Consequently, citizens are entirely justified in overthrowing any government that systematically violates these rights. Locke's thinking, which had a direct influence on the American and French Revolutions, encapsulated two core ideas of modern political thought: the viability of both popular revolutions and parliamentary democracy as the means of ensuring that political authority is grounded in citizens' consent.

Locke's approach to ethics and his conception of property rights are also noteworthy for their ecological implications. For Locke, ethical action entails the pursuit of pleasure. Because "man has property in his own person," he therefore owns whatever he mixes his labor with (1965: 328–9). Thanks to the invention of money, men can pursue pleasure by accumulating wealth without letting nature's goods spoil. Taking a less secular approach than Hobbes, Locke also grounds his understanding of individual property rights in Biblical injunction. Because He commanded man to "subdue the Earth," God gave the world "to the use of the Industrious and Rational" (333). Land that is left to nature, for Locke, is wasted. (Likewise, those who are not industrious and rational are not truly human and can therefore be justifiably treated as animals.) Given that communal ownership of land was the norm throughout most of the world at the dawn of modernity, the liberal theory of "possessive individualism" represented a major change requiring the sort of rhetorical justification offered by Locke. Combining the various strands of Locke's thought, political authority is premised upon the state's ability to guarantee property rights and thereby facilitate market relations, and ethical action involves both the conquest of nature and the pursuit of pleasure. Acting upon these premises in a world of finite resources will inevitably produce dire ecological consequences at some point in time. Thus, Locke's ideas on both political authority and the relationship between humans and nature have found a comfortable home in modernity.

Although the Westphalian order enthroned the right of princes to exercise political and ecclesiastical authority within specified jurisdictions, and to that extent gave birth to the modern system of mutually exclusive territorial states, the basis of that right was conceived as "divine right" rather than popular consent. From Hobbes onward, both in terms of political theory and the founding constitutions of states, the basis of state authority has been explicated in terms of citizens' consent. Historically, the material basis of that consent was conceived in terms of a range of goods that the state could be expected to provide, especially common defense and protection of property rights. Thus, the authority of the modern state derives from its role as guarantor of territorial integrity and wealth production. This does not preclude the possibility of states failing to fulfill these expectations, for many have so failed. Robert Jackson's analysis of "quasi-states" suggests that the authority of many Third World states derives more from their international recognition than from their indigenous capacity to facilitate wealth production (1990). Yet the fact that their authority comes more from external than internal sources does not diminish the crucial importance of the latter. It is precisely the deficit in indigenous capacity and consensual authority that engenders political instability in many of these countries.

Since the Great Depression, states' authority (at least in the West) has rested substantially on governments' ability to protect their citizens from the vagaries of markets, which in turn has required greater collaboration in the management of international economic transactions (Polanyi 1944). As a consequence of this shift in expectations, state authority has been internationalized to some extent (Ruggie 1993). Moreover, the persistence of rule-governed behavior in international relations offers strong circumstantial evidence for the proposition that international law and regimes are generally accepted as legitimate (Franck 1990). Nonetheless, the internal legitimacy of state authorities varies according to citizens' assessment of their performance. Elections are decided in large measure on the basis of key economic performance criteria: joblessness and economic growth. Edward Tufte (and others) find a tight correlation between incumbent electoral results and changes in real disposable income per capita (1974:139–148). Put bluntly, "It's the economy, stupid!" Whatever political leaders' commitments to international institutions and ethical responsibility might be, performance criteria remain crucial.

Authority, Political and Scientific

From the seventeenth century onward, and from left to right across the political spectrum, Western thought has been characterized by an overarching faith in science. The belief in the authority of science to improve human life is perhaps the quintessential hallmark of modernity, a belief that is reinforced by the material achievements of industrialization (Ezrahi 1990; Heineman 1994). During the second half of the twentieth century, that belief spread across the globe (Finnemore 1993).

The relationship between scientific and political authority is many-faceted. That the rise of liberal understandings of political authority during the seventeenth century paralleled the rise of modern science is not coincidental. Liberal political theory was informed by a mechanistic worldview that understood nature as composed of atomistic components. Indeed, the Newtonian image of particles in motion was the guiding metaphor in the emerging liberal conception of "possessive individualism" (MacPherson 1962). Consent was to be granted by atomistic individuals who "owned" the "property" of themselves. Thus, science and politics were grounded in the same ontological assumptions, even if their practices were conceived as distinct. The replicability of scientific experiments means that, at least in principle, knowledge can be obtained by anyone, regardless of class, nationality, or political persuasion. Thus, there is a strong link between democratic thought and modern science.

Interestingly, although the appeal of science throughout modernity has rested on its supposed access to objective truth, the liberal notion of consent also pervades science. Scientific truths are those that enjoy a consensus within a scientific community. Authoritative knowledge claims are those that enjoy a scientific consensus, suggesting that any capable scientist who applies the scientific method will reach the same conclusion. Science is conceived as functioning in a rather rarefied atmosphere, immune to the vagaries of political power and subjective opinion, but, as in politics, consensus stands as the touchstone of authority. The role of consensus, a social process, in generating authoritative knowledge claims raises the possibility that science might be tainted by nonscientific forces such as peer pressure, the power of tradition, the desire for funding, or socio-psychological identities (Kuhn 1962; Ziman 1968; Keller 1985).

Though science is an inherently social institution, the important point is that it is *perceived* as operating in a different realm and according to very different norms than politics. This perception, prevalent among both policymakers and the general public, is a crucial source of scientific authority. The dynamics of bargaining, coercion, and manipulation that characterize political practice contrast dramatically with the disinterested pursuit of truth, which is thought to characterize science. Therefore, if the authority of science depends upon its perceived isolation from social and political forces, then the deployment of scientific knowledge in the policy realm jeopardizes its legitimacy. The image of scientific knowledge as an objective and value-free source of competence makes it a powerful source of legitimation for all sides in a policy debate. In its application to policy problems, science thus finds itself in a double bind: In addressing socio-physical problems it must enter the political fray, but if it is to preserve its legitimacy it must remain isolated from politics. This dilemma is especially acute for environmental policy problems, which often depend upon science to both identify and address them.

The authority of science is inevitably undermined by uncertainty. Responsible policymakers, in order to make the best decisions, require as much certainty as possible, yet policy relevance typically has the ironic effect of increasing uncertainty. Scientific uncertainty is not an isolated dimension of environmental problems, for it casts its shadow across all aspects of a problem. Under conditions of uncertainty, the gravity of the problem is in dispute; actors cannot easily infer their preferences; proposed control measures may fail to alleviate the problem; and specific dramatic events may or may not be related to the issue at hand.

Uncertainty is far greater in certain fields than in others. Stephen Cole contrasts the *core* of a scientific discipline, which enjoys the greatest legitimacy, with research at the *frontiers* of the discipline (Cole 1992). Controversy, including policy-relevant controversy, generally involves science beyond the core. Eugene Rosa and Thomas Dietz (1998) add to Cole's typology the notion of scientific *horizons*—not simply an incremental extension from a disciplinary core to its frontiers, but a qualitative leap beyond the core. Horizon science, which is typically transdisciplinary, may involve discovery of a new problem or new tools to understand an old problem, or it may approach a problem at a wholly different level of abstraction. Because uncertainty is greatest for horizon science, its perceived legitimacy in policy-relevant questions should be especially low.

As Rosa and Dietz argue, global climate change qualifies as horizon science in several respects. It is certainly transdisciplinary. Since the world's climate involves a continually changing and highly complex set of relations, climate research faces severe obstacles in linking theory and empirical evidence. Climate science relies heavily on elaborate computer models, which convert fundamental laws from Newtonian mechanics and thermodynamics (core science) into long strings of mathematical equations, which are then applied to each of many thousands of cells of a planetary grid representing the earth's atmosphere. The most sophisticated of these models are General Circulation Models (GCMs), whose accuracy is tested by comparing their "predictions" of past global climate with historical data. Modeled predictions of future climate change are based upon incorporating current and projected greenhouse gas emissions into GCMs. Because of gaps in the data (e.g., cloud behavior; methane and emissions due to agricultural practices in developing countries; the ability of the oceans to absorb atmospheric CO_2), GCMs should be viewed as "heuristic devices rather than reality maps" (Elzinga 1997:79). Whether or not the models' predictions are valid cannot be known until sometime in the future, but they currently constitute the most authoritative knowledge available to guide climate change policy.

Science both renders the invisible visible and extends the temporal horizons of citizens and policy actors. As one long-time analyst of international environmental problem solving observes, "Science makes the environment speak. Without science, trees have no legal standing, ecosystems degrade unrecognized, and species are lost without our knowing" (Moltke 1997:265). Science interjects an intergenerational time frame into environmental policy discussions, especially with respect to climate change. Without scientists' predictions based upon computer models, climate change would not even exist as a political issue.

Because scientists do not expect the real impact of human-induced climate change to be felt until sometime towards the middle of the next century, action to ameliorate the problem therefore must be justified primarily on grounds of intergenerational responsibility. But, as I have argued above, the modern notion of political authority rests on consent of the governed, with performance criteria being largely focused on the promotion of economic well-being. Thus, the authoritative knowledge claims of climate science appear to impinge directly upon a significant source of state authority.

If, as argued above, social and political controversy erodes the authority of policy-relevant science, then this should be especially true for climate change science. Unlike past transnational environmental problems, such as acid rain, whaling, or ozone depletion, which involved relatively small segments of economic activity, the sources of climate change are seemingly ubiquitous. More importantly, the primary greenhouse gas, carbon dioxide (CO_2), is a by-product of fossil fuel consumption, which in turn has been positively correlated with economic growth for the past two hundred years. Since climate change uniquely touches the heart of industrial society, we may anticipate that states would strongly resist any proposals to reduce greenhouse gas emissions. Granted that the economic growth of some countries depends on fossil fuel use less than others, and that some countries (especially small island states) can expect to be more negatively affected than others, we would expect most states to protect their principal long-standing sources of wealth production. Furthermore, given the significant uncertainties in both the models and the data, we might expect some strong challenges to the authority of climate science—not just from interest groups like the automobile, coal, and petroleum industries, but also from states themselves.

Yet, as I argue below, an international political consensus has emerged that recognizes the authority of climate change science. Moreover, the precautionary principle, which affirms that in the face of scientific uncertainty, regulators should act to prevent harm rather than wait until damage occurs (Bodansky 1991), has figured prominently in international discussions of climate change, and has been formalized in the Framework Convention of Climate Change. This embryonic norm legitimated the negotiation of the 1997 Kyoto Protocol, the first international regulatory treaty addressing climate change. While statements about intergenerational responsibility are found in earlier documents, such as the 1992 Rio Declaration and Agenda 21, the Kyoto Protocol raises the bar because, once ratified, it is a binding treaty rather than a statement of principles or a guide to action.[5] Thus, the Kyoto Protocol offers some tentative evidence for the emergence of a new international norm of intergenerational responsibility, a norm that could have momentous implications for political authority in the twenty-first century.

Fossil Fuels, Wealth, and National Interests

The close correlation between economic growth and fossil fuel consumption is striking. In Europe and North America the first wave of industrialization was fueled by coal, with petroleum taking the lead in most Western countries during the twentieth century. Where abundant, coal is still widely used, but petroleum is the primary fuel of the world's economy because it is more easily traded and is used for transportation. Despite the fact that petroleum is relatively cleaner than coal, both in terms of local pollution and climatic effects, the exponential increase in its consumption contributed to a worldwide quadrupling of greenhouse gas emissions between 1950 and 1995. This corresponds to a quadrupling of Gross World Product during the same period (see Figures 1 and 2). Not surprisingly, given the close relationship between energy production and economic prosperity, governments have heavily subsidized the fossil fuel industry, albeit to a lesser degree in Western Europe than North America (Koplow 1993).

Nor, given the historical dependence of wealth production on greenhouse gas emissions, is it surprising that proposals to reduce the latter have encountered strong resistance. In 1988, scientists estimated that stabilizing atmospheric concentrations of carbon dioxide at then-current levels would mean reducing fossil fuel use by 50 to 80 percent, bringing it back to 1950 levels (Flavin 1990:20). Two years later, U.S. economist William Nordhaus put the cost to the United States alone of halving greenhouse gas emissions at $180 billion (Nordhaus 1990a; 1990b), a calculation that figured prominently in a subsequent National Academy of Sciences study (NAS 1991). While the most detailed analyses have been done for the United States, most country studies suggest that the costs of reducing greenhouse gas emissions will be substantial (Grubb et al. 1991). Even the small emissions reductions adopted in the Kyoto Protocol, ranging from 5 to 8 percent, have caused alarm in some quarters. According to critics, "if implemented, the treaty would force the most productive societies on earth—the ones that have led the way in making human life comfortable, safe, and prosperous—to slow their economic growth and degrade their standard of living" (Jacoby 1998). While certain state governments have an especially strong interest in opposing greenhouse gas reductions (e.g., OPEC

---

[5] I am grateful to Matthew Auer for clarifying this point.

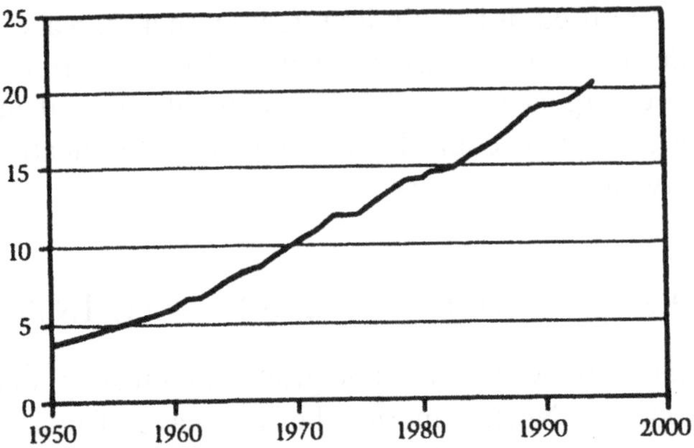

Source: Lester Brown, Nicholas Lenssen, Hal Kane, *Vital Signs 1995*. New York: Norton, 1995.

FIGURE 1. Gross World Product, 1950–94 (in trillions of 1987 U.S. dollars)

countries and the highest per capita consumers), *all* countries are utterly dependent on fossil fuels. Thus, in the absence of scientific claims about climate change, no country would have an obvious interest in reducing its use of fossil fuels.

At first glance, the Kyoto Protocol's requirement that industrialized countries reduce their greenhouse gas emissions by 5 to 8 percent by 2012 may seem minimalist. Yet this would be a serious misreading of the treaty's practical and symbolic significance. Given that projected emissions would have been 30 per-

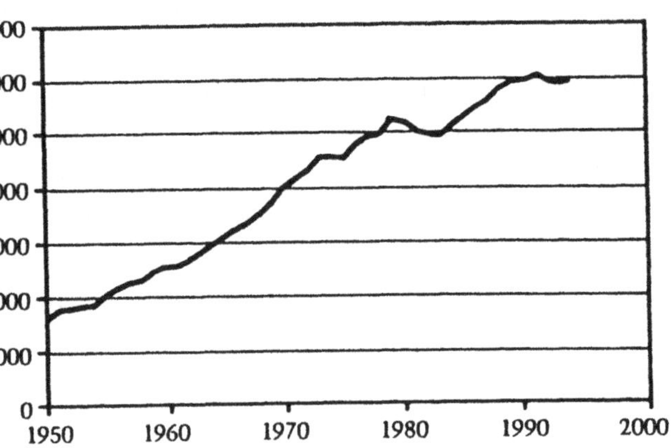

Source: Lester Brown, Nicholas Lenssen, Hal Kane, *Vital Signs 1995*. New York: Norton, 1995.

FIGURE 2. World Carbon Emissions from Fossil Fuel Burning, 1950–94 (in millions of tons)

cent higher, the protocol actually requires meaningful reductions from where they would have been (Bolin 1998). Moreover, the Kyoto Protocol should not be viewed as the last word, but rather as an important first step. From toxic waste trade to ozone depletion, global environmental regimes have been negotiated and amended on an incremental basis. Thus, Kyoto sets the course for future developments. Given the close correlation between wealth production and fossil fuel consumption, explanations of the climate change regime based upon traditional economic interests cannot account for the general willingness of industrialized countries to commit themselves to reducing greenhouse gas emissions. That willingness, even for the most reluctant countries like the United States, can only be explained on the basis of scientific authority.

The International Authority of Climate Change Science

Although the theory of the "greenhouse effect," caused by the radiation-trapping properties of certain gases, is one of the oldest and most widely accepted theories in the atmospheric sciences, global warming has only recently become an international policy problem (Elzinga 1997). As early as 1896, the Swedish scientist Svante Arrhenius calculated that a doubling of carbon dioxide would increase average global temperatures by 6°C, an estimate that was remarkably close to those of today's computer models (Rodhe et al. 1997). Until 1957, however, most scientists believed that the oceans would absorb virtually all anthropogenic CO_2. In that year, two scientists concluded that only half of the CO_2 produced by humans was being absorbed by the oceans. In an oft-repeated phrase, they declared that "mankind is conducting a great one-time geophysical experiment" (Revelle and Suess 1957:27). This dire warning, however, attracted neither policy attention nor research funding until the emergence of environmentalism in the 1970s (Hart and Victor 1993). Concern was amplified in the 1980s by the discovery that other trace gases, including methane, chlorofluorocarbons (CFCs), and nitrous oxides, would nearly double the warming trend expected from CO_2 alone (Kellogg 1987).

The level of political involvement by climate change scientists is unprecedented in global environmental politics, a fact that could arguably decrease the authority of their knowledge claims. While scientists were responsible for putting acid rain, ozone depletion, and climate change on the political agenda, only on the last issue have they spoken out in large numbers—even in the face of significant uncertainties. Beginning in the mid-1980s, scientific conferences generated a plethora of declarations in favor of serious, concrete efforts to reduce greenhouse gas emissions. Prior to the formation of the IPCC, scientific conferences in Villach and Bellagio during the 1980s called for a rapid reduction in the use of fossil fuels, for increasing energy efficiency by 50 percent, and for a cessation of deforestation, with the objective of limiting the rate of global warming to 0.1°C per decade (WMO 1985). At the Toronto Conference on the Changing Atmosphere, over three hundred scientists and policymakers called for reducing carbon dioxide emissions by 20 percent of 1988 levels by 2005. Although the declaration was considered quite sweeping, the 20 percent target, which scientists believed would fall far short of stabilizing the atmosphere, was a matter of political feasibility (WMO 1988). The U.S. EPA, for instance, estimated that stabilizing atmospheric concentration of CO_2 at 1988 levels would require reducing greenhouse gas emissions by 50 to 80 percent, putting them at 1950s levels (Flavin 1990:20).

Given the persistence of significant uncertainties, this intensity of political activism by scientists is somewhat surprising. The puzzle can be explained in terms of the *character* of the scientific uncertainties and the *precautionary values* of the scientists. First, for the most part, the uncertainties revolve around the *timing* and the *degree* of anticipated climate, not *whether* climate change will occur. The models differ somewhat in their predictions of future climate, and (until the mid-1990s) most climate experts declined to pinpoint the precise timing in order to avoid the embarrassment of having to explain the inevitable cold years. Nonetheless, there has been a broad consensus for over a decade that humanity is moving the climate into uncharted territory. Second, the values implicit in scientists' policy recommendations reflect an underlying precautionary approach—a belief that it is unwise to tamper with the global climate system in ways that might induce conditions with which the human species has no experience. One important set of uncertainties, "climate change surprises," could include disturbances of the gulf stream and possible triggering of an ice age in the Northern Hemisphere (Kerr 1998).

Within months of the Toronto conference, the IPCC was established in 1988 by the WMO and UNEP, with a twofold mandate reflecting its existence in two worlds: 1) to assess both available scientific information on climate change (Working Group [WG1]) and the environmental and socioeconomic impacts of climate change (WGII); and 2) to formulate "realistic response strategies" for managing climate change (WGIII). The IPCC assessment reports, peer-reviewed and prepared by international expert communities, also include user-friendly executive summaries for the policy community. In 1990, the First IPCC Assessment Report was accepted as the scientific basis for international negotiations. Shortly thereafter, the UN General Assembly established the International Negotiating Committee for a Framework Convention on Climate Change (FCCC).

The first IPCC assessment, which drew on the work of over three hundred scientists, only accepted as certain the greenhouse effect and that human activities were increasing atmospheric concentrations of greenhouse gases; that mean global temperatures had risen between 0.3°C and 0.6°C during the twentieth century; and that predicted global warming of 1.5°C to 5.0°C would occur sometime towards the middle of the next century. As for environmental effects, only sea level rise was predictable with any certainty, and even then the range was quite sizable: between 20 and 140 centimeters as a result of thermal expansion. The observed warming was consistent with the modeled predictions, but it also fell within the range of natural variability (IPCC 1990:2–5). Since the effects of global warming will be local and regional, but the models generate global averages, there is even greater uncertainty surrounding environmental and socioeconomic predictions. Paradoxically, it is simpler to predict what will happen to the planet, a closed system, than to make forecasts for specific regions. Similarly, scientists are more certain about what will happen over the long term than over a shorter one. While they can predict with confidence that, over the next several hundred years, continued use of fossil fuels will "dramatically alter the Earth's climate in ways that will impact nearly every living thing," predictions for the next fifty years are less certain (Kasting 1998:16). Thus, the complexity and uncertainties of climate change science make it extremely difficult for policy actors to ascertain costs and benefits, and also lend credence to those who would question its authority.

Nonetheless, the stated objective of the FCCC, which was signed at the 1992 Earth Summit in Rio and entered into force in 1994, is the "stabilization of greenhouse gas concentrations in the atmosphere at a level that would prevent dangerous anthropogenic interference with the climate system" (Article 2). More importantly, Principles 1 and 3 declare that the parties "should protect the climate system for the benefit of present and future generations of humankind, on the basis of equity and in accordance with their common but differentiated responsibilities and respective capabilities" and that they should "take precautionary measures to anticipate, prevent, or minimize the causes of climate change and mitigate its adverse effects" (Article 3). These commitments, which served as the basis for the ensuing negotiations towards a regulatory protocol, offer evidence for two notable normative innovations with respect to the interaction of scientific and political authority. First, science can serve as an important source of international authority—even in the face of significant uncertainties, even when scientists involve themselves in the policy realm, and even when the recommended policies entail action that might seem to undercut one of the traditional bases of state authority. Second, scientific authority, despite all these factors, can also serve as the basis for an evolving norm of intergenerational accountability.

The IPCC released its second assessment report late in 1995, concluding that "the balance of evidence, from changes in global mean surface air temperature and from changes in geographical, seasonal, and vertical patterns of atmospheric temperature, suggests a discernible human influence on global climate"

(IPCC 1996:5). Once climate change was scientifically documented as empirical reality rather than modeled prediction, the stage was set for negotiation of a legally binding regulatory agreement. The Kyoto Protocol, signed in December 1997, mandates reductions in overall greenhouse gas emissions by thirty-nine industrialized countries by 5.2 percent of 1990 levels by the year 2012. The targeted reductions are not the same for all, with most European countries bound by 8 percent targets, the United States by 7 percent, and Australia permitted to increase emissions by 8 percent. The Kyoto Protocol also authorizes tradeable permits, enabling countries to buy "credits" from other countries whose emissions levels are below the 1990 level. The treaty allows countries to count forests as carbon "sinks," so that their overall reductions in actual emissions could be somewhat lower than the mandated targets. Developing countries are not bound by any formal regulations, but do commit themselves to a "clean development mechanism."

The United States, accounting for about 25 percent of the world's greenhouse gas emissions, is a crucial player. Yet, as home to five of the seven major oil companies and the center of global automobile production, it has a powerful incentive to oppose international regulatory action. The Global Climate Coalition (GCC), the largest industry group involved in the climate change issue and closely tied to the fossil fuel industry, has been especially influential in the United States, where its member companies are among the largest contributors to congressional campaigns. In opposing a regulatory protocol, the fossil fuel industry has made tremendous efforts to contest the scientific authority of the IPCC. The tactics of industry groups, especially the GCC and the American Petroleum Institute, include sponsoring their own studies that dispute the IPCC findings and going directly to the mass media with their criticisms (Levy and Egan 1998).

Yet, as David Levy and Daniel Egan argue, industry's influence since Rio has been much greater in the United States than at the international level. In comparison to the governmental apparatus of states, international institutions are relatively more insulated from the structuralist pressures of capital. Ironically, "the very lack of democratic accountability within international institutions that worries some observers also serves to insulate [international institutions] from popular concerns about jobs and fuel prices" (1998:347). In other words, because the political authority of international institutions is not rooted in popular consent, they need not be so preoccupied with economic performance. Thus, industry groups like the GCC enjoy their greatest influence at the national level. Indeed, NGOs appear to have the upper hand in the international arena. Most noteworthy is the transnational Climate Action Network, which has distributed daily newsletters to the delegates to every Conference of the Parties since Rio. Unlike industry groups, NGOs have used the IPCC science as the basis for their positions. Nonetheless, industry groups may well be successful in preventing ratification of the Kyoto Protocol by the U.S. Senate, a development that could seriously hamper implementation elsewhere.

Given the 1988 "Toronto Target" of a 20 percent cut in greenhouse gas emissions, which itself was set more on the basis of political feasibility than rational prevention, the Kyoto Protocol represents only a small first step. Yet from the perspective of the interaction between political and scientific authority, it represents a significant development. On the basis of an international scientific consensus that human activities are poised to alter the earth's climate, states have acted upon that authority by committing themselves to reducing emissions which have traditionally been a by-product of economic growth. Whatever its tangible results in terms of the Earth's climate, the Kyoto Protocol provides evidence for a growing commitment of political leaders to the authority of climate science, even if that authority might encroach on a central dimension of their political authority—their ability to promote economic growth.

Conclusions

Before drawing any conclusions about the reconfiguration of political authority in the international system, we should consider alternative readings of this story. I have argued that a central feature of modernity is the notion that political authority rests upon consent of the governed, that elections are a key mechanism through which consent is granted or retracted, that election results are determined in large measure by economic performance criteria, and that fossil fuels historically have driven economic productivity. With an emerging scientific consensus that fossil fuel consumption must be decreased if the earth's climate system is to be stabilized, the authority of science presents a challenge to a key source of the state's political authority: its role as guarantor of wealth production.

One interpretation is that governments have accepted the authority of science to such an extent that they are willing to risk diminishing economic productivity against the wishes of their citizens. This would represent the strongest polarization between the authority of science and consent-based political authority. The facts, however, support only a more nuanced interpretation. Cross-national polling data indicate that citizens of both industrialized and developing countries generally view climate change as a serious problem (Dunlap 1998), suggesting that governments may be acting with the implicit consent of their citizens in agreeing to reduce fossil fuel consumption.

This suggests a second interpretation: that citizens do consent to government action to reduce the risk of climate change for future generations, even at the risk of decreasing their own wealth. In this case, the apparent tension between political and scientific authority would be resolved by popular acceptance of the latter. Given the widespread media coverage of global warming, especially prior to the 1992 Earth Summit in Rio (Mazur and Lee 1993), citizens (and not just governments) may have accepted the authority of climate science and consequently became willing to reduce their fossil fuel consumption. Yet the polling data also reveal a good deal of misinformation and confusion about the issue, as well as substantial ambivalence towards the prospect of making material sacrifices to address it. Moreover, the link between climate change and fossil fuel consumption in the public mind is not at all clear (Kempton 1997). This implies that the tension between scientific and political authority persists for two reasons. First, if citizens fail to understand even the basics of the issue, it cannot be said that they have granted consent on the basis of their acceptance of scientific authority. Second, and more importantly, governments at least run a real risk of antagonizing their publics when they agree to reduce greenhouse gas emissions. It is one thing for people to believe that climate change is "a serious problem"; it is quite another for them to be willing to incur economic sacrifices in order to address it. Thus, the tension persists. The authority of science poses a challenge to a crucial basis of the state's political authority: its role as guarantor of wealth production.

A third interpretation is that while the Kyoto Protocol commits industrialized countries to reduce their greenhouse gas emissions, either the levels of reductions are meaningless in terms of their impact on fossil fuel consumption or else states have no intention of making good on their commitments. In either case, the treaty's requirements could be interpreted as merely symbolic, representing no substantial reorientation of political authority on the basis of science. Yet neither argument is compelling. While the reductions mandated by the Kyoto Protocol, ranging from 5 to 8 percent for industrialized countries by 2012, do not appear to be substantial, they should be viewed in light of *projected* rather than existing emissions. In that light, the reductions represent roughly a 30 percent decrease in the expected emissions. Referring back to Figure 2, such a decrease would mean a negative slope to a curve climbing steadily since 1950, save for brief disruptions caused by the oil crises of the 1970s. Thus, the Kyoto-mandated reductions in greenhouse gas emissions are far from meaningless. The second argument is also questionable. While it is difficult to know governments' "intentions," this may be beside the point. The history of international environmental regime building indicates that once states have committed themselves to specific targets, they will face enormous pressure from environmental NGOs to live up to those commitments. Moreover, most environmental regimes have proceeded from relatively weak framework conventions, such as the FCCC, to increasingly stringent regulatory protocols, which are amended in light of new scientific information. If history is any guide, then governments, in signing the Kyoto Protocol, have started down a slippery slope towards greater reductions of greenhouse gas emissions. Thus, the argument that climate science poses no challenge to consent-based political authority because the agreed-upon reductions of greenhouse gas emissions are meaningless does not hold up to scrutiny.

A fourth plausible reading is that, in agreeing to the Kyoto mandate, governments have not necessarily accepted the authority of climate science, but rather have acted out of economic self-interest. The argument has been made that EU countries, which have taken the lead in pushing for sharp reductions of GHG emissions, have an interest in doing so because of their extreme dependence upon foreign energy sources. This claim is dubious. If EU action on climate change were driven purely by narrow economic interests, then we would expect EU countries to take a more activist stance when oil prices are high rather than at an all-time low as they have been in recent years. Moreover, given Europe's greater efficiency as a result of measures taken after the oil crises of the 1970s, further reductions in GHG emissions will be comparatively more demanding for the EU countries than for more energy-intensive economies. This does not mean that interests play no role in states' positions on the climate change issue. A strong regulatory protocol, for instance, might help France to expand its exports of nuclear technology. Both Germany and Britain are weaning themselves from their coal dependency, thereby reducing their GHG emissions anyway. Yet, the steep reductions (20 percent and beyond) promoted by these countries will likely require some economic sacrifice. Given the close correlation between wealth production and fossil fuel consumption, explanations based upon traditional economic interests cannot account for the general willingness of industrialized countries to commit themselves to reducing GHG emissions. That willingness can only be explained on the basis of scientific authority.

A fifth interpretation, and one that offers the greatest challenge to the argument presented in this paper, is that governments have agreed to reduce greenhouse gas emissions because they believe that wealth production can be decoupled from the use of fossil fuels. If this belief is true, then perhaps we are seeing a significant shift in the material foundations of economic productivity, but not any challenge to consent-based political authority. The fact that global emissions of carbon dioxide fell in 1998—for the first time during a year in which economic growth was strong—offers some support for this belief (Kirby 1999). But whether governments actually subscribe to such a belief is dubious. The persistence of many tax and spending policies that encourage fossil fuel consumption calls this interpretation into question. More to the point, there is little historical support for the belief that economic prosperity can be decoupled from fossil fuel emissions, at least in the near term. While it is true that the economies of most OECD countries have moved towards the services sector in the past two decades, greenhouse gas emissions in all of those countries have continued to rise. This can be explained by various developments, most importantly the phenomenal growth of emissions in the transportation sector, especially energy-intensive air travel. Moreover, there is no evidence that citizens in the "postindustrial" wealthy countries are consuming fewer manufactured goods. Rather, industrial production is being shifted to the developing world, so that the affluent lifestyles of the so-called "industrial" countries are increasingly accompanied by emissions in the developing countries. While the link between greenhouse gas emissions and jobs may be weakening, the link between emissions and prosperity would be much harder to break. Thus, if they do subscribe to a belief that prosperity can be decoupled from greenhouse gas emissions, then governments' willingness to reduce their emissions represents a kind of leap of faith. The only apparent reason for taking that leap is a strong scientific consensus that burning fossil fuels will cause global climate change sometime in the next century, bringing us back to the central argument of this paper.

Finally, we should be clear about the fact that the state does not *lose* legitimacy if it accepts the authority of science. Indeed, the rational legal state has a long history of using scientific evidence to solve problems. In a more fundamental vein, the epistemological basis of leadership in Western political thought since Plato has linked political authority to knowledge about what is good for society (Jones 1993:122). Rather, the *basis* of its authority shifts from liberal notions of consent to a different sort of authority, one based upon scientific expertise. The fact that such a shift can be perceived with respect to international responses to climate change does not mean that a wholesale reconfiguration of political authority is under way.

Perhaps more important in the long run will be the normative commitments to intergenerational responsibility entailed in the climate change regime. Prevailing accounts of political authority rooted in liberal notions of consent do not take into account the "consent" of future generations, but only the sanction of contemporary self-interested citizens who evaluate their government's performance in terms of enhancing security and prosperity. Yet efforts to address climate change, the real impact of which will not be felt until well into the next century, hinge upon the notion of intergenerational responsibility. Indeed, the normative implications of the precautionary principle suggest that states are moving in this direction, albeit haltingly.

References

ANDERSON, PERRY. (1974) *Lineages of the Absolutist State*. London: Verso Press.

ARENDT, HANNAH. (1968) "What is Authority?" In *Between Past and Future*. New York: Viking Press.

ARENDT, HANNAH. (1970). *On Violence*. New York: Harcourt Brace Jovanovich.

BODANSKY, DANIEL. (1991) The United Nations Framework Convention on Climate Change: A Commentary. *Yale Journal of International Law* **18** (Summer):52–79.

BOLIN, BERT. (1998) The Kyoto Negotiations on Climate Change: A Science Perspective? *Science* **279**(16) January:328–332.

BULL, HEDLEY, AND A. WATSON, EDS. (1982) *The Expansion of International Society*. Oxford: Clarendon Press.

COLE, STEPHEN. (1992) *Making Science: Between Nature and Society*. Cambridge, MA: Harvard University Press.

CONCA, KEN. (1994) Rethinking the Ecology-Sovereignty Debate. *Millennium* **23**:701–711.

CONNOLLY, WILLIAM. (1993) Democracy and Territoriality. In *Rhetorical Republic: Governing Representations in American Politics*, edited by F. M. Dolan and T. L. Dunn. Amherst: University of Massachusetts Press.

CUTLER, A. CLAIRE. (1999) Locating "Authority" in the Global Political Economy. *International Studies Quarterly* **41**(1) March:59–81.

DUNLAP, RILEY E. (1998) Lay Perceptions of Global Risk: Public Views of Global Warming in Cross-National Context. *International Sociology* **13**:473–498.

DWORKIN, R. M. (1990) "Obligations of Community." In *Authority,* edited by Joseph Raz, pp. 218–239. New York: New York University Press.

ELZINGA, AANT. (1997) From Arrhenius to Megascience: Interplay Between Science and Policymaking. *Ambio* **26**:72–80.

EZRAHI, YARON. (1990) *The Descent of Icarus: Science and the Transformation of Contemporary Democracy*. Cambridge, MA: Harvard University Press.

FINNEMORE, MARTHA. (1993) International Organizations As Teachers of Norms: The United Nations Educational, Scientific, and Cultural Organization and Science Policy. *International Organization* **47**(4) Autumn:565–597.

FLAVIN, CHRISTOPHER. (1990) Slowing Global Warming. In *State of the World 1990*, edited by Lester Brown, pp. 17–38. New York: Norton.

FRANCK, THOMAS M. (1990) *The Power of Legitimacy Among Nations*. Oxford: Oxford University Press.

FRANCK, THOMAS M. (1992) The Emerging Right to Democratic Governance. *American Journal of International Law* **86**(1) January:46–91.

FRIEDMAN, R. B. (1990) On the Concept of Authority in Political Philosophy. In *Authority,* edited by Joseph Raz, pp. 56–91. New York: New York University Press.

GREEN, L. (1990) "Commitment and Community." In *Authority*, edited by Joseph Raz, pp. 240–267. New York: New York University Press.

GREENWALT, K. (1990) Promissory Obligation: The Theme of Social Contract. In *Authority*, edited by Joseph Raz, pp. 268–299. New York: New York University Press.

GRUBB, MICHAEL J., ET AL. (1991) *Energy Policies and the Greenhouse Effect, Volume II: Country Studies and Technical Options*. Aldershot: Royal Institute of International Affairs.

HART, DAVID M., AND DAVID G. VICTOR. (1993) Scientific Elites and the Making of U.S. Policy for Climate Change Research, 1957–1974. *Social Studies of Science* **23**:643–680.

HEINEMAN, ROBERT. (1994) *Authority and the Liberal Tradition: From Hobbes to Rorty*. New Bruswick: Transaction Publishers.

HELD, DAVID. (1995) *Democracy and the Global Order: From the Modern State to Cosmopolitan Governance*. Stanford: Stanford University Press.

HOBBES, THOMAS. (1976 [1651]) *Leviathan*. New York: Dutton.

HUNTINGTON, SAMUEL. (1991) *The Third Wave: Democratization in the Late Twentieth Century*. Norman: University of Oklahoma Press.

INTERNATIONAL LAW DATABASE. (*http://www.tufts.edu/fletcher/multi/texts/historical/westphalia.txt*).

IPCC (INTERGOVERNMENTAL PANEL ON CLIMATE CHANGE). (1990) *IPCC First Assessment Report*. Geneva: World Meteorological Organization and United Nations Environment Programme.

IPCC (INTERGOVERNMENTAL PANEL ON CLIMATE CHANGE). (1996) *IPCC Second Assessment Report*. Geneva: World Meteorological Organization and United Nations Environment Programme.

JACKSON, ROBERT H. (1990) *Quasi-States: Sovereignty, International Relations, and the Third World*. Cambridge: Cambridge University Press.

JACOBY, JEFF. (1998) Scientists Don't Agree on Global Warming. *Boston Globe*, 5 November:A27.

JAMES, ALAN. (1986) *Sovereign Statehood: The Basis of International Society*. London: Allen and Unwin.

JONES, KATHLEEN B. (1993) *Compassionate Authority: Democracy and the Representation of Women*. London: Routledge.

KASTING, JAMES F. (1998) The Carbon Cycle, Climate, and the Long-Term Effects of Fossil Fuel Burning. *Consequences* **4**(10):15–27.

KATZENSTEIN, PETER J., ED. (1996) *Culture of National Security: Norms and Identity in World Politics*. New York: Columbia University Press.

KECK, MARGARET, AND KATHRYN SIKKINK. (1998) *Activists Beyond Borders: Advocacy Networks in International Politics*. Ithaca: Cornell University Press.

KELLER, EVELYN FOX. (1985) *Reflections on Gender and Science*. New Haven: Yale University Press.

KELLOGG, WILLIAM W. (1987) Mankind's Impact on Climate: The Evolution of Awareness. *Climatic Change* **10**:110–21.

KEMPTON, WILLETT. (1997) How the Public Views Climate Change. *Environment* **39**(9) November: 12–22.

KERR, RICHARD. (1998) Warming's Unpeasant Surprise: Shivering in the Greenhouse? *Science* **281** July 10:156–58.

KIRBY, ALEX. (1999) "World Carbon Pollution Falls." BBC News, Wednesday, July 28 (http://news.bbc.co.uk/low/english/sci/tech/newsid_405000/405973.stm)

KOPLOW, D. N. (1993) *Federal Energy Subsidies: Energy, Environmental, and Fiscal Impacts*. Washington, D.C.: Alliance to Save Energy.

KUEHLS, THOM. (1998) Between Sovereignty and Environment: An Exploration of the Discourse of Government. In *The Greening of Sovereignty in World Politics*, edited by Karen T. Litfin. Cambridge, MA: The MIT Press.

KUHN, THOMAS. (1962) *The Structure of Scientific Revolutions*. Chicago: University of Chicago Press.

LEVY, DAVID L., AND DANIEL EGAN. (1998) Capital Contests: National and Transnational Channels of Corporate Influence on the Climate Change Negotiations. *Politics and Society* **26**(3) September:337–361.

LINCOLN, B. (1991) *Authority: Construction and Corrosion*. Chicago: University of Chicago Press.

LINKLATER, ANDREW. (1982) *Men and Citizens in the Theory of International Relations*. London: Macmillan Press.

LIPSCHUTZ, RONNIE D., WITH JUDITH MAYER. (1996) *Global Civil Society and Global Environmental Governance: The Politics of Nature from Place to Planet*. Albany: State University of New York Press.

LITFIN, KAREN T. (1994) *Ozone Discourses: Science and Politics in Global Environmental Cooperation*. New York: Columbia University Press.

LITFIN, KAREN T. (1997) Sovereignty in World Ecopolitics. *Mershon International Studies Review* **41**:167–204.

LOCKE, JOHN. (1965) *Two Treatises of Government*. New York: New American Library.

MACPHERSON, C. B. (1962) *The Political Theory of Possessive Individualism: Hobbes to Locke*. Oxford: Clarendon Press.

MAZUR, A., AND J. LEE. (1993) Sounding the Global Alarm: Environmental Issues in the U.S. National News. *Social Studies of Science* **23**:681–720.

MCCORMICK, JOHN. (1989) *Reclaiming Paradise: The Global Environmental Movement*. Bloomington: Indiana University Press.

MERCHANT, CAROLYN. (1990) The Death of Nature: *Women, Ecology and the Scientific Revolution*. San Fransisco: Harper Collins.

MOLTKE, KONRAD. (1997)

NATIONAL ACADEMY OF SCIENCES. (1991) *Policy Implications of Greenhouse Warming*. Washington, D.C.: National Academy Press.

NORDHAUS, WILLIAM D. (1990a) Greenhouse Economics: Count Before You Leap. *The Economist*, July 7:19–22.

NORDHAUS, WILLIAM D. (1990b) "Global Warming: Slowing the Greenhouse Express." In *Setting National Priorities*, edited by H. Aaron. Washington, D.C.: Brookings Instititution.

PATEMAN, CAROLE. (1980) Women and Consent. *Political Theory* **8**:149–168.

PATEMAN, CAROLE. (1988) *The Sexual Contract*. Stanford: Stanford University Press.

PETERSON, M. J. (1992) Transnational Activity, International Society, and World Politics. *Millennium* **21**:371–388.

POLANYI, KARL. (1944) *The Great Transformation*. New York: Farrar and Rinehart.

PUTNAM, R. D. (1988) Diplomacy and Domestic Politics: The Logic of Two-Level Games. *International Organization*. **42**(3):427–460.

RAZ, JOSEPH. (1990) Introduction. In *Authority*, edited by Joseph Raz, pp. 1–19. New York: New York University Press.

REVELLE, R. AND H. E. SUESS. (1957) Carbon Dioxide Exchange between Atmosphere and Ocean and the Question of an Increase of Atmospheric CO_2 during the Past Decades. *Tellus* **9**:18–27.

RODHE, H. R. CHARLSON AND E. CRAWFORD. (1997) Svante Arrhenius and the Greenhouse Effect. *Ambio* **26**(1):2–5.

ROSA, EUGENE A., AND THOMAS DIETZ. (1998) Climate Change and Society: Speculation, Construction, and Scientific Investigation. *International Sociology* **13**.

ROSENAU, JAMES. (1990) *Turbulence in World Politics: A Theory of Change and Continuity*. Princeton: Princeton University Press.

RUGGIE, JOHN G. (1993) Territoriality and Beyond: Problematizing Modernity in International Relations. *International Organization* **47**:144–173.

SCHNEIDER, STEPHEN H. (1989) The Greenhouse Effect: Science and Policy. *Science* **243** (February 10):771–781.

SHIN, DOH CHULL. (1994) On the Third Wave of Democratization: A Synthesis and Evaluation of Recent Theory and Research. *World Politics* **47**(1) October:135–170.

SPRUYT, HENDRIK. (1994) *The Sovereign State and Its Competitors: An Analysis of Systems Change*. Princeton: Princeton University Press.

STOKKE, OLAV SCHRAM. (1997) Regimes as Governance Systems. In *Global Governance: Drawing Insights from the Environmental Experience*, edited by Oran Young, pp. 27–63. Cambridge, MA: MIT Press.

STRANGE, SUSAN. (1996) The Retreat of the State: The Diffusion of Power in the World Economy. New York: Cambridge University Press.

THOMSON, JANICE E. (1995) State Sovereignty in International Relations: Bridging the Gap between Theory and Empirical Research. *International Studies Quarterly* **39**:213–233.

TUFTE, EDWARD. (1974) *Data Analysis for Politics and Policy*. Englewood Cliffs, NJ: Prentice-Hall.

WAPNER, PAUL. (1996) *Environmental Activism and World Civic Politics*. Albany: State University of New York Press.

WEBER, MAX. (1946) Politics as a Vocation. In *From Max Weber: Essays in Sociology*, edited by H. H. Gerth and C. W. Mills, pp. 77–128. New York: Oxford University Press.

WEBER, MAX. (1947) *The Theory of Social and Economic Organization*, translated by A. M. Henderson and Talcott Parsons. New York: Oxford University Press.

WEISS, EDITH BROWN. (1989) *In Fairness to Future Generations: International Law, Common Patrimony, and Intergenerational Equity*. Tokyo: United Nations University.

WENDT, ALEXANDER. (1992) Anarchy Is What States Make of It: The Social Construction of Power Politics. *International Organization* **46**:391–425.

WIGHT, MARTIN. (1977) *Systems of States*. Leicester: Leicester University Press.

WMO. (1985) Report of the International Conference on the Assessment of the Role of Carbon Dioxide and of Other Greenhouse Gases in Climate Variations and Associated Impacts? Geneva: WMO-661.

WMO. (1988) The Changing Atmosphere: Implications for Global Security. Conference held in Toronto, June 27–30.

WOLFF, R. P. (1990) The Conflict between Authority and Autonomy. In *Authority*, edited by Joseph Raz, pp. 20–31. New York: New York University Press.

ZIMAN, JOHN. (1968) *Public Knowledge: An Essay Concerning the Social Dimension of Science*. Cambridge: Cambridge University Press.

Sovereignty Bargains in Regional Integration

Walter Mattli

Department of Political Science, Columbia University

Introduction

The Westphalian state is commonly defined as a system of political authority based on territory and autonomy. Territoriality implies that political authority is exercised over a defined geographic space, and autonomy means that no external actor enjoys authority within the borders of the state (Krasner 1990:115–116). As recently noted by Stephen Krasner (1990), breaches of the Westphalian model—through conventions, contracting, coercion, or imposition—have been an enduring characteristic of the international environment.[1]

An increasingly prominent type of international contractual arrangement that frequently violates the Westphalian model, even though it remains consistent with a legal understanding of sovereignty, is the creation of regional economic and political unions. The violation occurs when these unions establish authority structures that supersede territorial boundaries and transgress autonomy by conferring control to supranational actors. A recent example is the European Union (EU). It possesses the most far-reaching supranational institutions of any recent regional integration scheme. The Commission, for example, is both the executive and the main administrative body of the EU. It has the 'right of initiative,' that is, the right to draft EU legislation. It also discharges an important monitoring task, seeing that member states do not act in ways that run counter to EU law. It can take a member state to task by demanding termination of an infringement, or by taking the matter to the European Court of Justice (ECJ) for a final decision. The Court, too, plays a key monitoring and enforcing role. Most notably, it has improved the effectiveness of the EU enforce-

[1] See also Krasner (1993).

Published by Blackwell Publishers, 350 Main Street, Malden, MA 02148, USA, and 108 Cowley Road, Oxford OX4 1JF, UK.

ment mechanism through two judge-made doctrines: supremacy and direct effect. The supremacy doctrine holds that EU law has primacy over national legislation, and the direct effect doctrine provides that EU law is directly applicable to the citizens of the member states without prior intervention by their governments (Burley and Mattli 1993). In a significant step to further the Court's effectiveness, the EU empowered the ECJ to impose heavy penalties upon member states that fail to comply with Court rulings.

Driving regional integration is the assumption or belief that the benefit of integration, namely increased national prosperity, is worth the cost in terms of diminished national policymaking autonomy and power. British Prime Minister James Callaghan echoed this theme in the late-1970s while debating whether the United Kingdom should become a member of the European Monetary System (EMS): "When we joined NATO we removed some powers from ourselves but it was the general view of the House, continued for a quarter of a century, that in removing these powers we increased our security. That is surely the test that one needs to apply to this sort of proposal. If it means less power in order to increase prosperity, the House would have to take a decision whether it wished to remain poor and independent or whether it was willing to sacrifice some powers and be more prosperous" (Ludlow 1982:144).

Prosperity, however, is not the only benefit of regional integration. Participation in a regional union may increase the influence that any one member has over others, thereby helping it to attain certain policy objectives more directly. For example, when British Eurosceptics demanded that Britain leave the EU in protest over the refusal of the French government to lift its ban on imports of British beef, the current British Prime Minister Tony Blair reminded them that it is only thanks to UK membership that he is able to sue France, adding: "Where we have difficulties with Europe we will sort them out . . . [and] I will not give up [the UK]'s influence in Europe" (Preston 1999:5).

This example highlights the relevance of the concept of 'sovereignty bargains'—a term recently coined by Karen Litfin—to the study of regional integration (Litfin 1997:167–204). States engage in sovereignty bargains in which they voluntarily accept some limitations in exchange for certain benefits. "It is more accurate to say that states engage in sovereignty bargains . . . than [to say that they] ced[e] some monolithic principle of sovereignty" (Litfin 1997:169). In this view, sovereignty becomes an aggregated concept that varies according to historical and social circumstances. Its constituting elements are autonomy, control, and legitimacy. Autonomy refers to independence in policymaking and action; control is the ability to produce an effect; and legitimacy refers to the recognized right to make rules. In a sovereignty bargain, control may be enhanced by sacrificing autonomy; or increased control may undercut a state's legitimacy. For example, developing countries may find their autonomy and certain elements of control and internal legitimacy diminished by their participation in international environmental regimes, whereas capabilities and external legitimacy may be promoted. Conversely, industrialized countries may find their autonomy diminished by the expectation that they should pay for conservation in developing countries, even as their external legitimacy may be increased by such trends (169). In sum, Litfin's argument is that sovereignty has been reconfigured over time and that this process, induced by pressure from both below and above the state, can only be grasped by disaggregating the key elements that constitute the term. While sovereignty bargains reconfigure sovereignty, they do not necessarily diminish it; reduced autonomy, for example, may be the price to pay for enhanced control or legitimacy.

This study argues that a multidimensional conceptualization of sovereignty, similar to the one proposed by Litfin, is a fruitful way of gaining an analytical understanding of the trade-offs that outsider countries face when debating whether or not to join an economic union. Litfin correctly notes that states enter sovereignty bargains that impose limitations in exchange for certain benefits. The following analysis pays considerable attention to the costs and benefits of membership in an economic union. The study, however, also extends Litfin's work by carefully specifying the background conditions of sovereignty bargains, thus introducing a temporal or dynamic element into the analysis. That is, it seeks to specify the factors that affect states' assessment of the costs and benefits of membership.

Membership in a union may have advantages but it often exacts a heavy toll in terms of foregone policymaking autonomy, especially if the union is economically successful. For example, membership in the European Union requires that an applicant be willing and able to accept the so-called *acquis communautaire*, a body of rules that comprises not only union law as enshrined in the Treaty of Rome but also a very extensive body of secondary law as defined in the European Union's directives and regulations. Membership in the North American Free Trade group is similarly costly. A Latin American applicant must accept what John Williamson dubs the "Washington Consensus," which includes reducing fiscal deficits, shifting expenditure priorities, tax reform, interest rate reform, exchange rate adjustment, liberalization of rules governing foreign direct investment, privatization, deregulation, and protection of property rights (Williamson 1990:7). Or consider a nineteenth-century example: Prussia required prospective members of the Zollverein, the German customs union, to adopt Prussian customs law, tariffs, and auditing procedures. In some cases, Prussia even demanded that a newcomer agree to restrict its participation in future changes of the common legislation as well as in negotiations of commercial treaties between the Zollverein and neighboring states.

Despite this heavy price, membership may be worth the candle, especially in times of economic decline. The analysis assumes that leaders value both policymaking autonomy and material resources (tax revenues, etc.). It also assumes that politicians' ability to hold on to political power depends on their relative success in managing the economy. Leaders who fail to maintain relatively high levels of economic growth will be ousted.[2]

These postulates imply that leaders in outsider countries that prosper economically may have little incentive to join a union since the price of integration is substantial while the expected marginal benefits from integration in terms of improved reelection chances (or more broadly, the leaders' chances of staying in office) is minimal during a period of relatively rapid national economic growth. In hard times, leaders may be more willing to embrace pro-integration agendas. The reason is that the expected marginal value from integration is likely to increase as the economy declines. And as this value grows larger than the price of integration, rational outsiders will seek to become union insiders (Mattli 1999). Frequently, the economic difficulties in outsiders' economies is attributable, in part, to the negative economic effects of regional integration among neighboring states. These effects can take the form of trade and investment diversions; that is, outsiders may face temporary or lasting discriminatory trade policies, and rapid economic growth within a union as well as the large size of its single market may attract a larger share of international capital at the expense of outsiders. Some new investment may be triggered by the need to get around the union's external tariff. Furthermore, improved competitiveness of the industries in a union could lead to increased production and lower prices, thus putting producers outside the union at a competitive disadvantage and resulting in a reduction of external trade.

Evidence of the logic of the autonomy-prosperity trade-off that determines outsiders' decisions to join unions is presented from two cases: the enlargement of the EU and the Zollverein. In sum, the analysis finds that eighteen out of twenty applications for EU membership by eleven West European states were submitted in times of sustained economic difficulties. Similarly, the results from the Zollverein show that the rulers of the many German kingdoms, electorates, and duchies clung to their sovereign rights and obstructed proposals for economic unification until economic crisis and empty treasuries forced them to seek membership in the Zollverein. The general pattern is that these outsiders sought no integration when there was no performance gap with the union, and sustained performance gaps always eventually triggered moves toward integra-

[2] For evidence on the link between economic performance and reelection chances, see Erikson (1989, 1990), Norpoth et al. (1991), and Eulau and Lewis-Beck (1985).

tion. Countries that failed to experience such a gap saw no reason to pay the price of integration and thus opted to stay out.

Relative prosperity, however, is not the only benefit of integration. Co-decision and participation in collective problem solving will offer former outsiders a voice in (and thus some control over) the affairs of the union. For example, the members of the Zollverein sent representatives to the General Congress. This political platform provided them with a formal channel to express their policy preferences and to participate in the management of the union. The Congress acted as legislative body, settled accounts, and solved problems arising from the common administration of the Zollverein. Important decisions were always taken by consent. Similarly, the UK came to realize in the early 1960s that membership in the EU would not only help her restore economic health but also give her an effective way to influence the course of European integration. Small countries may also gain control by joining a union. For example, when the candidate members from Central and Eastern Europe join the EU, they will increase the collective political weight of the group of poor member states, which includes Greece, Ireland, Portugal, and Spain.

In conclusion, it is worth noting that sovereignty bargains are many; or as Litfin put it: "[S]overeignty bargains are structured differently for different states" (1997:196). Switzerland, whose powerful multinational corporations operate all over Europe and beyond and derive up to 95 percent of their revenues from international business, may be less worried about market access to the EU than say Romania, a predominantly agricultural state. Further, as one of the wealthiest countries, Switzerland would be a net contributor to the budget if it became a EU member state—a consideration that, in isolation, militates against membership. Romania, however, sees one of the biggest attractions of membership in the generous transfer payments that it would be entitled to as one of the poorest countries in the EU. Finally, Switzerland possesses the technical expertise to adjust its laws unilaterally to EU norms to avoid regulatory discrepancies that may adversely affect its economy. Romania, in contrast, has neither the infrastructure nor the expertise to keep up with regulatory developments in the Union, but as a candidate country it would receive extensive financial and technical support to establish a modern administrative and judicial apparatus capable of implementing and enforcing Union rules. The more general point is that very poor outsiders have a strong preference to join successful unions because membership is likely not only to boost economic growth but also to help bridge the glaring income gap between them and insiders. Rich outsiders, however, will be more reluctant to join since the costs will weigh more heavily. But in times of relative economic decline, even wealthy states may find membership in a union economically advantageous.

Before proceeding, I would like to preempt some possible criticism. The analysis of sovereignty bargains proposed in this study gives pride of place to economic variables. Some readers may find such a focus too narrow and the framework too parsimonious. I do not wish to imply that other variables, such as security or domestic politics, are irrelevant or that economic variables are all that matter. Nevertheless, a few broad questions about the external dimension of integration are formed within a context of unchanging military alliance patterns or domestic political structures. In such a context, economic variables may take us a long way towards explaining puzzling aspects of integration. Second, the study looks at sovereignty bargains primarily from the perspective of the applicant country. It assumes that the union is interested in enlargement. At times, however, a union may have no interest in accepting new members. If an outsider is not a desirable candidate in the sense of being able to make a net positive contribution to the union (e.g., through net payments into the common budget, or by offering obvious commercial advantages), the union is unlikely to accept it, unless exclusion of such a candidate is costlier to the union than accepting it.[3]

The study is organized as follows: Section 2 examines sovereignty bargains in the context of the German Zollverein, highlighting the context of the bargains and discussing the price and benefits of membership. Section 3 looks at sovereignty bargains that resulted in the first few rounds of EU enlargements, focusing primarily on the trade-off between autonomy and prosperity and the basic logic of the enlargement process from the point of view of the applicant. Section 4 spells out the elements of the sovereignty bargain for very poor countries. It analyzes the costs and benefits of potential EU membership for Central and East European countries. Conclusions are drawn in Section 5.

Sovereignty Bargains and the German Zollverein

In the early years of the nineteenth century, Germany was fragmented into over three hundred independent kingdoms, electorates, duchies, imperial cities, ecclesiastical territories, and estates of imperial kings (Henderson 1958:1). These territories had enjoyed increasing independence ever since the close of the Middle Ages, but were able to claim full sovereignty only with the abolition of the Holy Roman Empire in 1806 (Price 1949:12–19). After the defeat of Napoleon in 1815, Germany's political entities were consolidated into thirty-eight states,

---

[3] A union may have an interest in accepting "undesirable" candidates when negative externalities originating in outsider countries threaten to disrupt the union's prosperity, stability, and security. See Mattli (1999:94–99).

which grouped themselves into the German Confederation (*Deutscher Bund*).[4] This union of sovereign states (*Staatenbund* as opposed to *Bundesstaat*), where unanimity was required for joint action, proved utterly inadequate to provide for either economic or political unity. Political jealousies and the desire for autonomy by each state blocked any attempt at economic unification. In a period where income taxes were nonexistent, and customs and excise duties were the main sources of state revenues, the submission to a common customs system with an independent customs administration would have amounted to giving away a vital part of sovereignty (Price 1949:97). Not surprisingly, the many conferences of the postwar period that were convened to discuss the rationalization of the German economy came to nought. Price notes: "It is . . . almost unbelievable that negotiations were kept up for so many years, and it is easily understood why they failed in their purpose. . . . [E]verybody was thinking first of his own state and hardly anybody ever considered the interests of the union they were going to establish, took broad views, or pursued a farsighted policy. . . . [A]ll of them refused to give up an iota of their own sovereignty" (90). Benaerts likewise observes that the formation of an integrated German market was not the spontaneous national movement that German legend ascribed to it (Benaerts 1904:63). He points out that, on the contrary, the rulers of the many kingdoms, electorates, and duchies exhibited the most narrow-minded spirit of *Kleinstaaterei*, clinging to their sovereign rights and obstructing proposals for economic unification till empty treasuries forced them to seek membership in the Zollverein (Benaerts:63–72; Roussakis:16).

The first step towards an improvement of Germany's antiquated economic structure was taken by Prussia when it announced a customs reform in 1818 that abolished internal duties, established one single customs line along the boundaries of the monarchy, and replaced the chaotic system of over sixty different rates of customs and excises by a standardized tariff (Marriott and Robertson 1915:290). In addition, transit dues were introduced in the eastern and western parts of Prussia, which lay on important European trade routes.[5] This new customs law put Prussian state finances back on a sound basis, aided

---

[4] See Oncken and Saemisch (1934, volumes 1–3). See especially volume 1, section 2, entitled "Die Verhandlungen am Bundestag, die Wienner Konferenzen und die süddeutschen Einigungsbestrebungen," pp. 297–548. For a carefully detailed study of the Vienna Final Conferences, see Aegidi (1865).

[5] Prussia's eastern possessions stretched from the Memel at the mouth of the Vistula to Muhlhausen in the south of the Harz mountains. They comprised East Prussia, Posen, Pomerania, Brandenburg, Saxony, and Silesia. The western possessions included Westphalia and the Rhineland Province (from 1824). Prussia was divided by Hesse-Cassel, Brunswick, and the southern portion of Hannover.

Prussian industry and commerce, and thus consolidated Prussian monarchy (Roussakis and List 1968:46–60; Hahn 1984:20–27).[6]

The Cost of Exclusion and the Price of Membership

The construction of a single Prussian market, however, had negative effects on surrounding territories. Prussia's external tariff contributed to the economic weakening of neighboring territories by raising the prices on imported manufactured goods on which they heavily depended and by limiting the access of their exports to the large Prussian market. Thus isolated and destitute, these small countries faced the unenviable choice of remaining poor and autonomous or trading some of their sovereignty for market access and prosperity.

Hesse-Darmstadt was the first state to wake up to the inevitable. Its linen industry and viticulture were badly injured by the loss of Prussian markets. Cheap foreign manufactured articles grew scarce (Henderson 1958:50). The introduction in 1824 of a boundary tariff system failed to stem the economic decline. Owing to the length of the frontier, the cost of maintaining the new customs line absorbed most of the collected revenues. Smuggling began to flourish and seriously compete with legitimate trade (Price 1949:203). Hesse-Darmstadt approached Prussia in 1825 for an economic agreement. Three years later, a treaty was signed establishing a joint Customs Union.[7] This greatly benefitted Hesse-Darmstadt's state finances through increased customs revenues and provided a much-needed boost to its economy. In return, Hesse-Darmstadt agreed to pay the price of membership in terms of foregone autonomy; this meant adoption of Prussian customs law, tariffs, and auditing procedures. It was allowed to administer the collection of customs duties in its own territory but only according to Prussian practices. Inspections were designed to assure uniformity. Secret treaty articles further limited Hesse-Darmstadt's sovereign rights: Its participation in future changes of the common legislation was restricted, and the Prussian customs inspectors at Darmstadt were given wider powers than those laid down in the principal treaty (Oncken and Saemisch 1934, volume 2:207–211). In addition, Prussia undertook all important negotiations with foreign countries on behalf of the union, and it distributed the customs revenues.

---

[6] A good measure of the relative efficiency of the new law is reflected by the fact that it reduced administrative costs in Prussia to only 14 to 15 percent of total receipts (see Price 1949:121). This contrasts with rates well over 50 percent for most other states. See also Von Waltershausen 1923:1–69.

[7] The best discussion of the causes and consequences of the adhesion of Hesse-Darmstadt and the remaining Middle German states to the Prussian Zollverein is Hans-Werner Hahn (1982:145–246). See also Schmitt (1926) and Eckert (1902).

The creation of the Prussia–Hesse-Darmstadt union was received with great apprehension in neighboring states. The British envoy Milbanke wrote to the Earl of Dudley from Frankfurt-am-Main on March 14, 1828: "The news of this negotiation [between Prussia and Hesse-Darmstadt] has created . . . no small alarm among the merchants and others connected with the trade in this part of Germany who will undoubtedly suffer considerably by it, as the Prussian custom house establishment is conducted with the utmost severity and the adoption of that system in the dutchy of Hesse-Darmstadt will have the effect of raising the duties upon a great number of articles of commerce" (Henderson 1958:53). Unsurprisingly, the sequence of events by which most other German states acceded to the Prussian Customs Union followed the pattern of the Hesse-Darmstadt case: first, loss of easy access to the large market, then economic deterioration (at times combined with social unrest) and, finally, resignation to the inevitable, that is, economic merger with Prussia. The terms of membership were essentially the same as those that Hesse-Darmstadt had accepted. In some cases, however, unwillingness to pay the price of membership led affected outsiders to search for substitute export markets or to organize rival commercial unions (the second integrative response). Only after these efforts had failed did these outsiders approach Prussia. Three such temporary unions were established: a customs union between Bavaria and Württemberg, the Middle German Commercial Union, and the Tax Union (*Steuerverein*).

The Bavaria-Württemberg customs union came into force in July of 1828 in response to the Prussian treaty with Hesse-Darmstadt. Bavaria and Württemberg were, however, too small and their economies too much alike to form a powerful and efficient union. The customs revenues per head of population were only 9.5 silver groschen; Prussia collected 24 silver groschen. Administrative costs absorbed 44 percent of receipts which compared poorly to Prussia's 14 percent (Benaerts 1904:46).

The Middle German Commercial Union (*Mitteldeutscher Handelsverein*) was set up in September of 1828, only a few months after the Bavaria-Württemberg union. It comprised Hannover, Saxony, Hesse-Cassel, Nassau, Brunswick, Oldenburg, Frankfurt-am-Main, Bremen, the Saxon duchies, the Reuss principalities, Hesse-Homburg, Schwarzburg-Rudolfstadt, and the Upper Lordship (*Oberherrschaft*) of Schwarzburg-Sonderhausen. The oppositional or anti-Prussian character of this union was unmistakable. The union prohibited its members from concluding individual customs or trade agreements with nonmembers and sought to keep open the North–South main trade routes from Hamburg and Bremen to Frankfurt-am-Main and Leipzig, but to restrict the traffic on the West–East routes in so far as they ran through Prussian lands (Henderson 1958:68).

Efforts to turn this counterunion into a true common market foundered, as did attempts to use the union as a collective bargaining agency in negotiations with neighboring states (Hahn 1984:43–51). The economies of their members exhibited little complementarity, and lack of clear leadership rendered consensus elusive. Furthermore, the economic conditions in the member-states of the Middle German Commercial Union deteriorated rapidly and gave rise to widespread revolts in 1830. The Union's demise had begun. Sachse-Weimar was the first to defect, followed by Hesse-Cassel, which joined the Prussian Customs Union in 1831 on essentially the same terms as Hesse-Darmstadt.[8] Most of the remaining states now considered themselves at liberty to approach Prussia. Prussia signed treaties in 1833 with the Thüringen States,[9] Saxony, Bavaria, and Württemberg. These all came into force on January 1, 1834, and on that day the German Zollverein was born. Thirty years after its foundation, Gustav Fischer wrote that "the elder generation can still remember how joyfully the opening hour of the year 1834 was welcomed by the trading world. Long trains of wagons stood on the high roads, which till then had been cut up by tax barriers. At the stroke of midnight every turnpike was thrown open, and amid cheers the wagons hastened over the boundaries, which they could thenceforward cross in perfect freedom. Everyone felt that a great object had been attained" (Fischer 1865:375).

Baden, an agricultural state that traditionally exported wine, tobacco, hemp, hops, and cattle, joined the Zollverein in 1835 when it became clear that substitute trade with Switzerland and Holland was no adequate compensation for the loss of German markets (Wallschmitt:1–75). It was shortly followed by Nassau and the Free City of Frankfurt-am-Main, where commercial isolation was threatening utter ruin.[10]

The only states to demur further were Hannover and Brunswick. They formed the Tax Union (*Steuerverein*) in 1834, which Oldenburg joined in 1836. Unlike the Middle German Commercial Union, this *Steuerverein* was a genu-

---

[8] Hesse-Cassel agreed, in addition, to introduce the same excise duties as those imposed in Prussia on wine, cider, and tobacco.

[9] The Thüringen States included Sachse-Weimar, the smaller Saxon duchies, the Reuss principalities, the Prussian district of Erfurt, Schleusingen, and Ziegenrück, and the Hesse-Cassel district of Schmalkalden.

[10] Henderson (1958:110–121). A dispatch to the British Foreign Office from the British envoy to the German Diet of December 1834 reads: "[H]emmed in by a line of Customs Houses all round the gates of the town. . . [, Frankfurt's] commercial intercourse with the interior of Germany was greatly harassed and restricted. . . . [I]ts commerce and trade had already fallen off considerably, and . . . great apprehensions were entertained that its fairs would be irretrievably injured unless the union with Prussia was speedily effected; . . . the British houses[,] . . . finding their old customers deterred from frequenting the fairs and their buyers diminish, had themselves become the advocates of the union with Prussia." Quoted in Viner (1950:62).

ine customs union with a common tariff, a joint customs administration, and common excise duties. In its early years it obtained a revenue of a thaler per head of population from these duties, which was a third more than was raised by the Zollverein (Henderson 1958:88). With no domestic manufacturing industry to protect, the *Steuerverein* pursued a policy of free trade to obtain English clothes, colonial goods, and wines as cheaply as possible in exchange for its agricultural goods. It also turned a blind eye on the smuggling of foreign merchandise into the Zollverein (Arning 1930). By 1840, the revenue differential between the Zollverein and the Tax Union had disappeared (Henderson 1958:88). In 1841, Brunswick announced its decision to leave the Tax Union for the Zollverein.[11] Exasperated at Brunswick's desertion, Hannover entered into negotiations with the Zollverein but failed to reach an agreement because Prussia was not prepared to grant the far-reaching concessions demanded by Hannover. A few years later, plagued by severe financial troubles, Hannover reopened talks and agreed to Prussia's terms.[12] It duly signed a treaty with the Zollverein in 1851. Oldenburg joined in 1852.

The Benefits of Membership

How did the states fare as members of the German customs union? In a nutshell, overwhelmingly well. Bavaria, for example, had drawn about 2.1 million florins from the revenues of its customs union with Württemberg in 1831; it obtained 3.86 million florins in its first year of membership in the Zollverein (Henderson 1958:141). Frankfurt-am-Main reported excellent business at its first fair after accession to the Zollverein, and watched with satisfaction the decline of its arch-rival Offenbach (121). Agriculture revived in Baden and sugar refining was introduced under the protection of the Zollverein. Similar examples abound. In general, the extension of the market, along with improved communications by road, inland waterways, and railways, permitted the expansion of existing manufacturers and the development of new ones. Tax collection costs fell from an overall German average of 44 percent of total receipts prior to the Zollverein to 9 percent in the late-1830s. Tax revenues increased by

---

[11] According to Hilde Arning, Brunswick refused to renew its membership in the Steuerverein after Hannover turned down a request by Brunswick to discontinue the construction of a road from Uelzen to Salzwedel connecting Prussia and Hannover. Brunswick feared that this road would compete with its own trade road to Hamburg (Arning 1930:42–43). The prospects of sharing the rapidly growing revenues of the Zollverein arguably also played an important role in Brunswick's decision.

[12] The extent of Hannover's financial and economic difficulties is detailed in Arning (1950: 74–78. See also Benaerts (1904:180).

71 percent between 1834 and 1843 while population increased by only 21.7 percent.[13]

The Zollverein also brought Germany a broad institutional framework in which technological improvements of the industrial revolution could flourish. The executive body of the Zollverein was the 'annual' General Congress, which met each time in the capital of a different member state.[14] It was composed of official delegates from the member states, thus offering the various states some voice in the management of the Zollverein. The Congress solved problems arising from the common administration of the Zollverein, settled the accounts, and acted as legislative body.[15] To be sure, Prussia played a leading role in these institutions. Two factors explain this: first, Prussia was by far the largest and wealthiest state in the Customs Union. Second, Prussia always served as recipient of requests for union membership. This gave it considerable freedom in defining the terms and conditions under which a new state became a member. Nevertheless, despite its political preponderance, Prussia cannot be said to have abused its position. Its fellow members joined the union voluntarily and were free to leave as they pleased. No state ever left; all remained members and had strong material incentives to do so. Bowden, Karpovich, and Usher write: "[Their] financial return made an end of any hostility that might [have been] felt towards Prussia. The gains in revenue soothed the pain of losing complete independence" (Bowden et al. 1970:338).

Prussia distributed the proceeds of the customs in proportion to the population of the various states. This was highly favorable to nearly all the other membes of the union because their per capita consumption was considerably smaller than the Prussian average. At times, this arrangement imposed important financial costs on Prussia. For example, Prussia experienced a decline in receipts following the establishment of the Zollverein, while the other member states registered strong gains. Its revenue per capita was 20 silver groschens in 1833. It then declined to 15.5 groschens and reached the 1833 level again only in 1838 (Henderson 1958:141–142). Nevertheless, Prussia remained the region's paymaster throughout the existence of the Zollverein, despite occasional mis-

---

[13] Another measure of success is the fact that German mercantile tonnage doubled between 1835 and 1855; in 1870 it was three and a half times the level of 1835. See Hoffmann (1963:104–105).

[14] Only fifteen General Congresses were held between 1834 and 1863.

[15] After the Seven Weeks' War of 1866, the old General Congress was replaced by a federal customs council. In addition, a popularly elected customs parliament was introduced that was called in session when business required it to be or when one-third of the customs council demanded a meeting.

givings by Prussian officials[16] and despite some changes to the system of revenue distribution over the years.

Participation in the Zollverein brought another benefit to many German rulers, namely control of the smuggling problem. Prior to the Zollverein, smuggling had contributed to the weakening of the financial health of several treasuries, particularly in Southwestern Germany. A Prussian commissioner reported in 1835 that "smuggling on a very large scale takes place from Frankfurt to all the neighboring parts of the Zollverein. . . . Open smuggling is done partly by carriers . . . and partly by vehicles, particularly coaches, which travel in large numbers every day between Frankfurt and Offenbach; large quantities of goods are smuggled in the vehicles and in the clothes and on persons of the passengers. Secret smuggling is generally done by means of forged customs-seals with the cooperation of those who issue certificates of origin" (Henderson 1958:114). Much smuggling occurred also through forests and mountainous terrain. With the creation and the gradual enlargement of the Zollverein, smuggling ceased to be a major problem because the single customs line was shorter relative to the size of the common market and easier to control. For example, the first few enlargements gave the Zollverein an easily guarded river frontier in the Southwest in place of a difficult frontier in the hills of the Black Forest. Likewise, the adhesion of Nassau and Frankfurt-am-Main eliminated convenient pockets for smuggling in Southwestern Germany. Finally, contraband trade in the Harz mountains along the Hanoverian frontier with Prussia disappeared when Hanover joined the Zollverein.

Sovereignty Bargains and the Early Enlargements of the EU

The logic of enlargement of the EU is quite similar to the one of the Zollverein. Membership, however costly in terms of foregone national policymaking autonomy, was often viewed as the most effective means by which to remedy economic malaise. In the case of the Zollverein, the main cause of relative economic decline of outsiders' economies was the loss of easy access to the rapidly growing single German market. Faced with sagging economic fortunes, outsiders

---

[16] In a memorandum of December 22, 1839, for example, the Prussian government complained: "Although Prussia fully recognizes that its subjects have shared in the general advantageous results of the customs union . . . the position is quite different when viewed from the financial standpoint . . . Prussia . . . has good reasons for having considerable misgivings if it is to hold no other prospect save that of new financial sacrifices in the future while all other members of the union look forward to a permanent increase of customs revenue." Quoted in Henderson (1958:142).

became willing to trade much of their autonomy for market access, prosperity, and some measure of control. In the case of the EU, outsiders' economic difficulties have also often been triggered or aggravated by negative economic effects due to trade and investment diversions.[17] In some instances, export-oriented firms in non-EU countries were faced with discriminatory trade policies in the community; in others, outsiders suffered because international investors pulled capital out and channelled it into the large common market. Finally, outsiders may also be adversely affected because integration puts some of the domestic producers in outsider economies who do not benefit from new market efficiencies (due to economies of scale and greater competition) at a competitive disadvantage, reducing their exports to the union.

As illustrated below, when these negative economic effects were strongly felt, outsiders were compelled to seek closer links with the EU. Sovereignty bargains, however, were structured differently for different states. The UK, for example, stood to gain economically from membership, but it was also determined to use its political clout as a major power to influence the pace and nature of European integration. The poorer candidate countries were hoping for a big boost in foreign private capital, generous aid packages in support of regional and social development policies, solidification of democratic principles, and greater political stability. Finally, the small but mostly wealthy European neutrals also sought closer ties with the EU in times of economic difficulties. Their greater reticence towards membership may be attributable, in part, to an attachment to the principle of neutrality, or—perhaps more persuasively—to an aversion to becoming net contributors to the common budget or a concern about gaining only a trifling voice in the union.

The following section will primarily focus on the trade-off between autonomy and prosperity and describe the basic logic of the enlargement process from the point of view of the applicant.

Trading Autonomy for Prosperity

The Treaty of Rome, which established the European communities, came into force on January 1, 1958. It committed the EC-Six (Germany, France, Italy, the Netherlands, Belgium, and Luxembourg) to a far-reaching exercise in economic integration that envisaged free movement of goods, services, capital, and labor, aided by common policies in agriculture, transport, regional devel-

[17] Integration may of course benefit outsiders when positive income effects pull in greater amounts of trade than it diverts. The argument here is not to say that this is a rare event but to point out that in cases where integration has overall negative effects on outsiders, these countries will have an incentive to respond in ways that bring them closer to the union.

opment, external commerce, economic cohesion, and other domains. By the end of the transition period in 1969, the basic ingredients of the customs union—elimination of internal tariff and quotas and erection of a common external tariff—were established. The member-states agreed to deepen integration on two further occasions: in the mid-1980s by signing the Single European Act, and in the early 1990s by agreeing to the Maastricht Treaty on European Union.

The United Kingdom, Sweden, Norway, Denmark, Austria, Switzerland, and Portugal were among the outsiders of European integration. At first, they reacted to the formation of the European Community by establishing the European Free Trade Association (EFTA) on January 4, 1960.[18] This rival organization with a minimalist integrative program committed its members to establishing free trade in industrial goods only. The economic rationale for integration among EFTA countries, however, was not particularly compelling. These countries were strewn in a loose circle around the EC and traded primarily with EC members rather than with each other.

Unsurprisingly, foreign investors considered the European Community more promising than EFTA and redirected their capital accordingly. For example, the percentage of the value of U.S. direct investment in Western Europe which was apportioned to EC countries rose from 40.5 percent in 1957 to 44.7 percent in 1964. Yannopoulous relates this increase to a diversion of the flow of U.S. investment from the non-EC countries of Western Europe, particularly the United Kingdom, to members of the EC (Yannopoulos 1990:366). Numerous other studies have likewise concluded that the EC attracted significantly more of the growth in total U.S. foreign direct investment than EFTA countries.[19]

This investment diversion undoubtedly contributed to the UK's worsening economic condition. The UK grew in the late fifties and early sixties well below the EC average. To stem economic losses, the United Kingdom formally announced in 1961 that it had decided to apply for full membership in the EC. Startled by the sudden reversal of British policy and deeply worried about the possibility of economic isolation, most other EFTA countries rushed to submit separate applications for association with the EC. Negotiations dragged on until January 13, 1963, when General de Gaulle declared at a Paris press conference that Britain was not ripe for membership. Two weeks later, all negotiations were adjourned indefinitely.

Continuing poor economic performance relative to that of the EC-Six led the British Prime Minister, Harold Wilson, to announce in May of 1967 that the

---

[18]Finland signed an association agreement with EFTA in 1961.

[19]Schmitz (1970); Schmitz and Bieri (1972); Lunn (1980, 1983); and Scaperlanda and Balough (1983). For a useful review of the empirical studies, see Yannopoulos (1990:238–247).

United Kingdom had decided to submit its second application.[20] Ireland, Denmark, and Norway followed suit. Negotiations were immediately initiated, but only a few months later de Gaulle, in one of his famous press conferences, declared that full membership for Britain would lead to the destruction of the EC. This closed the door to entry yet again. Events in May 1968 led to the resignation of de Gaulle, and under President Pompidou, France no longer objected in principle to British membership. The United Kingdom, along with the three other applicants, were invited back to the negotiating table.[21] The United Kingdom, Ireland, and Denmark continued to grow at rates substantially below the EC average after the resumption of talks. This trend narrowed or reverted only as the three acceded to membership in 1973.

Norway's planned membership in the EC was vetoed by a national referendum held in October 1972. Why? Norway was the only country of four applicants where the performance gap of the years 1968–70 had completely disappeared in 1971–72, thus possibly giving Norwegians the impression that membership was no longer worth the cost. This is not a far-fetched conclusion considering that membership entails not only a relative loss of policymaking autonomy but usually also net contributions to the EC's budget by wealthy members.[22] The reversal of Norway's economic fortune can be attributed to a stroke of good luck. In 1969, the first commercially important discovery of petroleum on Norway's continental shelf was made at the Ekofisk field, just as foreign oil companies were about to give up after four years of exploratory drilling. Later major finds have included the Frigg field, one of the largest offshore natural gas deposits, and the huge Statfjord field. The estimated reserves below the sixty-second parallel alone ensured an annual production for twenty years that is several times Norway's domestic consumption of petroleum products.[23]

Nevertheless, in the early 1970s Norway and other outsiders, including Austria, Portugal, Sweden, Switzerland, and Iceland, signed agreements with the European Community for free trade in industrial goods. A decade later, a joint EC-EFTA ministerial meeting in Luxembourg produced a declaration which sought to continue, deepen, and extend cooperation between the EC and the

---

[20] For a lucid study on the economic performance gap between the EC-Six and the EFTA countries, see Breuss (1990).

[21] For an overview of this enlargement process, see Preston (1997:23–45).

[22] Christopher Anderson and Shawn Reichert write: "[P]ublics in . . . member states . . . that are considering membership . . . will be more reluctant to support integration if they will be net payers" (Anderson and Reichert 1996:246).

[23] See country report on Norway in the Encyclopaedia Britannica (Macropaedia), 1992, pp. 1082–1096.

EFTA with the aim of creating a dynamic European Economic Area (EEA) (Nell 1990). The dialogue on the EEA intensified, and in 1992 a treaty signed by the two organisations established a European free trade zone in goods, services, labor, and capital. The EEA came into force on January 1, 1994.[24] Clearly, therefore, while not officially applying for EC membership, outsider countries have demonstrated a recognition of the benefits of association with the successful regional grouping.

Besides trade agreements, outsiders resorted to policy mimicry (i.e., unilateral adoption of rules, regulations, and policies forged outside their jurisdiction) to narrow the institutional gap with the EC and thus mitigate the negative effects of European integration on their economies. For instance, in 1988 the Swiss government introduced the "Europe Clause" requiring all proposed legislation or amendments to be examined for compatibility with EC rule (Senti 1991:220). In 1993 the Swiss government announced plans to press ahead on harmonizing its laws and regulations with those of the EC, even though it did not consider membership (Bundersrat 1993). In the same year, Switzerland introduced a value added tax as a further step to align its fiscal and economic policies with those of the European countries.

In Norway, steps were taken as early as 1987 to create a new Secretariat in the Foreign Ministry, together with a Committee of Permanent Secretaries, in order to ensure better coordination of European policies. These agencies were mandated to scrutinize all new EC directives and to seek to involve a wider range of bodies in European affairs. Legislative adaptation proceeded on a wide scale in various ministries, in close consultation with export industries, labor and employers' organizations, and other interest groups (Saeter and Knudsen 1991:189). It is telling that these steps were taken at a time of rapid economic decline in Norway. World crude oil prices fell to $8 a barrel in 1985–86, delivering a severe blow to Norway's economy from which it took a long time to recover. The reduction in petroleum revenue slashed Norway's spendable real income by 9 percent. By the late-1980s registered unemployment climbed to nearly 6 percent, the highest suffered in Norway for over sixty years.[25]

In Sweden, an extraordinary decree was adopted by the government in June 1988 that required every expert inquiry or Royal Commission proposing a policy in fields related to the internal market or European integration to evaluate the policy's compatibility with corresponding EC legislation and EC commission proposals. The burden of proof of compatibility rested on the proposer and every proposal that diverged from EC legislation had to

---

[24] In a referendum held in December 1992, Switzerland rejected the EEA by a narrow majority.

[25] See survey on Norway in Financial Times, June 2, 1992, Section IV.

be justified. EC compatibility also needed to be considered in the judicial review of government bills (Stalvant and Hamilton 1991:203). Furthermore, a secretariat for integration questions was established, which was responsible for internal adjustments and the implementation of domestic integration policy (202). Sweden unilaterally adopted and implemented more than twenty directives by the end of 1989. At the same time, it enlarged its value added tax base in line with that of the EC, changed its somewhat restrictive banking and currency laws, and undertook some deregulation.[26]

In the monetary domain, acts of mimicry were also quite common. For example, in the 1980s and early 1990s neither Austria nor Switzerland nor Sweden were members of the EMS. Yet their respective central banks pegged their currencies to the deutschmark, the EMS's anchor currency.[27]

In short, even before seeking formal membership European outsider states went a long way down the road of unilateral adaptation to EC law and policies to avoid being effectively left out. Their national policymaking autonomy remained intact de jure, but de facto it had lost much of its value.[28]

Yet, despite rapid progress towards an EEA and despite sweeping policy mimicry, outsiders were unable to reverse relative economic decline in the late-1980s and early 1990s. Corporate pressure on governments to move towards full membership grew intense in those years. Big firms became increasingly discontented with the uncertainty and lack of transparency of many of the measures taken by their governments to bridge the institutional gap with the EU. They argued that such measures did not provide conditions favorable enough to successfully compete with the big firms within the common market. In particular, they felt that their

---

[26] Finland also followed the beat of legislative calibration to Community norms. See Antola (1991).

[27] A Swedish diplomat was quoted in the *Washington Post* as saying: "How long can anyone remain 'independent' vis-à-vis a decision by the *Bundesbank* to change the interest rate or the value of the German Mark? About 20 minutes?" Quoted in an article by Hoagland (1992).

[28] Nell (1990:352). An interesting example of the logic of policy mimicry in a different historical era can be found in Spruyt (1994:527–557). Spruyt writes that "sovereign states proved better at mobilizing their societies and enhancing their domestic economies [than the cities of the Hanseatic league]. Territorial units gradually encroached on the independence of the cities. . . . The German princes thus started to *mimic the administrative processes and legal framework of territorial states*. . . . When political elites recognized the consequences of localism and the lack of economic integration in their city-states, they turned to the territorial rules of Frederick and Catherine the Great as models worthy of emulation. . . . [I]ndividuals had reasons to mimic those successful institutions. . . . [They] emulated what they perceived to be successful arrangements in order to reduce uncertainty and gain legitimacy" (546 and 550, emphasis added).

governments could not commit themselves to implement EC policies as credibly as EC governments (Stalvant and Hamilton 1991:208). This created lingering doubts about the comprehensiveness and thoroughness of policy mimicry and also made outsiders vulnerable to discriminatory treatment by the EC in several domains, such as research and development and public procurement. As a result, multinationals in outsider countries began to invest more and more of their resources away from home, within the EC. This enabled them to lower production costs and get a stronger foothold in the European market (Fioretos 1997:312).

In Sweden, the result of this process was a striking gap between outward investment and inward investment in the late-1980s. Disinvestment of such magnitude came at a particularly inopportune time. Sweden was grappling with its most severe recession since the 1920s.[29] The recovery package that the government had designed was to a large extent dependent on retaining Swedish companies. In dire need to improve the investment climate, the Swedish government was left with no option but to apply for full EC membership. Even after the application was filed in 1991, Swedish firms kept pressing government officials for rapid membership negotiations, repeatedly issuing explicit threats of exit.[30] Fioretos concludes unequivocally: "The engine of Sweden's integration . . . has been its large multinational corporations. . . . [T]he Swedish government had little option but to secure access for Swedish firms to the Union if it was to retain domestic investment, promote growth and employment, as well as make Sweden an attractive site for foreign investment in the future" (Fioretos 1997:313).

The Austrian case is similar to the Swedish one. In a recent case study, Tim Büthe summarized the key motives of Austrian membership application as follows: "Austria—first some of its firms, eventually its government on behalf of Austria's economic growth perspective—had sought EC membership to insure access to the EC market for Austrian exports and . . . to insure competitiveness" (Büthe 1995:22). The membership issue was first brought up in Austria by export-oriented firms in the mid-1980s, during the period of negotiations for the Single European Act. The textile industry of Vorarlberg in Western Austria felt increasing discrimination from the EC, despite free trade agreements (Luif 1991:135). The Federation of Austrian Industrialists was the first important interest group to endorse the demands for EC membership made by the textile industry. In 1987 it issued an "urgent appeal to the Federal Government to do everything so that full membership in the EC can be accom-

---

[29] Sweden's economy declined by 1.2 percent in 1991 and 1 percent in 1992.

[30] (Moses and Jenssen 1998:217). The two authors also note that in public opinion polls conducted in the run-up to the referendum, a majority of Swedes thought that EU membership would improve domestic economic fortunes. In contrast, only 28 percent of Norwegians felt that membership would be an advantage to Norway's economy.

plished at the earliest possible moment" (Vereinegug Oesterreichischler Industrielle 1987)[31] The idea of membership was also endorsed by the Federal Chamber of Commerce and quickly enjoyed widespread popularity. Such positive public response is best understood against the backdrop of an Austrian economy in distress. Paul Luif notes: "In November 1985, Austria's large state-owned industry was on the brink of bankruptcy and the federal government had to come to the rescue, but the already high budget set limits for such intervention. The nationalized industry had to abandon one of its most cherished policies and to dismiss workers and employees on what was, for Austria, a massive scale. These problems were only one indication of the precarious state of the Austrian economy, which in the mid-1980s was growing more slowly than . . . the EC economies taken as a whole" (Luif 1991:135). On July 17, 1989, Austria submitted its EC application to the Commission—an application that had been authorized by a 95 percent majority of the lower chamber of the Austrian Parliament (Büthe 1995:7).

Like big firms in Sweden, firms in Austria strongly preferred full EC membership over membership in the EEA (Kurzer 1993). They felt that EEA membership alone would neither provide a sufficient guarantee against EC discrimination nor create the right investment climate. Büthe notes, for example, that investments in Austria which were financed on international capital markets in 1994 still cost a premium over investments in the EU, despite Austrian membership in the EEA (Büthe 1995:23). Only EC membership seemed to offer big Austrian business the necessary safeguards and advantages to compete effectively with EC firms.

The more general expected gains from full membership on Austria were illustrated in a series of influential studies published in the early 1990s by the Austrian Institute of Economic Research. The studies predicted that GDP would be 2.8 percent higher by the year 2000 if Austria were a full EU member instead of simply belonging to the EEA (Arndt 1998:260–261). Persuaded by such arguments, two-thirds of Austria's voters endorsed EU membership in a 1994 referendum. The strong vote in favor of membership was possibly influenced by renewed economic difficulties in the early 1990s. Austria's recession peaked in 1993 when GDP declined by about 0.25 percent. Along with Sweden and Finland, Austria joined the European Union on January 1, 1995.

---

[31] Note that most of Austria's trade has always been with Community members. In 1985, for example, the EC countries received 56.1 percent share of Austrian total exports whereas the EFTA countries got only 10.5 percent. At the same time, Austria imported 62.1 percent of goods from the EC and only 7.6 percent from EFTA countries. See IMF (1970–1998).

The Swiss case is, at least in part, consistent with the logic of integration. In the early 1990s, Switzerland entered into a recession that lasted for several years.[32] At the same time, internationalized sectors of the Swiss economy, most notably the engineering and chemical industries, began to lobby for EU membership. In 1988, engineering exports represented 28.3 percent of total Swiss exports to the EC market. Products by the chemical industry accounted for 21.4 percent of total Swiss exports to the EC (Plavsak 1996:32). These industries expressed concern about negative externalities from the deepening process of European integration, particularly in the form of discrimination in the areas of technical harmonization, public procurement, and research and development. In light of growing economic unrest, the Swiss government declared its intention to seek EU membership in October 1991. It sent a formal application to the EC on May 18, 1992. How did it justify such a move, considering the 'sacredness' of Swiss neutrality? In a 1993 foreign policy report, the Swiss government explained that neutrality had never been an end in itself but merely a means of preserving Swiss independence. In the post–Cold War world, Swiss independence was threatened more by not having a say in EU matters than by any hostile military power. Prosperity through integration became the declared objective of Swiss foreign policy (Bundesrat 1993).

Unexpectedly, however, 50.3 percent of Swiss opposed EEA membership against 49.7 percent favorable votes in December 1992, thus in effect also barring any further talks on EU membership. The economic cost of the 'no' vote was estimated to be high. Several studies suggested that by not joining the EEA, investments in Switzerland would grow at a rate of only 0.5 percent instead of 3.5 percent. As a result, GNP would rise by less than 1 percent, compared to 2.3 percent, and unemployment would double (Schwok 1994:34). The prolonged period of economic difficulties of the Swiss economy in the wake of the 'no' vote seems to have confirmed many of these predictions (Hall 1997:27).

Why this negative vote? The theoretical argument developed in Section 2 cannot explain it. This need not imply that the approach is wrong. First, many of the dynamics leading up to the referendum were well captured by the approach; further, the outcome of the referendum was extremely tight, thus it is not an outcome that convincingly 'falsifies' the approach. Nevertheless, it does suggest that, at least in the Swiss case, the type of economic calculus proposed in this study is *analytically* incomplete. But the approach remains useful because it provides a benchmark by which to assess the extent and impact of noneco-

[32] The Swiss economy started to move back into growth in the last quarter of 1993. The jobless rate rose to over 5 percent during the recession.

nomic motivations in deciding for or against integration. It thus suggests that a more fine-grained analysis is needed in the Swiss case that takes into consideration factors such as the country's sociopolitical characteristics, or elements that capture the peculiarity of Swiss political decisionmaking.[33]

Sovereignty Bargains and EU Enlargement to the East

Enlargement of the EU to the East is a process that started timidly in the early 1990s. The Central and East European Countries (CEECs) were moving from an era of communism and rigid command economies towards a goal of democratic pluralistic regimes with market economies. This transformation represented a gargantuan social experiment of uncertain outcome. Rising unemployment, food shortages, and a decline in the already precarious standard of living, combined with ethnic tensions and mounting criminality, posed a serious threat to the pace and scope of economic and political reforms.

The West responded to the plight in the East initially by offering technical assistance and advice in areas such as food distribution, privatization, banking, civil service reform, education, environment, and energy through the PHARE and the TACIS programs.[34] In addition, loans were provided by the European Investment Bank (EIB) and the European Bank for Reconstruction and Development (EBRD). Such traditional aid, however, proved insufficient. The attempted Soviet coup in August of 1991 signalled to the West that more effort was needed to avert chaos (Mortimer 1992:21).

Only the integration of Eastern and Western Europe seemed to offer a way of stimulating economic growth and producing sufficient political stability to mitigate the pressure for large-scale migration. Jackie Gower notes that "[u]ntil the summer of 1991 the prevailing view in Brussels was that none of the former Comecon states could realistically be regarded as candidate members of the Community until well into the next century. Indeed, it is arguable that the EU's overriding objective at this time was to avoid the question of membership." Gower concludes that the shock of the attempted Moscow coup changed the

---

[33] See, for example, Sciarini and Listhaug (1997).

[34] PHARE is the acronym for "Pologne, Hongrie: Activité pour la Restructuration Economique." (The word "phare" also means lighthouse in French.) The PHARE program now includes ten countries in Eastern Europe. It is funded by the EU budget and the money is given by way of grants. The total sum allocated to PHARE was raised to 1 billion ECU in 1992. (See Kramer 1993:221–226.) TACIS stands for Technical Assistance to the Commonwealth of Independent States. Its budget amounted to 450 million ECU in 1992.

EU's attitude towards enlargement (Gower 1993:289–290). Avoidance was simply no longer a sensible policy option.

Instead, the EU initiated negotiations on gradual integration with Czechoslovakia, Hungary, and Poland. On December 16, 1991, far-reaching association agreements (also called "Europe Agreements") were signed, under which the EU promised to remove its barriers to industrial imports from these three countries within five years. Each of the three states in turn committed itself to taking concrete steps towards a market economy and pluralist democracy.[35] Romania and Bulgaria signed similar association agreements with the EU in 1993.[36]

During the Copenhagen Summit in June 1993, the EU offered more formal political ties and greater market access. New vehicles for cooperation—"association councils" composed of foreign ministers of the Twelve and their counterparts in the "associate" states—were set up. Foreign ministers also agreed to an Anglo-Italian plan for formal cooperation at international conferences and joint foreign policy actions with the associate states.

Two years later, the EU issued a "white paper" on Eastern Europe. The three-hundred-page paper was addressed to Poland, Hungary, the Czech Republic, Slovakia, Bulgaria, and Romania; it constituted a road map for these countries on how to align their economies to the internal market as a step towards full membership of the European Union (Commission of the European Communities 1995). In 1997, the EU recommended the opening of accession negotiations with Poland, the Czech Republic, Slovenia, Hungary, and Estonia; the negotiations with these five countries and Cyprus began in late 1998. The EU also proposed pre-accession talks with Bulgaria, Slovakia, Romania, Latvia, and Lithuania in 1997; and in December of 1999 the EU agreed to launch accession negotiations with these five East European countries and Malta.

The Price of Membership

Membership in the prosperous and influential European Union exacts a heavy toll on newcomers in terms of foregone policymaking autonomy. Prospective

---

[35] Commission of the European Communities (1990, 1992). After the dissolution of Czechoslovakia, separate negotiations were conducted between the EU and the Czech and Slovak Republics.

[36] The association agreements sought to establish not only gradual market integration but also wide-ranging cooperation, such as industrial collaboration aimed at structural change, promotion of scientific research and technological development, support of vocational training and higher education, cooperation in the energy, environmental and telecommunications sectors, regional development, and joint undertakings in the fight against money laundering and drug trafficking. See Kramer (1993:229–230).

members are required to satisfy three sets of conditions, often referred to as the Copenhagen criteria, namely to ensure 1) the stability of institutions guaranteeing democracy, the rule of law, human rights, and respect for the protection of minorities; 2) the existence of a functioning market economy as well as the capacity to cope with competitive pressure and market forces within the Union; and 3) the ability to take on the obligations of membership, including adherence to the aims of political, economic, and monetary union; that is, candidate countries must bring their laws and regulations into line with the *acquis communautaire*—the rules developed and accepted by EU member states during the forty-two years since the six founder members signed the Treaty of Rome. These rules are sweeping in scope, covering virtually every aspect of a modern economy: science and research, education and training, small and medium-sized enterprises, cultural and audio-visual policy, telecommunications, industrial policy, common foreign and security policy, company law, statistics, consumer and health protection, fisheries, competition policy, free movement of goods, customs duties, external relations, social policy, monetary policy, free movement of capital, energy, transport, taxation, freedom to provide services, environment, agriculture, regional policy, free movement of persons, justice and home affairs, financial control, financial and budgetary provisions, and institutions.

The process of adopting this enormous body of EC rules, regulations, and policies by the candidate countries is closely monitored by the EU. The Commission published a first assessment of the progress made by candidate countries in 1998; a second report was issued in 1999 (Commission of the European Communities 1999). In the latter report, the Commission noted, for example, the sluggish pace of transposition of EU law in Poland and the Czech Republic and concluded that "the slow and piecemeal approach to alignment in these countries is not consistent with their political aspiration for rapid accession to the EU." The report lauded Latvia for progress in the sectors such as state aids and standards and certification, but urged it to devote more attention to general public administration and judicial reform. Hungary received high marks for having developed "a reasonably consistent track record in setting up and strengthening its institutions to implement and enforce the *acquis*," but Estonia's performance was criticized for being sketchy, "resulting in a situation where certain parts of the administration are well equipped to effectively implement the *acquis* while others have serious weaknesses." The report also stipulated that the opening of negotiations with Bulgaria was conditional on Bulgarian authorities offering acceptable closure dates for Soviet-designed reactors that cannot be upgraded to EU safety standards. Similarly, negotiations with Romania would start only if the government agreed to provide adequate resources to reform the institutional care system for some 100,000 orphan children.

The Benefits of Accession

The intrusiveness of many of the accession demands has been sweetened by the willingness of the EU to share the enormous costs of modernizing the economies of the candidate countries and aligning their laws and infrastructures with the *acquis communautaire*. The EU provides extensive financial and expert assistance through the PHARE program, which has been remodelled to become an accession-targeted instrument. The program's budget of 1.5 billion euros supports the effort of candidate countries to build strong administrative and judicial apparati capable of effectively implementing and enforcing the *acquis*. The EU's policies toward CEECs are also supported by the lending activities of the European Investment Bank (EIB). The Bank disbursed some 7 billion euros in the region between January 1997 and January 2000 (Commission of the European Communities 1999).

The EU also dispatches technical experts from ministries, regional bodies, public agencies, and professional organizations in the member states to counsel and instruct their homologues in the candidate countries. Regular high-level contacts between representatives of the CEE ministries and the various directorates of the European Commission, as well as a multitude of other meetings within the framework of several partnership programs, have established dense political and bureaucratic networks. These provide continuing legal guidance and technical support, and closely monitor the process of implementation of EU rules, regulations, and policies.

The gradual adoption of the Union's *acquis* is enhancing the transparency, stability, and predictability of the legal and regulatory environment in CEECs, thus mitigating the risks of investing in CEE economies. The result has been a rapid increase in the flow of transnational capital into the region—arguably the greatest economic benefit of the accession process.[37] Foreign direct investment (FDI) has grown from $3.6 billion in 1992 to $5 billion in 1994 and $11.3 billion in 1997.[38] Not surprisingly, the EU countries have been the most important source of foreign direct investment in CEECs. In 1997, for example, the EU accounted for 61 percent of the FDI stock in the Czech Republic, 63 percent in Hungary, and about 55 percent in Poland (United Nations 1998). Several recent studies predict that the influx of capital into the region will double or triple once the CEECs attain the status of full members of the EU.[39]

---

[37] See Mattli (1999:44–50, 105–108); Baldwin, et al. (1997:125–76); Lankes and Venables (1996:331–347); EIU (1999); and European Roundtable of Industrialists (1999).

[38] These figures are for FDI in Bulgaria, Czech Republic, Hungary, Poland, Romania, Slovakia, Slovenia, Latvia, Lithuania, and Estonia. See United Nations (1998).

[39] See, for example, Welfens (1997:18) and Brenton and Di Mauro (1998).

Full membership will offer other advantages: CEECs will have unrestricted access to the single European market and will no longer have to fear reversals of free trade in sensitive areas. In particular, agriculture, a large segment of CEE economies, is likely to see its exports boosted with accession. Both influx of capital and free trade will improve economic growth in the region, which, in turn, will attract more capital and further increase the volume of exports. And as prosperity spreads and tax revenues grow, the political leaders will have the means—propped up by generous EU transfer payments—to better control and guide the development of the national economies and to effectively attend to society's needs.

Finally, membership will not only help CEE leaders to augment their domestic control, but also their external control, that is, their influence in European matters. As members, CEECs will be represented in the key decisionmaking bodies of the Union. As they are for the most part small and poor countries, their entry into the Council and Commission will increase the collective political weight of the group of relatively poor EU member states, which currently includes Ireland, Greece, Portugal, and Spain. And even though the next Intergovernmental Conference (IGC) is likely to change the weighting and decisionmaking modus within EU institutions, it is not outside the realm of possibility that the group of poor countries may end up having a blocking minority in certain bodies, thereby gaining a political say that is disproportionate to their economic and population size.[40]

Conclusion

This study has examined the nature of sovereignty bargains in the context of regional integration. Drawing on and extending recent work by Karen Litfin, the study has described the types of trade-offs that countries contemplating membership in an economic union face, and has specified the factors that affect states' assessment of the costs and benefits of membership and thus the nature of sovereignty bargains. Membership in successful economic unions tends to exact a heavy toll in terms of foregone national policymaking autonomy. The most dramatic example is the EU, where an applicant must accept extraterritorial institutions and enforcement mechanisms as well as the *acquis communautaire*, a set of rules that comprises not only union law as enshrined in the Treaty of Rome but also a very extensive body of secondary law on issues as wide-ranging as competition, intellectual and commercial property, public procurement, banking, financial services, company accounts and taxes, indirect taxation,

[40] On this and related issues, see Baldwin et al. (1995); Mayhew (1998); Nicoll and Schoenberg (1998); and Preston (1997).

technical rules and standards, consumer protection, health and safety, transport, and the environment.

Despite such high a price, membership may be worth the candle. The scope and nature of the benefits from inclusion into a union vary depending on such factors as relative economic health of a state's economy, level of socioeconomic development, and size and political clout of a country. It is for this reason that no two sovereignty bargains are structurally identical. A large and rich newcomer will reap obvious economic gains but also quite possibly win considerable control over the pace and direction of integration. A small and poor country is unlikely to exert much political influence as a union member, but it still has much to gain; membership may help it attract foreign capital, improve the competitiveness of its economy, generate wealth across society, solidify domestic institutions, and contribute to political stability. Finally, wealthy but small countries may be more reluctant applicants since their costs are likely to weigh more heavily than those of poor countries. But in times of economic decline, even small and wealthy states may find it advantageous to seek closer ties with economic unions.

References

AEGIDI, KARL LUDWIG. (1865) *Aus der Vorzeit des Zollvereins. Beitrag zur Deutschen Geschichte*. Hamburg: Noyes and Geister.

ANDERSON, CHRISTOPHER, AND SHAWN REICHERT. Economic Benefits and Support for Membership in the EU: A Cross-National Analysis. *Journal of Public Policy* **15**:246.

ANTOLA, ESKO. (1991) "Finland." In *The Wider Western Europe: Reshaping the EC/EFTA Relationship*, edited by Helen Wallace, pp. 146–158. London: Pinter Publishers.

ARNDT, SVEN. (1998) "Alpine Contrasts: Swiss and Austrian Responses to the EU." In *Forging an Integrated Europe*, edited by Eichengreen and Frieden. Ann Arbor, MI: University of Michigan Press.

ARNING, HILDE. (1930) *Hannovers Stellung zum Zollverein*. Hannover: Culemannsche Buchdruckerei.

BALDWIN, RICHARD, J. FRANÇOIS, AND R. PORTES. (1997) The Costs and Benefits of EU Enlargement: The Impact on the EU and Central Europe. *Economic Policy* **24**:125–76.

BALDWIN, RICHARD, PERTTI HAAPARANTA, AND JAAKKO KIANDER, EDS. (1995) *Expanding Membership of the European Union*. Cambridge: Cambridge University Press.

BENAERTS, PIERRE. (1904) *Les Origines de la Grande Industrie Allemande*. Paris: Librarie Nouvelle de Droit et de Jurisprudence.

BOWDEN, WITT, MICHAEL KARPOVICH, AND ABBOTT PAYSON USHER. (1970) *An Economic History of Europe since 1750*. New York: AMS Press.

BRENTON, PAUL, AND FRANCESCA DI MAURO. (1998) "The Potential Magnitude and Impact of FDI Flows to CEECs." CEPS Working Document, no. 116.

BREUSS, FRITZ. (1990) *Integration in Europa and gesamtwirtschaftliche Entwicklung: EG- und EFTA-Staten im Vergleich*. Wien: Oesterreichisches Institut für Wirtschaftsforschung.

BUNDESRAT, (1993) *Bericht über die Aussenpolitik der Schweiz in den 1990er Jahren*. Bern: Bundesrat Press.

BURLEY, ANNE-MARIE, AND WALTER MATTLI. (1993) Europe Before the Court: A Political Theory of Legal Integration. *International Organization* **47**:41–76.

BÜTHE, TIM. (1995) "European Union and National Electorates: The Austrian Public Debate and Referendum on Joining the European Union in June 1994," Working Paper 5.8. Cambridge, MA: Harvard University, Center for European Studies.

COMMISSION OF THE EUROPEAN COMMUNITIES. (1990) *Association Agreements with the Countries of Central and Eastern Europe: A General Outline*. Brussels.

COMMISSION OF THE EUROPEAN COMMUNITIES. (1992) *Association Agreements with Poland, Czechoslovakia and Hungary: Background Briefs*. Brussels.

COMMISSION OF THE EUROPEAN COMMUNITIES. (1995) *White Paper on the Preparation of the Associated Countries of Central and Eastern Europe for Integration in the Internal Market of the Union*. Brussels.

COMMISSION OF THE EUROPEAN COMMUNITIES. (1999) *Composite Paper: Reports on the Progress Towards Accession by Each of the Candidate Countries*. Brussels.

ECKERT, CHRISTIAN. (1902) Zur Vorgeschichte des deutschen Zollvereins. Die preussisch-hessische Zollunion vom 14. Februar 1828, in *Jahrbuch für Gesetzgebung, Verwaltung and Volkswirtschaft im Deutschen Reich* 26, edited by Gustav Schmoller, pp. 51–102. Leipzig: Dunker and Humbolt.

EIU (ECONOMIC INTELLIGENCE UNIT). (1999) "Eastern Europe Economy: Costs/Benefits of EU Membership to FDI." The Economic Intelligence Unit—EIU Views Wire, 28 June 1999, http://www.viewswire.com/.

ERIKSON, ROBERT. (1989) Economic Conditions and the Presidential Vote. *American Political Science Review* **83**:567–576.

ERIKSON, ROBERT. (1990) Economic Conditions and the Congressional Vote: A Review of the Macrolevel Evidence. *American Journal of Political Science* **34**:373–399.

EULAU, HEINZ, AND MICHAEL LEWIS-BECK. (1985) *Economic Conditions and Electoral Outcomes: The United States and Western Europe*. New York: Agathon Press.

EUROPEAN ROUNDTABLE OF INDUSTRIALISTS. (1999) "The East-West Win-Win Business Experience," 12 December 1999, http://www.ert.be/.

FIORETOS, KARL-ORFEO. (1997) The Anatomy of Autonomy: Interdependence, Domestic Balances of Power, and European Integration. *Review of International Studies* **23**.

FISCHER, GUSTAV. (1865) "Über das Wesen und Bedingungen eines Zollvereins." In *Hildebrands Jahrbuch für Nationalökonomie und Statistik*, p. 375. Quoted in Henderson, *The Zollverein*, p. 94.

GOWER, JACKIE. (1993) "EC Relations with Central and Eastern Europe." In *The European Community and the Challenge of the Future*, 2d ed., edited by Juliet Lodge. New York: St. Martin's Press.

HAHN, HANS-WERNER. (1982) *Wirtschaftliche Integration im 19. Jahrhundert: Die Hessischen Staaten und der Deutsche Zollverein*. Göttingen: Vandenhoeck and Ruprecht.

HAHN, HANS-WERNER. (1984) *Geschichte des Deutschen Zollvereins*. Göttingen: Vandenhoeck and Ruprecht.

HALL, WILLIAM. (1997) Switzerland: Isolation Is Now Being Questioned. *Financial Times*. Survey (March).

HENDERSON, WILLIAM OTTO. (1958) *The Zollverein*, 2d ed. Chicago: Quadrangle Books.

HOAGLAND, JIM. (1992) A Bogeyman Theory of Government. *Washington Post*, June 2.

HOFFMAN, WALTER. (1963) "The Take-off in Germany." In *The Economics of Take-off into Sustained Growth*, edited by Walt Rostow. London: Macmillan.

IMF (INTERNATIONAL MONETARY FUND). (1970–1998) "Directions of Trade." Washington, D.C.: IMF.

KRAMER, HEINZ. (1993). The European Community's Response to the New Eastern Europe. *Journal of Common Market Studies* **31**:213–244.

KRASNER, STEVEN. (1995/96) Compromising Westphalia. *International Security* **20**(Winter).

KRASNER, STEVEN. (1993) "Westphalia and All That." In Ideas and Foreign Policy: Beliefs, Institutions, and Political Change, edited by Judith Goldstein and Robert Keohane, pp. 235–264. Ithaca: Cornell University Press.

KURZER, PAULETTE. (1993) *Business and Banking: Political Change and Economic Integration in Western Europe*. Ithaca: Cornell University Press.

LANKES, HANS-PETER, AND A. VENABLES. (1996) Foreign Investment in Economic Transition: The Changing Pattern of Investments. *Economics of Transition* **4**(2):331–347.

LITFIN, KAREN. (1997) Sovereignty in World Ecopolitics. *Mershon International Studies Review* **41**:167–204.

LUDLOW, PETER. (1982) *The Making of the European Monetary System: A Case Study of the Politics of the European Community*. London: Butterworth Scientific.

LUIF, PAUL. (1991). "Austria." *The Wider Western Europe: Reshaping the EC/EFTA Relationship*, edited by Helen Wallace. London: Pinter Publishers.

LUNN, JOHN. (1980) Determinants of U.S. Direct Investment in the EEC: Further Evidence. *European Economic Review* **13**:93–101.

LUNN, JOHN. (1983) Determinants of U.S. Direct Investment in the EEC: Revisited Again. *European Economic Review* **21**:391–393.

MARRIOTT, J. A. R., AND C. G. ROBERTSON. (1915) *The Evolution of Prussia*. Oxford: Clarendon Press.

MATTLI, WALTER. (1999) *The Logic of Regional Integration: Europe and Beyond*. Cambridge: Cambridge University Press.

MAYHEW, ALAN. (1998). *Recreation Europe: The European Union's Policy Towards Central and Eastern Europe*. Cambridge: Cambridge University Press.

MORTIMER, EDWARD. (1992) "European Security after the Cold War." Adelphi paper no. 271. London: International Institute for Strategic Studies.

MOSES, JONATHAN, AND ANDERS TODSE JENSSEN. (1998) Nordic Accession: An Analysis of the EU Referendums. In *Forging an Integrated Europe*, edited by Eichengreen and Frieden, pp. 211–246. Ann Arbor, MI: Univeristy of Michigan Press.

NELL, PHILIPPE. (1990) EFTA in the 1990s: The Search for a New Identity. *Journal of Common Market Studies* **28**(June):327–358.

NICOLL, WILLIAM, AND RICHARD SCHOENBERG, EDS. (1998). *Europe Beyond 2000: The Enlargement of the European Union towards the East*. London: Whurr Publishers.

NORPOTH, HELMUT, MICHAEL LEWIS-BECK, AND JEAN DOMINIQUE LAFAY. (1991) *Economics and Politics: The Calculus of Support*. Ann Arbor, MI: University of Michigan Press.

ONCKEN, HERMANN, AND F. E. M. SAEMISCH, EDS. (1934) *Vorgeschichte und Begründung des Deutschen Zollvereins 1815–1834. Akten der Staaten des Deutschen Bundes und der Europäischen Mächte*. Volumes 1–3. Berlin: Reimar Hobbing.

PLAVSAK, KRISTINA. (1996) "Why Do Small States Want to Join European Integration? Responses of Austria, Norway, and Switzerland to the EC Challenge." Unpublished paper. New York: Columbia University, Department of Political Science.

PRESTON, CHRISTOPHER. (1997) *Enlargement and Integration in the European Union*. London: Routledge.

PRESTON, ROBERT. (1997) *Enlargement and Integration*. London: Routledge.

PRESTON, ROBERT. (1999) "Beleaguered Blair Maintains Tough Line amid Attacks on European Policy." *Financial Times*, December 11/12.

PRICE, ARNOLD. (1949) *The Evolution of the Zollverein*. Ann Arbor: University of Michigan Press.

ROUSSAKIS, EMMANUEL. (1968) *Friedrich List, the Zollverein, and the Uniting of Europe*. Bruges: College of Europe.

SAETER, MARTIN, AND OLAV KNUDSEN. (1991) "Norway." In *The Wider Western Europe: Reshaping the EC/EFTA Relationship*, edited by Helen Wallace. London: Pinter Publishers.

SCAPERLANDA, ANTHONY, AND ROBERT BALOUGH. (1983) Determinants of U.S. Direct Investment in the EEC: Revisited. *European Economic Review* **21**:381–390.

SCHMITT, H. (1926) *Die Begründung des Preussisch-hessischen Zollvereins vom 14. Februar 1828*. Giessen: Philosophische Fakultät der hessischen Ludwigs Universität.

SCHMITZ, ANDREW. (1970) The Impact of Trade Blocs on Foreign Direct Investment. *Economic Journal* **80**:724–31.

SCHMITZ, ANDREW, AND JURG BIERI. (1972) EEC Tariffs and U.S. Direct Investment. *European Economic Review* **3**:259–70.

SCHWOK, RENE. (1994) "Switzerland: The European Union's Self-Appointed Pariah." In *Prospective Europeans: New Members for the European Union*, edited by John Redmond. New York: Harvester Whatsheaf.

SCIARINI, PASCAL, AND OLA LISTHAUG. (1997) Single Case or a Unique Pair? The Swiss and Norwegian "No" to Europe. *Journal of Common Market Studies* **35**(September):407–437.

SENTI, RICHARD. (1991) "Switzerland." In *The Wider Western Europe: Reshaping the EC/EFTA Relationship*, edited by Helen Wallace. London: Pinter Publishers.

SPRUYT, HENDRIK. (1994) Institutional Selection in International Relations: State Anarchy as Order. *International Organization* **48**(Autumn):527–557.

STALVANT, CARL-EINER, AND CARL HAMILTON. (1991) "Sweden." In *The Wider Western Europe: Reshaping the EC/EFTA Relationship*, edited by Helen Wallace. London: Pinter Publishers.

UNITED NATIONS (1998). "World Investment Report 1998: Trends and Determinants." New York: United Nations.

VEREINIGUNG OESTERREICHISCHER INDUSTRIELLER. (1987) "Europa—unsere Zukunft. Eine Stellungnahme der Vereinigung Oesterreichischer Industrieller zur Europäischen Integration." Vienna. Quoted in "Austria" by Paul Luif. In *The Wider Western Europe: Reshaping the EC/EFTA Relationship*, edited by Helen Wallace. London: Pinter Publishers.

VINER, JACOB. (1950) *The Customs Union Issue*. New York: Carnegie Endowment for International Peace.

VON WALTERSHAUSEN, AUGUST SARTORIUS. (1923) *Deutsche Wirtschaftsgeschichte 1815–1915*, 2d ed. Jena: Gustav Fischer.

WALLSCHMITT, FERDINAND. (1904) *Der Eintritt Badens in den Zollverein*. Hanau: Waisenhaus Buchdruckerei.

WELFENS, PAUL. (1997) *EU Eastern Enlargement and the Russian Transformation Crisis*. Berlin: Springer.

WILLIAMSON, JOHN, ED. (1990) *Latin American Adjustment: How Much Has Happened?* Washington: Institute for International Economics. STEVEN HAGGARD. (1995) *Developing Nations and the Politics of Global Integration*. Washington D.C.: The Brookings Institute, p. 79.

YANNOPOULOS, GEORGE. (1990) Foreign Direct Investment and European Integration: The Evidence from the Formative Years of the European Community. *Journal of Common Market Studies* **28**(March):366.

Changing the Rules: Reconceiving Change in the Westphalian System

Kurt Burch[1]

Department of Political Science and International Relations
University of Delaware

Is the Westphalian system changing? Disputes abound. This essay interprets the question of Westphalian change as a question about analytical vocabularies and frameworks. The essay seeks to inform a new vocabulary and to craft an analytical framework sufficiently robust and comprehensive to address large-scale change and to embrace the scope, scale, fluidity, and contested character of Westphalian practices. The method is "close reading" of prominent texts. The essay makes three contributions. First, it elaborates a vocabulary and taxonomy of rules and rule, crafts an analytic framework attentive to forms of social rule, and develops a rule-oriented form of constructivism. Second, the essay illustrates that a rules-orientation is intrinsic to many prevailing views on Westphalia and social change. Third, the essay applies the rules-orientation to material and ideational theories of social change. The essay concludes that one may understand large-scale change in terms of changes in the form of rule. Specifically, global relations among states and corporations increasingly rely upon coordination and collaboration rather than commands.

---

[1]I thank David Blaney, James Caporaso, Raymond Duvall, Chris May, Nicholas Onuf, Robert Wolfe, and participants in the Minnesota International Relations Colloquium for helpful comments. I presented an early version of this essay at the International Studies Association annual conference, February 1999, Washington, D.C.

Published by Blackwell Publishers, 350 Main Street, Malden, MA 02148, USA, and 108 Cowley Road, Oxford OX4 1JF, UK.

We are not very good as a discipline at studying the possibility of fundamental discontinuity in the international system . . . we lack even an adequate vocabulary.

—John Ruggie (1998b:174–175)

Interesting philosophy is rarely an examination of the pros and cons of a thesis. Usually it is, implicitly or explicitly, a contest between an entrenched vocabulary which has become a nuisance and a half-formed new vocabulary which vaguely promises great things. . . . I am not going to offer arguments against the vocabulary I want to replace. Instead, I am going to try to make the vocabulary I favor look attractive by showing how it may be used to describe a variety of topics.

—Richard Rorty (1989:9)

Is the Westphalian system changing? Questions of social change are "the most difficult" for social science to address, in part because answers depend upon the analytical vocabulary, framework, and foundations one uses (Appelbaum 1970:1–10; Randall and Strasser 1981:1–7, quotation at 11; Kratochwil 1989:59). Such frameworks and foundations often resemble "nineteenth century folk wisdom" (Tilly 1984:13). Scholars in international relations (IR) and international political economy (IPE) similarly lack adequate vocabulary and analytical frameworks sufficiently robust or comprehensive for addressing change (Linklater 1998:3–8, 215–217). Further, existing frameworks often predetermine answers due to their "theoretical and political dispositions" (Spruyt 1994:36). Thus, to ask about social change is also to ask about vocabularies and analytic frameworks. This essay seeks to fulfill Ruggie's demand and Rorty's promise (see epigrams) by informing a "new vocabulary" and, through that vocabulary, to secure an analytical framework for addressing large-scale change.[2]

Disputes abound about whether the Westphalian system is changing. For example, Susan Strange (1996:3, 4) asserts that the "stable and orderly world" of the Westphalian system has been swept away by a pace of technological change

[2] Any comprehensive treatment of systemic change must entail, in my view, five elements: (a) a baseline for judging change that identifies key systemic features, (b) an analytical framework that does not predetermine results, (c) a theory of how change occurs, (d) a theory of why change is occurring now, and (e) empirical evidence (Burch 1999a). The characteristic Westphalian form of rule is my baseline. The bulk of the essay seeks to craft analytical vocabulary and frameworks as a prelude to other work.

"more rapid than human society had ever before experienced." These changes are comparable to the previous neolithic and industrial revolutions (Strange 1994, 1996:51; Burke 1999:14–15). Failure to recognize these transformations indicates to Strange "serious intellectual myopia" (Strange 1996:186). In contrast, Stephen Krasner (1995:278) dismisses as "historically myopic" any claims that technological innovations fundamentally alter the state system, because no basic transformation has occurred: the Westphalian model "has not been replaced by some alternative conception of how the international system might be organized" (Krasner 1995/96:145; 1999:24, 238). In further contrast, John Ruggie (1998b: chapters 4 and 7) conceives gradual change. Since 1850, but especially since World War II, national rulers have willingly transferred authority to multilateral institutions to address "irreducibly transterritorial" problems (Ruggie 1998b:172). The authority of multilateral institutions may auger a profound transformation by negating exclusive territoriality (Ruggie 1998b:130, 190).

These authors talk past each other by employing different analytic frameworks, vocabularies, and premises. They talk of different subjects. Strange writes of technological change within an expanding global political economy (e.g., 1996:48; 1998). Ruggie writes of normative change and multilateral institutions; Krasner, of national authority and compromised sovereignty. Strange (1994:209; 1996:xv, 4) concludes there is a need to abandon IR and "to rethink some of the assumptions of conventional social science." Krasner (1994:17; 1999:6) holds that neorealism and neoliberalism are the "proper" ways to investigate global affairs. Ruggie (1998b:3) advocates constructivism as an alternative to the "blind spots and silences" of neo-utilitarian approaches. Each concedes that explaining change is difficult (Strange 1996:xii, 185–188; Krasner 1995/96:145; 1999:43–56; Ruggie, 1998b:23).

Also, each author understands social relations in terms of rules. For example, Krasner (1999:23, 43, 46, 48, 228–229) describes institutions, behavior, and theories in terms of rules. Strange is implicit; Ruggie, explicit. From their work I trace a rules-orientation to social relations, sketch a vocabulary of rules and rule, and outline a rules-oriented constructivism. To frame the effort I use Nicholas Onuf's (1989) taxonomy of rules and my elaboration of it (Burch, 1998:18–20).

I intend this essay as a *prise de position*, a broad statement to be explored subsequently. The essay makes three contributions. The first is to outline a rules-orientation by informing a vocabulary and taxonomy of rules and rule. I elaborate a rules-oriented form of constructivism distinct from forms of constructivism currently prominent in IR/IPE.[3] The second contribution is to illus-

[3] For descriptions and typologies of constructivism, see Adler (1997), Checkel (1998), Katzenstein et al. (1998:674–678), Price and Reus-Smit (1998), Ruggie (1998b:35–36), Walt (1998), Wendt (1999), and Burch (2000).

trate a rules-orientation not as an *alternative* framework, but as an approach *intrinsic* though implicit in prevailing views. I illustrate the taxonomy in the work of authors who differently address systemic change: Hendrik Spruyt, Stephen Krasner, and Susan Strange. The third contribution is to apply the "new" vocabulary and taxonomy to theories of Westphalian change.

I conclude that social change is not limited to change *of* and *within* systems. Rather, change in a system's form of rule also describes large-scale change.[4] Specifically, the prevailing form of rule in the global system changes as national and corporate agents increasingly rely upon coordination rather than commands.

I organize the essay in five subsequent sections. The first section informs a rules-oriented analytical framework. The next section informs the framework via "close readings" of three authors. The third section summarizes themes concerning rules-orientation and large-scale change. Section four applies a rules-orientation to theories of change. Conclusions follow.

Building an Analytical Framework: A Rules-Orientation, Constructivism, and a Typology of Rule

A Rules-Orientation

A *rules-orientation* conceives practices, agents, and social arrangement—including regimes, institutions, societies, and structures—in terms of social rules. Several rules-orientations currently circulate in IR/IPE. For example, James March and Johan Olsen (1984, 1989, 1998) and Elinor Ostrom (1990) treat states and institutions as systems of rules. Douglass North (e.g., 1981, 1990) studies the effects of social rules and institutions on economic-historical change. Christopher Lloyd (1993) encourages historians to investigate "structures of rules." Game theorists also address rules (e.g., Axelrod 1984; *Ethics* 1990). Although IR/IPE scholars appropriated these models, no IR/IPE scholars, other than Kratochwil and Onuf, study rules per se.[5] Rather, scholars encounter rules in their study of diverse subjects. Thus, rules and norms became

---

[4] Most accounts of change focus upon magnitude, time span, effect (process vs. structure), rate (or pace), periodization, direction, degree of violence, and scope of analysis (individuals, groups, societies). See, for example, Appelbaum (1970:7–10), Randall and Strasser (1981:16–20), Boudon (1986), and Linklater (1998). Braudel (1980) and Gould (1980) offer unique accounts of change. A rules-orientation describes sites of change and classifies the kinds of change that merit theorizing (Onuf, 1998b:189–190).

[5] See bibliography for Kratochwil; Kratochwil and Ruggie; and Onuf.

prominent foci in "rationalist" and constructivist studies. However, IR/IPE scholars commonly define rules and norms in circular terms: rules are normative constraints and norms are behavioral rules (e.g., Finnemore and Sikkink 1998:891, 892).

Despite confusion over terms, prevailing definitions convey how understandings of system, society, institution, and regime blur and dovetail, yet share "rules" as a common element. For example, the Westphalian system of interacting sovereign states comprises a "*governance system,*" "an institution that specializes in making collective choices on matters of common concern to the members of a distinct group" (Young 1994:26). As an *institution*, the Westphalian system exhibits "persistent and connected sets of rules, formal and informal, that prescribe behavioral roles, constrain activity, and shape expectations" (Keohane 1990:732). More generally, an "institution" is "a relatively stable collection of practices and rules defining appropriate behavior for specific groups of actors in specific situations. Such practices and rules are embedded in structures of meaning and . . . interpretation that explain and legitimize particular identities and the practices and rules associated with them" (March and Olsen 1998:948; also Finnemore and Sikkink 1998:891). Krasner (1982:186) similarly defines *regimes* as "sets of implicit or explicit principles, norms, rules, and decision-making procedures around which actors' expectations converge in a given area of international relations."[6] Kratochwil (1989:46), following Nardin (1983: chapter 1), describes regimes and societies as rule-shaped institutions. As such, Westphalian relations comprise a system, institution, regime, and *society*, a "congeries of regimes" that forms "the most inclusive regime [institution, society] of which states are members" (Onuf 1998b:175). Ensembles of rules constitute institutions, of whatever scope.[7]

Lewis Kornhauser (1996:204–207) sketches a tripartite taxonomy of rules: (a) regularities of behavior; (b) conventions [regimes] identifying an equilibrium solution to coordination games or collective action problems; and (c) "authoritative reasons for action," often called norms. Rules as regularities weakly describe correlated behavior, but offer no causal explanation. In IR/IPE, rationalists privilege conventions; constructivists emphasize norms.

For rationalists, rules are "features of the environment" that rational actors consider when calculating behavior (Katzenstein et al. 1998:679). Yet confusion ensues. Such rules, or "normative structures," arise from institutions, yet

---

[6] See critiques and elaborations by Kratochwil (1989:57–60) and Onuf (1989:143–154; 1998:174–177).

[7] Since the word "institutions" connotes both specific bodies (e.g., the UN) and broad relations (e.g., marriage, sovereignty, the Cold War), I henceforth use the label "social arrangements" as the umbrella term for "ensembles of rules."

institutions are ensembles of rules (e.g., Finnemore and Sikkink 1998:891; March and Olsen 1998:948; Krasner 1999:43). "Institutions are formal or informal structures of norms and rules that are created by actors to increase their utility" and material interests (Krasner 1999:43). Agents also instrumentally create norms (Katzenstein, Keohane, and Krasner 1998:680, 681). Normative and institutional conventions result. Yet for rationalists, power always shapes conventions (rules, institutions) (Krasner 1999:228).

To explain the instrumental reasons for forming conventions, rationalists often turn to game theory (e.g., Axelrod 1984; Katzenstein et al. 1998:679; Milner 1998:769–772, 776–779 and citations therein). To sustain the argument that material interests cause actors to create rules and institutions, four additional assumptions concerning the resulting convention must hold: the convention should represent an equilibrium condition, the parties should share beliefs, the solution should be a Nash equilibrium, and the solution should be a coordination equilibrium (Lewis 1969; Kornhauser 1996:204–206). However, according to Kornhauser (1996:210), a game theorist and law professor, this argument about conventions is simplistic and incomplete: "To identify a social rule [or institution] with a particular equilibrium in a game apparently gives little explanatory force to the social rule. The behavioral assumptions underlying the equilibrium concept carry most of the explanatory force. . . . The additional assumption of common knowledge . . . provides the rest of the explanation."[8] Seeking equilibrium and instrumental conventions, rationalists find them. Instead, analysts should explore the mechanism that promotes common knowledge (Kornhauser 1996:210). This mechanism is co-constitution.

In contrast to rationalists, constructivists regard rules as reasons for action. This view circulates in anthropology, sociology, philosophy, and legal studies (e.g., Hart 1961:88; Raz 1979:146; Kratochwil 1989:100–102; Habermas 1998:5).[9] Two views of rules-as-reasons circulate in IR/IPE. I call them *norm-oriented constructivism* (NOC) and *rule-oriented constructivism* (ROC).[10] They share several elements.

Rules communicate reasons for action by giving meaning, setting standards, and constituting conditions and agents. First, rules give meaning to human

---

[8] See Kornhauser (1996:211) and Kratochwil (1989:59) for criticisms of "narrow rationality" associated with rules-as-conventions.

[9] Among rationalists, Krasner (1999) is an exception. He declares that the Westphalian system is no convention because it "is not an equilibrium outcome" (1999:24, 68). However, rules remain reasons for action and they yield institutions (Krasner 1999:6, 46).

[10] I also distinguish structure-oriented constructivism (SOC), for which Alexander Wendt is the foremost advocate (Burch 2000). Yet Wendt (e.g., 1999) accords no prominence to rules.

action by communicating "shared understandings" that shape and orient behavior (Hart 1961; Kratochwil and Ruggie 1986:764; Kratochwil 1989:11; Hasenclever et al. 1997:163). In this sense rules (norms) shape normative and ideological frameworks that constitute stable patterns of interaction such as regimes and institutions. As such, rules also guide and regulate behavior. Thus, second, rules convey standards of conduct that tell us how to behave (Finnemore and Sikkink 1998:891; Onuf 1998a:59). Scholars call these "regulative rules" and assume that they "cause" actors to behave in particular ways. Rationalists share this conception of cause (e.g., Krasner 1999:46–47). However, not all reasons for action are causal (e.g., Hart 1961:54; Kratochwil and Ruggie 1986:767; March and Olsen 1989:23; Kornhauser 1996:206; Hasenclever et al. 1997:162–164; Ruggie 1998a:880). Common practice distinguishes regulative rules from "constitutive" ones. Constitutive rules "prestructure the domains of action" in which meaning, regulative rules, intention, and rational action occur (Kornhauser 1996:213; Ruggie 1998a:873, 879).[11] By extension, rules constitute not only normative frameworks and institutional settings, but also the immediate coordination game that precedes them, and "the larger game" of society, culture, and ideology in which the meanings, institutions, and games are embedded (Kornhauser 1996:213; Krasner 1999:63).

Rules and Social Construction

Rules as reasons lead to questions of social construction. A view that links rules and social construction shares much with "strong cognitivists," "critical constructivism," and "neoclassical constructivism" (Hasenclever et al. 1997:154–210; Katzenstein et al. 1998:676–677; Ruggie, 1998b:32–35, respectively). Ruggie and Kratochwil are foremost advocates: "constructivists view international structure as a social structure" or "normative structure" that constitutes agents who recognize and understand rules and who are subject to material and institutional constraints (Ruggie 1998a:879). I call this *norm-oriented constructivism* (NOC) for its attention to norms and collective understandings as causes that help explain cooperation, institutionalization, and norm entrepreneurship (e.g., Sikkink 1991; Price 1997, 1998; Keck and Sikkink 1998).[12]

---

[11] On constitutive rules more broadly, see Rawls (1955), Hart (1961), Giddens (1984:19–25, 258–262), Dessler (1989:453–456), Kratochwil (1989: chapter 2), Onuf (1989:50–52, 61–65), and Searle (1995:27–29, 43–51, 114–118).

[12] My view of rules shares with NOC a desire to make sense of intersubjectivity. Yet I explore the linguistic construction of agents, and regard rules, concepts, and discursive practices as ontologically primary, so share concerns with "postmodern constructivism." For contrasting views on postmodern constructivism, see Price and Reus-Smit (1998) and Krasner (1999:43–44).

For scholars investigating social construction, the foremost analytical problem is deciding how to cut into the process. Debates in IR/IPE question not whether social construction occurs, but how to accommodate its insights with rigorous social science and where to insert its insights into processes of co-constitution and rationality. In recent years IR/IPE scholars have transformed the problem of co-constitution into a problem of infinite regress. Rationalists posit agents with given interests. Constructivists argue that prior institutions and normative frameworks constitute actors and rationality. Rationalists counter that agents craft institutions to address problems of coordination and collective action. Constructivists reply that norms, such as "contract," must exist prior to agreements to create institutions (Ruggie 1998a:872). And so on. One solution is to explore social rules as the medium of co-constitution, as the social sinews connecting agents to social arrangements.

However, simultaneously considering rules, agents, and social arrangements—each perpetually changing in relation to the other two—replaces the problem of incompleteness with complexity. The problem of complexity has two solutions: postpositivist interpretation or a rules-orientation (Onuf 1997:8). Postpositivists may interpret the meanings that inform agents' worldviews and motivate choices. Another solution is to account systematically for how rules co-constitute agents and social arrangements and, in turn, how relations among agents and social arrangements constitute conditions of rule. This solution describes *rule-oriented constructivism* (ROC), the view I advocate.

Reduced to fundamentals, ROC comprises six premises (Onuf 1999:9). First, social relations arise from a continuous process of social construction via the simultaneous co-constitution of agents and social arrangements *and* of material conditions and ideas.

Second, speech acts and consequent rules (norms, principles, laws, procedures, policies) are the means of social construction and co-constitution. This claim, ROC's bedrock, represents a philosophically and analytically stronger version of rules-as-reasons. This version looks beyond the normative content of rules to the logic of their forms and expression (e.g., Von Wright 1963; Onuf 1989; Pettit 1990; Braybrooke 1996:3–4, 11–13).

Third, the distinction between regulative and constitutive rules is false. Addressing the distinction "is the necessary starting point for a constructivist social theory" (Onuf 1989:63). All social rules are simultaneously constitutive and regulative (e.g., Giddens 1984:17; Onuf 1989:50–52, 61–65; 1998b:173). For example, posted speed limits do not merely regulate traffic; obedience constitutes "good drivers." Conversely, the allegedly constitutive rule of sovereignty also regulates national behaviors such as intervention. Just as drivers often ignore speed limits, governments often violate prohibitions against intervention. And just as officers often tolerate highway speeds over the limit, so governments often tolerate a measure of intervention. As a result, the content of the rules changes. As drivers, we "know" that the tolerable speed limit is actually over the posted speed; U.S. officials "knew" during the Cold War that Russian military aircraft screaming toward Alaskan airspace and veering off near the border were probing U.S. reactions, but were not intervening. Ruggie's (1998a:872) lament that "social constructivists in international relations have not yet managed to devise a theory of constitutive rules" poses not the obstacle he imagines, because no unique theory is necessary.[13]

Fourth, change is "a pervasive and inevitable feature of social construction," so involves rules (Onuf 1998b:188; see also Ruggie 1998b:34). Gradual change occurs unendingly: as agents continuously make choices to reinforce, revamp, reject, or ignore social rules, these rules constantly accrete or erode. Consider speed limits and airspace.

Fifth, scholars miss the relationships among rules, rule, and resources: rules yield rule by shaping material conditions into social resources. "Rules are the social component, resources the material component of all human endeavor. . . . Resources are nothing until mobilized through rules, rules are nothing until matched to resources to effectuate rule" (Onuf 1989:64). In short, "Politics is about rule" (e.g., Spruyt 1994:34; Ruggie 1998b:178). Rule is about ruling. Ruling requires rules. Rules yield rule (Onuf 1989:49–52, 59–65; 1998b:172–173). Rules and rule always distribute advantages unequally. Rule arises because "human agents author rules and deploy resources in accordance with those rules so as to secure and ensconce advantages over other agents" (quotation from Onuf 1989:60; Burch, 1994, 1998, 1999b; Burch et al. 2000). Rule shapes social arrangements and frames authority (Onuf 1989: chapter 6). Alas, IR/IPE scholars narrowly conceive authority as "hierarchy."

Sixth, the unequal distribution of resources yields three forms of rule: hierarchy, heteronomy, and hegemony. Any instance of rule combines the forms.[14]

---

[13]Trapped by confining definitions, Krasner (1999:229) proclaims that "the international system . . . does not have constitutive rules." Yet it does have "persistent norms" (1999:58) that shape (constitute?) the system like a game in which "clubs can always trump" (1999:238). Do these norms not "constitute" his premise of anarchy? What point does he make when he declares that "[the] international system is not like the game of chess" (p. 229), but is like a game of bridge?! Also, why is the international system susceptible to geometric disproof whereby a counter-example falsifies initial claims? However, one easily praises Krasner's illustrations of social construction.

[14]For example, Burch (1998: especially 18–20, 146, 153–155) addresses the formation of early modern European states from a ROC perspective that illustrates that any particular instance of rule combines hierarchical, heteronomous, and hegemonic forms. The following section draws on this work.

A particular type of rule, each corresponding to a speech act, characterizes each form of rule.[15]

From these points comes a richer conception of rules: rules are "binding practices [normative constraints] that involve people in structures of motivation [reasons for action] for themselves and others [shared meanings] and in structures of social control [rule]" (Braybrooke 1996:12).[16] A typology of rules and rule follows.

Typology of Rule

Hierarchy. Max Weber is a premier theorist of hierarchical relations. In hierarchical contexts the ruler rules, sovereigns command. Hierarchy occurs when social relations are arranged vertically, as in bureaucracies and militaries. In such arrangements, superiors direct subordinates. Such commands—called directive-rules—inform agents how to behave, and specify the consequences for violations. Commands arrange relations by catalyzing agents. Since interstate relations comprise only informally hierarchical relations, authoritative directive-rules occur infrequently. Yet great powers often convey desires via directives. For example, consider Western commands to Serbian leaders about ceasing hostilities in Kosovo. Allied airstrikes (the penalty) in response to violated dictates (the rules) underscores these hierarchical relations.

Heteronomy. Immanuel Kant is the premier theorist of heteronomy. In heteronomous settings, no one or everyone appears to rule. Individual agents are subject to several different rules and rulers. In this sense Ruggie (1998b:179),

---

[15] The following table illustrates how categories (types) of rule derive from speech acts (see Onuf 1989: chapter 6; Burch 1996). A more elaborate table appears in Burch (1998:18–20, note 10).

Speech Acts	Categories of Rules	Expressions of the Rule	Forms of Rule
Directives	Directive-Rules	To request, order, command	Hierarchy
Assertives	Instruction-Rules	To name, declare, inform, assert	Hegemony
Commissives	Commitment-Rules	To promise, commit, oblige	Heteronomy

[16] Braybrook's definition captures central elements of March and Olsen's (1998:948, citing their earlier work) definition of "institution" and Onuf's (1989, especially 52–65, 205; 1997:15–17) attention to the relationship of rules and rule.

Spruyt (1994:36), and others describe feudalism as "heteronomous," entailing a decentralized system of fragmented, overlapping authority. In contrast to the vertical, linear character of hierarchy, heteronomy is diffuse. Heteronomous rule occurs when rights and duties dominate social relations, and agents perform multiple social roles, as in markets, the liberal-republican constitutional state, feudal relations, and characterizations of the Westphalian system. Agents reciprocally exchange rights and duties; they mutually exchange commitments. If accepted, such promises—called commitment-rules—create a nonlinear web of social relations. From an agent's view, authority seems fragmented, radiating from different sources. Promises convey an agent's intention to commit to an action by the act of promising or accepting a promise. Commitments order social relations by coordinating agents' activities.

Heteronomy describes contracts, alliances, market exchange, and diplomatic comity. Heteronomy defines international "anarchy" (Wendt 1992), though realists and liberals deny that, consequently, international relations are *ruled* relations. In this form of rule, no one agent or group appears to rule. The liberal preference for market influence over state intervention reflects a preference for rule by the invisible hand rather than by heavy-handed leaders. Both represent forms of rule. Thus, Adam Smith is a telling theorist of heteronomy. (Neo)liberals are more attentive to hierarchical repression than to heteronomous oppression because they conceive hierarchies as ruled, but imagine heteronomies as unruled (anarchy) and unruly (the market). In heteronomous rule, market anonymity masks social asymmetries as social equality. Yet, as Smith explains, heteronomous relations are ruled "at arms length," beyond an actor's intention or control. An invisible hand is still a controlling hand, if only metaphorically and fantastically.

Ruggie understands "heteronomy" differently but compatibly. For Ruggie (1998b:179–180), heteronomy is the antonym of homonomy. Heteronomy describes a social system composed of dissimilar units; homonomy represents interactions among like units. Yet, as Ruggie notes, dissimilar units must exchange mutually recognized commitments (vows, oaths, promises, duties) to each other in order to interact advantageously. While Ruggie pays foremost attention to interacting *units* and fragmented authority as markers of the institutional setting, Onuf attends to the social *relations*, the mediating rules, and the consequent form of rule.

Hegemony. Karl Marx and Antonio Gramsci are notable theorists of hegemony. Hegemonic relations prevail when ideas seem to rule. Neither commands nor promises are necessary to yield stable relations. Hegemonic agents assert conditions by identifying what counts as valuable and valueless. Such assertions—called instruction-rules—shape social relations by naming, claiming, and privileging. Policing becomes less necessary because agents recognize the values and rules, so "know" how to act appropriately.[17] Consider the values embedded in ruling class culture, ideology, and mores. Similarly, caste systems, professions, and theocracies function by identifying and disseminating specific principles and ideas that, by their character, shape behavior.

IR scholars use "hegemony" to signal a preeminent power that dominates the informal international hierarchy. This widespread use confuses two forms of rule. Hierarchy is already self-evident, as the term "great powers" suggests. However, observers recognize the "hegemony" of particular, especially Western, ideas. Since the fall of the Berlin Wall, decidedly Western conceptions of "democracy," "liberalization," and popular culture freely circulate with no pretense of being other than (allegedly) self-evidently compelling hegemonic ideas, even if the ideas are unclear, inconsistent, or incoherent (Dryzek 1996:3, 5). Leaders from China, India, Africa, and the Muslim world routinely resist the hegemonic character of Western culture, democratic political practice, liberalism, and human rights principles. Such leaders consistently protest that pressure for enactment of these principles represents a form of ruling and structural disciplining that occurs distinct from the mere circulation of ideas (Burch 1995). As Gramsci notes, hegemony always combines elements of coercion and consent, so blends hierarchy and heteronomy with hegemony. This point illustrates that all conditions of rule always mix the three ideal forms.

Illustrating a Rules-Oriented Analytic Framework

I closely read work by Spruyt, Krasner, and Strange in the same way many political theorists read the great texts. Such "close readings"—also called deconstruction, discourse analysis, exegesis, hermeneutics, immanent critique, or literary criticism—seek to reveal underlying meanings and motifs within the text. Why engage in close readings rather than discuss or investigate contemporary empirical problems? Because "it is by interpreting and reinterpreting 'classical' works that fundamental argument is conducted in the social sciences" (Alexander 1982:1). From such readings I discern in Spruyt, Krasner, and Strange

---

[17] A confusion arises because NOC scholars conflate types of rules. Finnemore and Sikkink (1998:892, citing Fearon) write that all social norms take a generic form: "Good people do (or do not do) Q in situations A, B, C. . . ." This is the form of a directive-rule, not of all rules (Burch 1998:18, note 10). By presuming that "good people" behave in manner Q, Finnemore, Sikkink, and Fearon simultaneously invoke the form of an instruction-rule: "x counts as y." Thus x (following directive-rules, doing Q) counts as y (being good persons).

elements of a rules-orientation that reproduce the typologies of rule and rely upon implicit constructivist premises. This orientation—embedded in their views rather than standing outside their analyses—illustrates how deeply and implicitly a rules-orientation permeates social worldviews, practice, and inquiry.

Rules and Rule in Hendrik Spruyt's work

Spruyt (1994) explores how trading leagues, city-states, and sovereign territorial states displaced feudal arrangements, the Roman Catholic Church, and the Holy Roman Empire. His classification of competing institutions illustrates a typology of rule; his attention to "systems of rule" indicates a rules-orientation. His analysis of the competition among institutions reveals premises congruent with constructivism.

Spruyt groups feudalism, Church, Empire, sovereign states, city-states, and trading leagues as "systems of rule" (pp. 35, 55, 154). In keeping with his claim that "politics is about rule" (p. 34), he could easily have distinguished among these six examples as forms of rule. "Feudalism was essentially a system of rule based on mutual ties of dependence without a clearly defined hierarchy" (p. 35). Thus, feudalism mixes heteronomy and hierarchy. Heteronomy arises from "mutual ties": "One's specific obligations or rights depended on one's place in the matrix of personal ties" (p. 35). Feudal relations were also undeniably hierarchical, embedded in the Great Chain of Being which located everyone in a fantastic pyramid of statuses surmounted by God. Consequently, "the status of the individual, the 'quality' of the person, became an important ingredient in maintaining social order" (p. 56). The confusing feature of feudalism was that the hierarchical relations involved "crosscutting jurisdictions" (p. 3) and overlapping claims. In this sense political authority was fragmented and "hierarchy was diffuse" (p. 56). The structure of secular rules resembled a butte, not a pyramid.

Commands to obey, to respect, and to perform particular service constitute hierarchies. That an individual might be simultaneously subject to two mutually exclusive commands does not change the form and character of the rules. Also, exchanged rights and duties foster heteronomy. Spruyt ably depicts this mixed form: "if the chieftain could not deliver his end of the bargain, the vassal could renounce his obligation to the superior" (p. 37). Spruyt concludes that feudal rule comprised two obligations: "reciprocal military obligations" (heteronomy) and "hierarchical, nonreciprocal" production relations (p. 38).

In contrast, the Church as a form of rule mixes hegemony and hierarchy. The Church, "with its clear perception of hierarchy, saw itself as a community of believers" (p. 35) linking individual worshippers through clerical officers to the Pope and God. As community members, Christians deferred to the powerful ideas of the faith, which defined secular and eternal life. To be obvious, the authority of the Church derived from the overawing power of Christian ideals and their significance for defining and constituting social relations. This power of ideas to shape social relations—to rule, in effect—defines hegemony. The Church effects its rule via intensive and extensive instruction: what counts as significant, virtuous, sinful, just, etc. By identifying fundamental values, the Church shapes culture and rules society. By conjoining the "teachings" of Jesus and the ten "commandments" from God, one understands the mix of hegemony and hierarchy.

The Holy Roman Empire represents competing hierarchical claims. The "emperor claimed superiority over all other rulers" (p. 35). However, the "duality of secular and religious legitimation [proffered by the emperor] led to the absence of clear hierarchical authority" (p. 56). Any pretense to simultaneous hegemonic significance was diluted because the emperor's "semireligious status" (p. 35) was less clear than the Pope's. Nonetheless, for Church and Empire "rule was per definition spiritual" (p. 47). Though the Pope was more hegemonically significant, the emperor tried similarly to effect rule and exercise authority. Thus, Spruyt (p. 51) approvingly cites Harold Berman: "The empire was not a geographical entity, but a military and spiritual authority." Imperial rule flowed from imperial dictates.

One can also account for territorial sovereign states, trading leagues, and city-states in terms of rules and rule. States are hierarchies: sovereigns command. Trading leagues are heteronomies: merchants exchange commitments and goods. City-states are remarkable. As republics, they are incompletely hierarchical; as merchant-polities, they are heteronomous; yet as centers of regional power, they are hegemonic. In practice, each *system* of rule was a mixed *form* of rule.

Rules and Rule in Stephen Krasner's work

Krasner (1993, 1994, 1995, 1995/96, 1999) sharply challenges many premises of globalization. "Globalization is not new. . . . Challenges to the authority of the state are not new. . . . Transnational flows are not new" (1994:13). Nor are effects attributed to globalization new since Westphalian premises have never accurately described states (1995/96:115). He claims that material and ideational factors have always compromised Westphalian sovereignty (1999:9). Krasner thus transforms the realist simile of states as billiard balls to states as whiffle balls, but most of the realist worldview endures.

Krasner (1999) explains that conventions, contracts, coercion, and imposition consistently compromise the Westphalian system. These compromises represent two forms each of heteronomy and hierarchy. Coercion and imposition illustrate hierarchical relations. Each "must involve power asymmetry" (p. 37). *Imposition* "occurs when the target is so weak that it has no choice but to accept the demands of the more powerful" or else be eliminated (p. 37). *Coercion* differs only because the target may choose a response to the "credible threats" of the other actor (the aggressor?). Krasner's vocabulary of "strong" and "weak" states, "targets," and "threats" informs a clear hierarchical picture.

In contrast, contracts and conventions illustrate heteronomy. Actors join agreements by forming *contracts* when they promise to do something in exchange for a benefit provided by the opposite party. This much is clear. *Conventions,* he tells us, occur when rulers enter into agreements from which they expect to reap a gain, but their commitments "are not contingent" on what other signatories do (p. 30). Krasner offers the example of human rights "accords." These examples illustrate the heteronomous exchange of mutual promises. Such is the dictionary definition of an agreement: "a mutual arrangement, an expression of assent, an exchange of promises."

Krasner does not directly address hegemony, but he considers the hegemony of select ideas. For example, the Westphalian model "has been a point of common reference" that shapes rulers' actions (1994/95:149). Against this standard agents make choices and judge the choices of others. This is hegemony. This is rules-oriented choosing. Both Spruyt and Krasner have difficulty identifying hegemony because they expound a hegemonic view, seeing it as right or proper. Indeed, Krasner (1993:264) becomes impatient when those with "wrong" ideas fail to see matters correctly. This too is hegemony. This too illustrates rule and (a) discipline at work.

Rules and Rule in Susan Strange's work

For Strange (1996), the place of rules and rule is implicit, but no less central. She seeks to confirm three hypotheses (pp. 13–14, 25, 189). First, the growing power of strong states represents hierarchy: "it is more 'power over' than 'power from' that matters" in global affairs (p. 25). She offers examples of U.S. directive-rules to forbid or command others (p. 25–26).

Second, the lateral shift in authority from states to nonstate actors illustrates heteronomous relations, illustrated by the "triangular diplomacy" in which "bargains were struck" among states, among firms, and between states and firms (p. xiv; Stopford and Strange 1991). Such bargains represent exchanges of mutual promises. Her treatment of the telecommunications industry illustrates firm–firm bargains, whether strategic alliances, joint ventures, or cooperative arrangements (p. 102–103). Similarly, private organizations and businesses may form their own cooperative regimes or cartels (p. 123). Strange illustrates state–state agreements with examples from international governmental organizations concerned with the global economy (p. 164–171). State–firm coordination appears in the corporatist literature and in the economic literature on "collaborative alliances" (e.g., Branscomb, Kodama, and Florida, eds. 1999).

Strange underscores heteronomy when she notes (p. 26) that power may be exercised, and rule effected, in the absence either of an intention or an actor. She writes "that 'power over' need not be confined to outcomes consciously or deliberately sought" (p. 26). With actor-oriented analyses, it becomes "much harder to think of power being exercised by one party over another unconsciously, without deliberate intent" (p. 26). However, structural analyses—especially when attentive to heteronomous or hegemonic relations—more easily illustrate how power and rule may arise without clear intention or a key actor. In such cases, power appears to have "evaporated" because "no one was exercising it" (p. 189). Indeed, "no one is responsible for authority functions, even though they may pretend to be" (Strange 1996:42).[18]

Strange addresses hegemonic rule by describing U.S. global influence radiating through regimes, which "cloak an American ideology" (p. 192). Though Strange's comments on U.S. power suggest hierarchical asymmetry, she also implies dominant liberal ideas transmitted by a transnational class (p. 162). Thus, "the secretariats of international institutions . . . are subliminally socialised into administering an international order that is by no means neutral either in its intentions []or its consequences" (p. xiv). Dependency exists "even when it is, so to speak, self-inflicted" (Strange 1994:215). For Strange, the power of liberal "beliefs," in conjunction with changes in technology and finance, explain the widespread adoption over the last decade of market-oriented economic policies. In this sense, U.S. global influence combines hierarchical and hegemonic rule as constituted by U.S. commands and liberal ideology, respectively. She describes "the soft velvet glove" of liberal, market-promoting international institutions encasing "the iron fist" of U.S. power (p. 162).

A Socially Constructed World of Continuous Flux, Dispute, and Material Change

From my readings I draw conclusions about rules-orientation, Westphalia, large-scale social change, and ROC.

---

[18] Compare Strange with Onuf (1998b:77): "An anarchy is ruled by no one in particular, and therefore by everyone is association, as an unintended consequence of their many, uncoordinated acts. . . . If anarchy is a condition of rule unrelated to any agent's intentions, then international relations is no anarchy. We need another term to indicate the form of rule in which agents intend that they be ruled by what seem to be unintended consequences of exercising their rights. *Heteronomy* is a better term." Krasner (1999) essentially makes this argument.

The work of Spruyt, Krasner, and Strange implicitly illustrates a vocabulary and typology of rules and rule. All forms of rule are mixed types, as suggested by Strange's example of American hegemony, by Krasner's example of Westphalian compromises, and by Spruyt's (e.g., 1994:35, 55) many examples. Rules are deeply implicated in these practices, though each accords rules a different significance. The authors agree that the Westphalia system is a social construction shaped by specific social practices; they imply that the Westphalian system represents a form of rule (Spruyt 1994:192; Strange 1994:4; Krasner 1999:58).

The authors offer competing views on epochal change.[19] Spruyt and Krasner are clear: change of units means change of system (e.g., Spruyt 1994:5, 188). Strange argues that technological change causes systemic change. More broadly, she declares that "change in the international political economy has so far been inadequately described and diagnosed" because "social scientists, in politics and economics especially, cling to obsolete concepts and inappropriate theories" (also Spruyt 1994:4; Strange 1996:xii, 3; Linklater 1998:34; Ruggie 1998b:173).

The authors illustrate how material conditions, ideas, and resources affect social change (Spruyt 1994:6, 184; Strange 1996:7–12; Krasner 1999:9). For example, although Strange (1996) writes primarily of technological change, she argues that such changes alter "the name of the game" (p. 9), and thus spark new "commonsense" understandings (p. 8; also Spruyt 1994:184). In dramatic instances, new institutions arise; more typically, existing institutions adapt. Varying prospects for adaptation spark Strange's anxiety, Krasner's confidence, and Spruyt's musings. Although Krasner (1999) argues that sovereignty is "organized hypocrisy," one might as easily conclude that the meaning of sovereignty varies and/or that the institutional framing of states and the Westphalian state system shift along the three axes of hierarchy, heteronomy, and hegemony.

These authors agree that material conditions spark social change, but they do not tell us how to reconcile their disagreements or how to apprehend a world of flux. Constructivism addresses such matters; ROC offers a vocabulary. Although the authors do not explicitly adopt each ROC premise, they implicitly confirm most.

For example, each author clearly indicates that change, flux, and process are central features of social life. Social relations are never fixed because *social construction occurs continuously*. Epochal, norm-transforming change occurs infrequently, but change is ever-present. Are these not the premises of social construction?

---

[19] As an illustration, note that their claims about change indicate three distinct instruction-rules in the form of "X (events, conditions) do [or do not] count as Y (epochal change)."

The second premise of ROC holds that *speech acts and rules are the means of social construction*. Krasner (1999:48–49, 50–51), the most thoughtful of the trio concerning social construction, does not invoke speech acts, but he accepts constructivist premises concerning discourse, and disputes the analytic weight of "shared understandings" (p. 51) versus power. However, Krasner approvingly cites an analysis of constructivism (1995) by Searle, a preeminent speech act theorist (e.g., 1969), who links speech, rules, and institutions. Relatedly, none of the authors view all *rules as simultaneously regulative and constitutive*.

A fourth premise holds that *social change involves social rules*. Each author argues that new powers will introduce new rules. Their references to property rights also indicate that social change occurs via changing content and purposes of rules. Thus, the authors confirm the ROC premise that *rules transform raw materials*, whether physical or ideational, *into social resources*. Although the authors directly consider material conditions, one easily infers from their arguments that ideas may also be crafted and mobilized as resources. Why else write books about profound questions?

Last, *rules yield rule*. I illustrate this point in the section above.

From my reading of several authors I discern rules, rule, aspects of social construction, and elements of rule-oriented constructivism. Indeed, I discern implicit typologies of rule, constructivist premises, and theories of change amenable to ROC analyses. I turn now to theories of change.

Theories of Change

Spruyt, Krasner, Strange, and Ruggie draw different conclusions about the character of Westphalian society, yet they share elements of a familiar theory of change. Since all, save Ruggie, emphasize material conditions, I start there. However, each author notes both material and ideational causes for change.

A General View: The "Classical Paradigm"

Spruyt, Krasner, and Strange assert that changing material conditions—whether innovation, technological change, or economic growth—affect normative attitudes, which then affect patterns of political authority and institutions. Andrew Janos (1986) calls this model the "classical paradigm" of social change, a bedrock foundation for Western social science (Janos 1986:147–154). The theory animating this model explains that innovation sparks change (e.g., Hamblin, Jacobsen, and Miller 1973).

Innovation affects material conditions, which affect agents' worldviews, self-conceptions, and interests. These factors influence behavior. Behavior, in turn, affects agents, ideas, and material conditions. Although innovation may first affect material conditions then ideas, ideas may shape material conditions.

One can readily interpret this model in terms of social rules and social constructivism. Material conditions become social resources via social rules. Innovation is the premier example of transforming, say, ore into metal. Material conditions, and the rules that constitute them, shape social rules (and arrangements) by which actors make choices. Agents' behavior affects actors, conditions, and patterned relations by affecting rules. This is social construction in action. Through rules ideas have social consequence.

One version of the "classical paradigm" emphasizes culture by attempting to explain innovation and changing material conditions not as discrete historical events, but as an "ongoing process that requires the steady reproduction of beliefs and symbolic systems" (Janos 1986:153). In many ways this argument mirrors constructivist claims. Problems hamper this cultural argument (151), because efforts to date "skirt some of the weightiest philosophical problems" (153). Yet ROC addresses many of Janos's concerns. What is absent is a theory of why change is occurring at a particular moment or era (see note 2).

A Theory of Change: Applying the "Classical Paradigm" of Material Conditions

Westphalian society will change because technological innovations expand economies of scale and make existing social systems more complex. Complexity and scale create incentives for agents to collaborate (Holland 1995); they also complicate the network of rules (Vogel 1996). Changing conditions spur actors to reinforce or resist the changes and/or to devise new arrangements (see Spruyt 1994:25–27, 30–33; Thomas and Tetreault, eds. 1999). For example, multinational corporations increasingly cooperate internationally to establish rules for behavior and institutional support because governments and international organizations are unwilling and unable to administer global commerce (Cutler et al., eds. 1999). Whether technological and institutional innovation precedes conceptual innovation is not the issue; rather, in either case, some form of innovation sparks social change and new demands for political rule (Janos 1986:3). As national governments increasingly enmesh themselves in diverse material and social systems, the Westphalian system changes from a dominant state-centered arrangement—a dominance derived primarily from hierarchical (national, vertical) rules—to a prominent institution that coordinates and meshes with other (nonstate) systems via diffuse heteronomous, collaborative rules.

The technologies that drive many transnational corporations require global economies of scale; traditional notions of national comparative advantage that inform trade theory are increasingly irrelevant for high-technology firms that operate beyond national control (Mowery, ed. 1988; Mowery and Rosenberg 1989, 1998; Lorange and Roos 1992; Greider 1997:186; Archibugi and Michie, eds. 1998). *The Economist* (1995) breathlessly reports this familiar sentiment:

> The benefits of size will encourage mergers. . . . The economies of scale and scope are such that, by the second quarter of the next century, only a handful of really big international providers may be left. The big operators in the rich world are getting ready to grab a share in the global market by forming alliances with partners in other countries. . . . What if, as privatisation and liberalisation progress, the concept of national operators becomes an anachronism?[20]

A similar story describes many industrial, financial, and service sectors. States, firms, and organizations coordinate affairs by enacting new rules and constituting subsequent arrangements. Examples include strategic alliances and mergers of transnational firms in pharmaceuticals, telecommunications, biotechnology, chemicals, banking, agribusiness, broadcasting and mass media, retail, corporate–university relations, airlines, and other sectors. Such collaboration also occurs among international organizations and nongovernmental organizations (e.g., WTO 1998:1; 1999:1). Further, consider the "triangular diplomacy" that brought about the WTO and its twin pillars, the Dispute Settlement Mechanism and Trade-Related Intellectual Property Rights protections (Hicks and Holbein 1997; Sell 1998; Hudec 1999:2–15; Burch 1999b; Burch et al. 2000).

States, firms, and organizations realize goals by exchanging promises with each other—establishing contracts, enacting treaties, forming alliances—rather than by compelling, commanding, or instructing. Thus the mix of rules shifts from the dominance of coercive command to collaborative cooperation. What is a "strategic alliance," for example, if not formal cooperation in which partners pool, exchange, or integrate resources for mutual gain (Lorange and Roos 1992:vi)? One study reports that over half of the growth companies in the United States plan to participate in some form of strategic alliance within the year and firms involved in strategic alliances grow 68 percent faster than non-allied peers (Canadian Consulate General 1999:1).

Examples abound. Again consider telecommunications and the "death of distance" they wrought. Schiller (1999:xiv, 1) heralds the era of "digital capitalism" by noting that telecommunications networks both widen and deepen the social and cultural ambit of global capitalism by fostering vast, intensive corporate alliances. Paradoxically, the plan requires "unremitting political intervention" (p. 2) and raises important public policy questions (Archibugi and Michie 1998:14–15). Thus began an era of close, selective government–corporate collaboration that, in turn, sparked more wide-ranging corporate alliances. Bell Atlantic, AT&T, British Telecom, Microwave Communication Incorporated (MCI), and Tele-Communications Incorporated (TCI), for example, are currently crafting alliances, consortia, and integrated networks.

---

[20] Quotation available on page 2 of: <www.mnemiopis.com/interne/tekno/the-economist/death-of-distance/tel8.html>

More broadly, pundits declare that U.S. global influence requires "soliciting cooperation" and the active pursuit of equitable partnerships (Wills 1999, quotation at 58). A policymaker warns that effective management of the global economy requires "close coordination among international financial institutions . . . [and] regulators of all countries should coordinate much more" (Garten, 1999:85–90, quotation at 86).

Claims about innovation-driven coordination rely upon the "classical paradigm" of change (Janos 1986), familiar claims about globalization and technological innovation (i.e., why is change occurring now), and voluminous evidence. These claims also entail unfamiliar elements: the character of social rule and an analytical framework of rule-oriented social constructivism.

A Theory of Change: Ideational Change

Material change is intricately interwoven with conceptual and ideological change. For example, conceptual innovation follows recent "triumphs" of neoliberal market principles and the associated ideological "monopoly of neoliberal" premises (Janos 1986:69). Also, the collapse of the Soviet Union precipitated rethinking about global life. "With the death of the USSR it is now possible to envisage a transformation of the rules of the world game without . . . a widespread military confrontation" (Laidi 1998:91). This transformation compels agents to identify and establish "new linkages between meaning (identity) and power (resources)" (p. 98). In the wake of such transformation, new relations and practices arise and "a new global social system [is] being born" (p. 98).

The engines of contemporary change are large-scale economic activity and technological progress (p. 99), thus linking current conditions to the "classical paradigm" of change. Yet more profound is the "crisis of meaning," the loss of "common meaning" and clear identities (p. 100–101). Since the state has lost the monopoly of giving meaning and providing identity (p. 104–107), agents have lost the "natural reference space" that constitutes identity, so "identity has to be renegotiated" (p. 104). Relatedly, states too have lost their traditional identities and roles. States—"no longer the controllers of the international system" (p. 111)—encounter a world no longer arranged in sharply "hierarchical" terms. The challenge is not to build a world order, because it will be "constituted" without our direct effort. Rather, we must "regulate the birth of a global social system" (p. 111). Rules are the means. Ideological and technological imperatives foster cooperation as an end.

> It is therefore necessary to try to organize international regulation on the basis of . . . collaboration between associate rivals rather than on a hierarchical relationship between the dominant and the dominated, and in a way which would take account of the loss of control by states of certain sections of international reality. (Laidi 1998:116)

Such cooperation does not now occur. If it will, it must produce meaning, identify and harness resources, and create new "rules or ways of proceeding," as well as new constitutive principles and rules.

Laidi teaches us three points. First, ideational change creates incentives for large-scale cooperation. Second, ideational change is intimately related to material change. Third, a rules-orientation ably captures both dynamics. *Whether* the cooperation Laidi foresees occurs in a planned, coordinated way, in a haphazard fashion, or not at all is a matter for future inquiry. *How* it occurs is ably captured by a rules-orientation and ROC.

Conclusions

This essay interprets the question of Westphalian change as a question about analytical vocabularies and frameworks. The essay seeks to inform a new vocabulary and to craft an analytical framework sufficiently robust and comprehensive to address large-scale change and to embrace the scope, scale, fluidity, and contested character of Westphalian practices. The essay makes three contributions. First, it elaborates a vocabulary and taxonomy of rules and rule, then crafts an analytic framework based upon these concepts. From this "new vocabulary" I sketch an analysis of systemic change attentive to social rules and consequent forms of rule.

Second, a rules-orientation is intrinsic to many prevailing views on Westphalia and social change. I discern several implicit ROC premises in the work of notable, nonconstructivist scholars. This is a significant conclusion because for over a decade many observers have labeled constructivism as an external, paradigmatic rival to the prominence/dominance of traditional neorealist theories and positivist-utilitarian foundations. Now, however, one can interpret familiar works as examples of a rules-orientation and constructivism. This effort refines social constructivism by orienting it to social rules, understood as the medium of social construction, and by extending the range of (rule-oriented) constructivist analyses.

Third, the essay applies the rules-orientation to material and ideational theories of social change. One may read each theory in terms of rules, rule, and ROC.

The essay concludes that large-scale change comprises changes in the mix of social rules and the consequent form of rule. Specifically, I suggest how and why global relations among states and corporations increasingly rely upon coordination and collaboration rather than commands.

References

Adler, Emanuel. (1997) "Seizing the Middle Ground: Constructivism in World Politics." *European Journal of International Relations* **3**:319–363.

ALEXANDER, JEFFREY C. (1982) "Theoretical Logic in Sociology." In Vol 2: *The Antinomies of Classical Thought: Marx and Durkheim*. Berkeley, CA: University of California Press.

APPELBAUM, RICHARD P. (1970) *Theories of Social Change*. Chicago, IL: Markham Publishing Company.

ARCHIBUGI, DANIELE, AND JONATHAN MICHIE. (1998) "Trade, Growth, and Technical Change: What Are the Issues?" In *Trade, Growth, and Technical Change*, edited by D. Archibugi and J. Michie, pp. 1–15. New York, NY: Cambridge University Press.

ARCHIBUGI, DANIELE, AND JONATHAN MICHIE, EDS. (1998) *Trade, Growth, and Technical Change*. New York, NY: Cambridge University Press.

AXELROD, ROBERT. (1984) *The Evolution of Cooperation*. New York, NY: Basic Books.

BOUDON, RAYMOND. (1986) *Theories of Social Change: A Critical Appraisal*. Berkeley, CA: University of California Press.

BRANSCOMB, LEWIS M., FUMIO KODAMA, AND RICHARD FLORIDA, EDS. (1999) *Industrializing Knowledge: University-Industry Linkages in Japan and the United States*. Cambridge, MA: The MIT Press.

BRAUDEL, FERNAND. (1980) *On History*, translated by S. Matthews. Chicago, IL: University of Chicago Press.

BRAYBROOKE, DAVID. (1996) "The Representation of Rules in Logic and Their Definition." In *Social Rules: Origin, Character, Logic, Change*, edited by D. Braybrooke, pp. 3–19. Boulder, CO: Westview Press.

BURCH, KURT. (1994) "The 'Properties' of the State System and Global Capitalism." In *The Global Economy as Political Space*, edited by S. Rosow, M. Rupert, and N. Inayatullah, pp. 37–59. Boulder, CO: Lynne Rienner Publishers.

BURCH, KURT. (1995) Intellectual Property Rights and the Culture of Global Liberalism. *Science Communication: An Interdisciplinary Social Science Journal* **17**(2) December: 214–232.

BURCH, KURT. (1996) Illustrating Constructivism: George Kennan and the Social Construction of the Cold War. *Swords and Ploughshares: A Journal of Peace Research and International Politics* **6**(1) Fall; 3–22.

BURCH, KURT. (1998) *'Property' and the Making of the International System*. Boulder, CO: Lynne Rienner Publishers.

BURCH, KURT. (1999a) The Promise and Practice of Restructuring Social Theory. Manuscript currently under review.

BURCH, KURT. (1999b) "Intellectual Property Rights and Dispute Settlement: Critiquing Central Institutions of International Trade." Paper presented at

ISA annual convention, March, Washington, D.C. Under review as "Complaints, Police, Prosecutors, and Protesters: Intellectual Property Rights and Political Poverty in the World Trade Organization."

Burch, Kurt. (2000) Forthcoming. "Toward a Constructivist Comparative Politics." In *Constructivist Comparative Politics* edited by D. Green. Armonck, NJ: M. E. Sharpe.

Burch, Kurt, P. J. Smith, and P. W. Wheatley. (2000) Divergent Incentives to Protect Intellectual Property: A Political Economy Analysis of North-South Welfare. *Journal of World Intellectual Property* **3**(2):169–195.

Burke, James. (1999) *The Knowledge Web*. New York, NY: Simon and Schuster.

Canadian Consulate General. (1999) Website devoted to attracting strategic alliances among U.S and Canadian businesses. Searched September 14. Available at: <www.canadaonlinechicago.net/english/strategicalliance.html>

Checkel, Jeffrey T. (1998) The Constructivist Turn in International Relations Theory. *World Politics* **50**:324–48.

Cutler, Claire, Virginia Haufler, and Tony Porter, eds. (1999) *Private Authority and International Affairs*. Albany, NY: State University of New York Press.

Dessler, David. (1989) What's at Stake in the Agent-Structure Debate? *International Organization* **43**:441–473.

Dryzek, John. (1996) *Democracy in Capitalist Times: Ideals, Limits, and Struggles*. New York, NY: Oxford University Press.

The Economist. (1995) Telecommunications Survey: The Death of Distance. September 30.

Ethics. (1990) A special issue on rules and game theory. **100**(4) July.

Finnemore, Martha, and Kathryn Sikkink. (1998) International Norm Dynamics and Political Change. *International Organization* **52**(4) Autumn:887–917.

Garten, Jeffrey E. (1999) Lessons for the Next Financial Crisis. *Foreign Affairs* **78**(2) March/April:76–92.

Giddens, Anthony. (1984) *The Constitution of Society*. Berkeley, CA: University of California Press.

Gould, Stephen J. (1980) *The Panda's Thumb*. New York, NY: W. W. Norton.

Gramsci, Antonio. (1971) *Selections from the Prison Notebooks*. New York, NY: International Publishers.

Greider, William. (1997) *One World, Ready or Not: The Manic Logic of Global Capitalism*. New York, NY: Simon and Schuster.

HABERMAS, JÜRGEN. (1998) *Betwen Facts and Norms*. Cambridge, MA: The MIT Press.

HAMBLIN, ROBERT L., R. B. JACOBSEN, AND J. L. L. MILLER. (1973) *A Mathematical Theory of Social Change*. New York, NY: Wiley and Sons.

HART, H. L. A. (1961) *Concept of Law*. New York, NY: Clarendon Press.

HASENCLEVER, ANDREAS, PETER MAYER, AND VOLKER RITTBERGER. (1997) *Theories of International Regimes*. New York, NY: Cambridge University Press.

HICKS, LAURINDA L., AND JAMES R. HOLBEIN. (1997) Convergence of National Intellectual Property Norms in International Trading Agreement. *American University Journal of International Law and Policy*. **12**(5):769–814.

HOLLAND, JOHN H. (1995) *Hidden Order: How Adaptation Builds Complexity*. Reading, MA: Addison-Wesley Publishing Company, Inc.

HUDEC, ROBERT E. (1999) The New WTO Dispute Settlement Procedure: An Overview of the First Three Years. *Minnesota Journal of Global Trade* **8**(1) January:1–53.

JANOS, ANDREW C. (1986) *Politics and Paradigms: Changing Theories of Change in Social Science*. Stanford, CA: Stanford University Press.

KATZENSTEIN, PETER, ROBERT KEOHANE, AND STEPHEN KRASNER. (1998) International Organization and the Study of World Politics. *International Organization* **52**(4) Autumn:645–685.

KECK, MARGARET, AND KATHRYN SIKKINK. (1998) *Activists beyond Borders: Advocacy Networks in International Politics*. Ithaca, NY: Cornell University Press.

KEOHANE, ROBERT O. (1990) Multilateralism: An Agenda for Research. *International Journal* **45**(4):731–764.

KORNHAUSER, LEWIS. (1996) "Conceptions of Social Rule." In *Social Rules: Origin, Character, Logic, Change*, edited by D. Braybrooke, pp. 203–216. Boulder, CO: Westview Press.

KRASNER, STEPHEN D. (1982) Structural Causes and Regime Consequences: Regimes as Intervening Variables. *International Organization* **36**(2):185–205.

KRASNER, STEPHEN D. (1993) "Westphalia and All That." In *Ideas and Foreign Policy*, edited by J. Goldstein and R. Keohane, pp. 235–264. Ithaca, NY: Cornell University Press.

KRASNER, STEPHEN D. (1994) International Political Economy: Abiding Discord. *Review of International Political Economy* **1**(1) Spring:13–19.

KRASNER, STEPHEN D. (1995) "Power Politics, Institutions, and Transnational Relations." In *Bringing Transnational Relations Back In: Non-State Actors,*

Domestic Structures, and International Institutions, edited by T. Risse-Kappen, pp. 257–279. New York, NY: Cambridge University Press.

KRASNER, STEPHEN D. (1995/96) Compromising Westphalia. *International Security* **20**(3) Winter:115–151.

KRASNER, STEPHEN D. (1999) *Sovereignty: Organized Hypocrisy*. Princeton, NJ: Princeton University Press.

KRATOCHWIL, FRIEDRICH. (1984) The Force of Prescriptions. *International Organization* **38**:685–708.

KRATOCHWIL, FRIEDRICH. (1988) Regimes, Interpretation, and the 'Science' of Politics: A Reappraisal. *Millennium* **17**:263–284.

KRATOCHWIL, FRIEDRICH. (1989) *Rules, Norms, and Decisions*. New York, NY: Cambridge University Press.

KRATOCHWIL, FRIEDRICH. (1993a) "Contract and Regimes: Do Issue Specificity and Variations of Formality Matter?" In *Regime Theory and International Relations*, edited by V. Rittberger. Oxford, England: Clarendon Press.

KRATOCHWIL, FRIEDRICH. (1993b) "Norms versus Numbers: Multilateralism and the Rationalist and Reflexivist Approaches to Institutions—A Unilateral Plea for Communicative Rationality." In *Multilateralism Matters: The Theory and Praxis of an Institutional Form*, edited by J. Ruggie. New York, NY: Columbia University Press.

KRATOCHWIL, FRIEDRICH, AND JOHN RUGGIE. (1986) International Organization: A State of the Art on an Art of the State. *International Organization* **40**:753–775.

LAIDI, ZAKI. (1998) *A World without Meaning: The Crisis of Meaning in International Politics*. New York, NY: Routledge.

LEWIS, DAVID. (1969) *Convention*. Cambridge, MA: Harvard Univeristy Press.

LINKLATER, ANDREW. (1998) *The Transformation of Political Community: Ethical Foundations of the Post-Westphalian Era*. Columbia, SC: University of South Carolina Press.

LLOYD, CHRISTOPHER. (1993) *The Structures of History*. Oxford, England: Blackwell.

LORANGE, PETER, AND JOHAN ROOS. (1992) *Strategic Alliances: Formation, Implementation, and Evolution*. Cambridge, MA: Blackwell Publishers.

MARCH, JAMES G., AND JOHAN P. OLSEN. (1984) The New Institutionalism: Organizational Factors in Political Life. *American Political Science Review* **78**:734–749.

MARCH, JAMES G., AND JOHAN P. OLSEN. (1989) *Rediscovering Institutions: The Organizational Basis of Politics*. New York, NY: The Free Press.

MARCH, JAMES G., AND JOHAN P. OLSEN. (1998) The Institutional Dynamics of International Political Orders. *International Organization* **52**(4) Autumn:943–969.

MILNER, HELEN. (1998) Rationalizing Politics: The Emerging Synthesis of International, American, and Comparative Politics. *International Organization* **52**(4) Autumn:759–786.

MOWERY, DAVID C., ED. (1988) *International Collaborative Ventures*. Cambridge: Ballinger.

MOWERY, DAVID C., AND NATHAN ROSENBERG. (1989) *Technology and the Pursuit of Economic Growth*. New York, NY: Cambridge University Press.

MOWERY, DAVID C., AND NATHAN ROSENBERG. (1998) *Paths of Innovation: Technological Change in 20th Century America*. New York, NY: Cambridge University Press.

NARDIN, TERRY. (1983) *Law, Morality, and the Relations of States*. Princeton, NJ: Princeton University Press.

NORTH, DOUGLASS. (1981) *Structure and Change in Economic History*. New York, NY: W. W. Norton and Company.

NORTH, DOUGLASS. (1990) *Institutions, Institutional Change, and Economic Performance*. New York, NY: Cambridge University Press.

ONUF, NICHOLAS G. (1985) Do Rules Say What They Do? From Ordinary Language to International Law. *Harvard International Law Journal* **26**(2) Spring:385–410.

ONUF, NICHOLAS G. (1989) *World of Our Making: Rules and Rule in Social Theory and International Relations*. Columbia, SC: University of South Carolina Press.

ONUF, NICHOLAS G. (1991) Sovereignty: Outline of a Conceptual History. *Alternatives* **16**(4) Fall:425–446.

ONUF, NICHOLAS G. (1994) The Constitution of International Society. *European Journal of International Law* **5**(1):1–19.

ONUF, NICHOLAS G. (1995) "Intervention for the Common Good." In *Beyond Westphalia?: State Sovereignty and International Intervention*, edited by G. M. Lyons and M. Mastanduno, pp. 43–58. Baltimore, MD: Johns Hopkins University Press.

ONUF, NICHOLAS G. (1997) "A Constructivist Manifesto." In *Constituting International Political Economy*, edited by K. Burch and R. Denemark, pp. 7–17. Boulder, CO: Lynne Rienner Publishers.

ONUF, NICHOLAS G. (1998a) "Constructivism: A User's Manual." In *International Relations in a Constructed World*, edited by V. Kubalkova, N. Onuf, and P. Kowert, pp. 58–78.

ONUF, NICHOLAS G. (1998b) *The Republican Legacy in International Thought*. New York, NY: Cambridge University Press.

ONUF, NICHOLAS G. (1998c) Everyday Ethics in International Relations. *Millennium* **27**(3): 669–693.

ONUF, NICHOLAS G. (forthcoming, 2001) "Worlds of Our Making: The Strange Career of Constructivism in International Relations." In *Visions of International Relations* edited by D. Puchala. Columbia, SC: University of South Carolina Press.

OSTROM, ELINOR. (1990) *Governing the Commons*. New York, NY: Cambridge University Press.

PETTIT, PHILIP. (1990) The Reality of Rule Following. *Mind* **99**(393):1–21.

PRICE, RICHARD. (1997) *The Chemical Weapons Taboo*. Ithaca, NY: Cornell University Press.

PRICE, RICHARD. (1998) Reversing the Gun Sights: Transnational Civil Society Targets Land Mines. *International Organization* **52**:613–644.

PRICE, RICHARD, AND CHRISTIAN REUS-SMIT. (1998) Dangerous Liaisons?: Critical International Theory and Constructivism. *European Journal of International Relations* **4**(3) September:259–294.

RANDALL, SUSAN C., AND HERMANN STRASSER. (1981) "Conceptualizing Social Change: Problems of Definition, Empirical Reference, and Explanation." In *An Introduction to Theories of Social Change*, edited by H. Strasser and S. C. Randall, pp. 11–35. Boston, MA: Routledge and Kegan Paul.

RAWLS, JOHN. (1955) Two Concepts of Rules. *Philosophical Review* 44:3–32.

RAZ, JOSEPH. (1979) *The Authority of Law: Essays on Law and Morality*. New York, NY: Clarendon Press.

RORTY, RICHARD. (1989) *Contingency, Irony, and Solidarity*. New York, NY: Cambridge University Press.

RUGGIE, JOHN G. (1998a) What Makes the World Hang Together?: Neo-Utilitarianism and the Social Constructivist Challenge. *International Organization* **52**(4) Autumn:855–885.

RUGGIE, JOHN G. (1998b) *Constructing the World Polity: Essays on International Institutionalization*. New York, NY: Routledge.

SCHILLER, DAN. (1999) *Digital Capitalism: Networking the Global Market System*. Cambridge, MA: The MIT Press.

SEARLE, JOHN. (1969) *Speech Acts.* New York, NY: Cambridge University Press.

SEARLE, JOHN. (1979) *Expression and Meaning.* New York, NY: Cambridge University Press.

SEARLE, JOHN. (1995) *The Construction of Social Reality.* New York, NY: The Free Press.

SELL, SUSAN. (1998) *Power and Ideas: North-South Politics of Intellectual Property and Antitrust.* Albany, NY: State University of New York Press.

SIKKINK, KATHRYN. (1991) *Ideas and Institutions: Developmentalism in Brazil and Argentina.* Ithaca, NY: Cornell University Press.

SPRUYT, HENDRIK. (1994) *The Sovereign State and Its Competitors: An Analysis of Systems Change.* Princeton, NJ: Princeton University Press.

STOPFORD, JOHN, AND SUSAN STRANGE. (1991) *Rival States, Rival Firms: Competition for World Market Shares.* New York, NY: Cambridge University Press.

STRANGE, SUSAN. (1994) Wake up, Krasner! The world has changed. *Review of International Political Economy* **1**(2) Summer: 209–219.

STRANGE, SUSAN. (1996) *The Retreat of the State: The Diffusion of Power in the World Economy.* New York, NY: Cambridge University Press.

STRANGE, SUSAN. (1998) *Mad Money: When Markets Outgrow Governments.* Ann Arbor, MI: University of Michigan Press.

THOMAS, KENNETH P., AND MARY ANN TETREAULT, EDS. (1999) *Racing to Regionalize: Democracy, Capitalism, and Regional Political Economy.* Boulder, CO: Lynne Rienner Publishers.

TILLY, CHARLES. (1984) *Big Structures, Large Processes, Huge Comparisons.* New York, NY: Russell Sage Foundation.

VOGEL, STEVEN K. (1996) *Freer Markets, More Rules: Regulatory Reform in Advanced Industrial Countries.* Ithaca, NY: Cornell University Press.

VON WRIGHT, GEORG HENRIK. (1963) *Norm and Action.* New York, NY: Humanities Press.

WALT, STEPHEN. (1998) One World, Many Theories. *Foreign Policy* **110**:29–46.

WENDT, ALEXANDER. (1992) Anarchy Is What States Make of It: The Social Construction of Power Politics. *International Organization* **46**(3) Summer: 391–425.

WENDT, ALEXANDER. (1999) *Social Theory of International Politics.* New York, NY: Cambridge University Press.

WILLS, GARRY. (1999) Bully of the Free World. *Foreign Affairs* **78**(2) March/April:50–59.

WTO (World Trade Organization). (1998) "Ruggiero Announces Enhanced WTO Plan for Cooperation with NGOs." Press release. July 17. Available at: <www.wto.org/wto/new/press107.htm>

WTO. (1999) "WTO High-Level Symposia on Trade and Environment and Trade and Development". Press release. March 1. Available at: <www.wto.org/wto/press/press123.htm>

Young, Oran. (1994) *International Governance: Protecting the Environment in a Stateless Society*. Ithaca, NY: Cornell University Press.

Printed and bound by CPI Group (UK) Ltd, Croydon, CR0 4YY
16/09/2026
14963386-0001